Trauma
Journalism

Trauma Journalism

On Deadline in Harm's Way

Mark H. Massé

continuum

Continuum International Publishing Group
80 Maiden Lane, New York, NY 10038
The Tower Building, 11 York Road, London SE1 7NX
www.continuumbooks.com

Library of Congress Cataloging-in-Publication Data
Massé, Mark H., 1952-
Trauma journalism : on deadline in harm's way / by Mark Massé. – 1st ed.
p. cm.
Includes bibliographical references and index.
ISBN-13: 978-1-4411-8463-4 (pbk. : alk. paper)
ISBN-10: 1-4411-8463-5 (pbk. : alk. paper)
ISBN-13: 978-1-4411-0540-0 (hardcover : alk. paper)
ISBN-10: 1-4411-0540-9 (hardcover : alk. paper) 1. War–Press coverage.
2. War correspondents–Mental health. 3. Violence–Press coverage.
4. Psychic trauma–Press coverage. 5. Journalism–Objectivity.
6. Journalism–Psychological aspects. 7. Journalists–Mental health.
8. Journalists–Violence against. 9. Journalists–Crimes against. I. Title.
PN4784.W37M38 2011
070.4'49–dc23
2011018858

ISBN: HB: 978-1-4411-0540-0
PB: 978-1-4411-8463-4

Typeset by Newgen Imaging Systems Pvt Ltd, Chennai, India
Printed and bound in the United States of America

*To trauma journalists worldwide for their
courage and commitment
To my late pal Craig "Mac" McAfee for his
loyalty and support
To my wonderful wife, Mykie, for her
love and devotion*

CONTENTS

FOREWORD

We have to believe in what we do, or we couldn't do it.

During the recent uprisings in Tunisia and Egypt, I logged onto the Al Jazeera English (AJE) news channel for online coverage as often as ten times a day. Al Jazeera's reporting far surpassed that of any American television network, with its focus on people passionately committed to toppling repressive regimes. As a journalist and journalism professor, it was natural that I focused on the brave and stubborn souls determined to show the world what was happening. Mostly Egyptians or other Arabs, with a scattering of Westerners, these men and women faced arrest, harassment, beatings, and in some cases torture for disseminating the news. I especially single out the Al Jazeera correspondents. Their offices were burned, their equipment confiscated, and their internet access shut down. Still, they kept that vital story "on the air" for weeks.

This is what journalists do, when they are doing their job the way it is supposed to be done. Get the story and get it out, no matter what the obstacles, no matter what the threats. Many die in that effort. Many others suffer, either directly, as autocrats use all in their power to stifle them, or indirectly, from the psychological effects of witnessing, close-up, day after day, the awful suffering of others. I have many memories that will never go away. Counting bodies in South Korea or Lebanon, so the Associated Press (AP) could report accurately the number of dead in this clash or that battle. "Counting" doesn't mean numbers to me, it means seeing close-up the torn bodies of men and women and children lying in the sun, and smelling the never-forgotten, sweetly horrible smell of human decomposition. Watching, notebook in hand, as dedicated doctors fight unsuccessfully to keep alive a young boy, covered with burning pits from phosphorus shrapnel, and interviewing those exhausted, shaken doctors afterward.

Why do we do this? How can we do it? Are we some kind of monsters, without feeling, without empathy? On the contrary, most journalists who cover violence, at least the ones I know, are sensitive, caring, idealistic people. They try not to show their emotions. They can't. They have to do their job and do it again tomorrow and next week, in other crises, with other dead. And they might not get the next important assignment if their bosses think they're "burning out." That's important to them, not for the money or the fame, but for the same reasons they started doing this in the first place: the powerful, driving need to find and tell the truth about war and violence, and the price it exacts.

It is only in the last twenty years or so that the trauma community began looking at the price the journalists themselves pay in their work. Like firefighters, police officers, and emergency medical techs, journalists are hard interviews—they don't like to talk about themselves, at least not on that subject. Mark Massé's work is part of a small but growing lexicon. I hope it will help to counter the unfortunately common view of news people as uncaring, careless voyeurs exploiting others' pain for shallow reasons. We have to believe in what we do, or we couldn't do it.

Terry Anderson
March 2011

PREFACE

Several years ago, when I first embarked on this journey to write about trauma journalism, I contacted literary agents to determine their interest. Perhaps my enthusiasm for the subject blinded me to the harsh realities of the publishing industry. Though as a longtime freelance writer, I was certainly no stranger to rejection. But I was struck by the blunt response of one East Coast agent who stated: "I suspect that there's little concern by John Q. Public for the emotional and psychological impact of traumatic news events on journalists."

Undeterred, I continued my research and reporting, motivated by the accounts compiled from journalists around the world, men and women who put themselves at risk physically and psychologically so others could be informed. I was also drawn to the reform efforts underway within the news media to challenge traditional practices and precepts. Still, as time passed, I wondered if the skeptical literary agent had been right. Did the "average person" really care about the lives of reporters covering conflict, tragedy, and trauma?

One way to answer that question would be to conduct a random survey of a cross-section of people. That would certainly provide quantitative data. But as a storyteller I believe in the power of a personal narrative to transform one's perspective. In February 2011, during the revolution in Egypt, compelling news accounts spoke of journalists who were hunted by gangs, beaten by mobs, and threatened with death. One female correspondent was brutally sexually assaulted in Cairo's chaotic Tahrir Square. The intimidation of international news media was part of a concerted effort by authorities to systematically target reporters and destroy their equipment and facilities in order to halt dissemination of news. These dramatic reports attracted global attention not only by print, broadcast, and online audiences, but also by governmental officials and organizations in several nations. Quite simply, people *did* care about the impact of traumatic events on journalists. Further, I maintain that people *are* interested in learning of the effects of hazardous coverage on news media workers who regularly confront stress and danger. Their stories have inspired me through the years to write this book.*

---

*Interviews in this book were conducted with sources at varying times during more than five years of research. Unless otherwise noted, people's ages are listed as of the year they were initially contacted. The eight individuals profiled as "Faces of Trauma Journalism" were interviewed in 2010–11.

"HIGH WIRE"

by Terry Anderson

The high-wire artist risks his life
To please the crowd, for fame,
The thrill of danger, and the pleasure
Of performing feats that few can do.
We risk our lives, and souls,
For motives much the same, plus
The heady feel of being next to power,
Even wielding some ourselves.
We take as many casualties, maybe more.
The names of those who die,
In gold and silver, are posted on the
Press club wall. Others we carry
Quietly, or just ignore until
They are encountered in the bar—
Burned-out relics of too many wars.
You see, you cannot go on bathing
In the world's violence unscathed,
Touch so many people's pain and grief
And not be burned. Tell me you could
Look into a hundred children's eyes,
Dark, huge with uncomprehending
Pain and hunger, and purge yourself
Of all you feel in a thousand words or so.
So we grow our shells. Those who can't
Don't last. Some grow them all too well—
The cynical, abrasive ones who
Cannot feel. Perhaps they never could.
They count their coups in front-page
Headlines, and pay in other ways.
Most of us just try to keep our balance,
Like the man up on the wire,
Eyes fixed straight ahead,
Never daring to look down.

TERRY ANDERSON, "HIGH WIRE," *DEN OF LIONS*
(REPRINTED WITH AUTHOR'S PERMISSION)

CHAPTER ONE

Tracking a Media Movement

Journalists' symptoms of traumatic stress are remarkably similar to those of police officers and firefighters who work in the immediate aftermath of tragedy, yet journalists typically receive little support after they file their stories. While public-safety workers are offered debriefings and counseling after a trauma, journalists are merely assigned another story.

— AL TOMPKINS, "HELP FOR JOURNALISTS UNDER STRESS," *POYNTERONLINE*[1]

It has taken the media industry far too long to realize that it is perfectly natural for journalists, like other people, to feel the effects of trauma. . . . The media need to wake up to traumatic stress as a subject worthy of debate.

— CHRIS CRAMER, GLOBAL EDITOR, MULTIMEDIA, THOMSON REUTERS, AS QUOTED IN *TRAGEDIES & JOURNALISTS: A GUIDE FOR MORE EFFECTIVE COVERAGE*[2]

I'm building a career on the misery of others.

— ANDERSON COOPER, *DISPATCHES FROM THE EDGE: A MEMOIR OF WAR, DISASTERS, AND SURVIVAL*[3]

For centuries, journalists worldwide have risked their health, safety, and lives while confronting conflict, tragedy, and trauma. They have borne witness to violence, destruction, and loss so that their audiences may be informed, enlightened, or compelled to action. When disaster strikes, journalists are often the first responders, sometimes arriving on the scene before law enforcement, firefighters, emergency medical technicians, or military personnel.

Reporters, photographers, videographers, and other news media workers explore the grim realities of war, genocide, terrorism, crime, catastrophes, and accidents, documenting their observations and experiences. But trauma journalism also reflects coverage of seemingly less dramatic events and issues, such as chronicling the courageous fight of a child stricken with cancer, the rehabilitation of a disabled war veteran, or the recollections of a family whose loved one has been killed in an auto accident.

Although war correspondents, crime reporters, and those drawn to covering conflict and crisis may be described as adrenaline junkies, adventure seekers, or a "different breed," journalists are not detached from scenes of terror, grief, or horror no matter how calm or collected they may appear on screen. No matter how efficiently they complete their stories and produce their images to meet deadlines. The fact is journalists, like other people, have varying emotional thresholds when it comes to confronting trauma.

Empathy and Objectivity

Comparing his actions to the clinical role of surgeon and noting that he is able to treat his reporting on tragedy, such as the genocide in Darfur and other atrocities across Africa, "with a certain amount of professional distance," Nicholas Kristof, Pulitzer Prize-winning reporter and columnist for the *New York Times*, states:

> In a career of reporting I've heard a lot of really wrenching stories about murder and rape and everything else. And at this point, I'm not really proud of it. I'm even a little embarrassed about it. I can listen pretty dispassionately to the most inhuman stories, and they, most of the time, don't really bother me.[4]

More than sixty years earlier, Marguerite Higgins, the esteemed war correspondent and photojournalist, listed similar responses to Kristof's in her memoir (*News is a Singular Thing*) in which she described her reactions when experiencing the liberation of the German concentration camp at Buchenwald at the end of World War II:

> How did all this affect me personally? The truth is that at the time I felt no strong emotional reaction to the things I heard or saw. My condemnation and disgust were of the mind. And I believe that is generally true that a journalist covering a war, a train wreck, a concentration camp, or some other disaster, tends to compartmentalize his emotions and isolate them from professional reactions. He feels no more personal involvement

than does a surgeon performing a delicate operation or a regimental commander ordering a comrade into battle.[5]

In one of several newscasts after the massive January 12, 2010, Haitian earthquake, CNN's Gary Tuchman described the horror on the streets. He talked of bloated corpses, the dead and injured beneath the rubble, widespread misery and desolation. Tuchman delivered his report professionally under devastating conditions. He focused on the story and not on himself. But how did his reporting affect him personally? And what was the impact of this coverage on his cameraperson and the editors back in the United States?

Psychiatrist Anthony Feinstein, a noted researcher on the effects of trauma on journalists, states: "Resilience in the face of adversity is not, however, synonymous with immunity."[6] Crisis coverage often has a dramatic, lasting effect on news gatherers. How print and broadcast reporters, photographers, and videographers cope under challenging circumstances is a critical question in trauma journalism research.

In a 1999 article ("Distancing Yourself from the Story, a Help or Hindrance?"), veteran journalist and author Jim Willis, who covered the Oklahoma City bombing in 1995 among other tragedies in his long career, offered reflections on his emotional detachment years earlier:

> I wondered have I been in this business too long? Am I becoming so hardened that I can't experience a normal rush of emotions in witnessing tragedy? Or have I just become so good at burying those feelings so I can go about my daily routine of distancing myself from life so I can report on it accurately?[7]

Willis is cited in Jody Santos' 2009 book, *Daring to Feel: Violence, the News Media and Their Emotions*, along with Denver Post reporter Miles Moffeit, who in 2004 reported on rapes in the US military.[8] Moffeit noted that by becoming personally engaged in his coverage, he was able to understand the story on a deeper, more meaningful level. Santos urged journalists to be keenly aware of their feelings when reporting and to understand the intersection of trauma and emotional injury, thereby becoming more empathetic with sources.

Terry Anderson, author of *Den of Lions*, a survivor of terrorism and a hostage in Lebanon from 1985 to 1991, says that being a disciplined professional journalist does not preclude passion or empathy for a given subject or source. While he believes journalists should utilize the tools of their craft and strive for balance and fairness, not all stories have the obligatory two sides. For example, he notes that when covering the Rwandan genocide, there was only one side to consider—the truth. Like others who have experienced tragedy and trauma firsthand (Anderson was a Marine correspondent in Vietnam), he does not believe that being detached is the proper perspective for a reporter. Being in touch with one's feelings when reporting on a difficult story, Anderson believes, will enable that journalist to write a more accurate, realistic, and dramatic account.

Former BBC (British Broadcasting Corporation) reporter Kate Adie speaks of being emotionally engaged in the craft of reporting. She is passionate about the role of journalists serving as witnesses, informing others about world events. That sense of conviction may also make one a better journalist, according to Adie, who wrote in her autobiography, *The Kindness of Strangers*: "Caring about what you see may well be the key to good reporting, for it means you look closer, and you look to find out why. The much-bruited idea that we are all damaged by grim experience is countered surely by the idea that we are all changed by experience, but not necessarily for the worse."[9]

Admittedly, the issue of objectivity in journalism extends beyond the world of trauma coverage. In their 2007 book, *The Elements of Journalism*, authors Bill Kovach and Tom Rosenstiel, claim that the discipline of the journalist's craft, the unity of his method (e.g., information gathering) and not his personal intent, philosophy, or style of presentation, is what should define objective news reporting:

> A stronger, more unified, and more transparent method of verifying the news would also be the single most important step that those who practice journalism could take to address and, if necessary, correct the rising perception that the work of journalists is marred by bias.[10]

The new age of converged, interactive, and social media has ushered in new rules governing objectivity and detachment on the part of reporters. Old ways are being replaced by immersive, collaborative, and intimate news coverage. Purists are offended, criticizing reporters for becoming too intimate with their stories, displaying their emotions on air, in print, or online. But audiences tend to respond positively when journalists act like "real people" when reporting on difficult stories. The lines, however, are blurring between information, advocacy, and opinion, between honest emotion and showmanship. Since the halcyon days of Murrow, Cronkite, and Woodward and Bernstein, the public's dissatisfaction (with the antics and insensitivities of journalists) and mistrust of the news media, as measured in surveys by organizations such as the Pew Research Center, continue to increase. Some believe that in response to such negative public opinion (and in the quest for ratings, ad revenues, and circulation), news outlets are overreacting during crises, such as the Haitian earthquake, and resorting to coverage dominated by "compassion and self-congratulation" as noted in a January 15, 2010, *New York Times* essay by Alessandra Stanley.[11]

Response to Trauma Coverage

Although several trends intersect in any contemporary analysis of the news media, my focus is on the characteristics, motivations, training, and coping skills of trauma journalists—that is, those in the news media who cover war, conflict, disaster, and tragedy.

One significant trend in recent years is the enhanced awareness of the need for greater physical protection of journalists in dangerous situations through weeklong hostile-environment training, provision of safety equipment, and assignment of private security guards. According to CNN's Anderson Cooper in his 2006 book, *Dispatches from the Edge: A Memoir of War, Disasters, and Survival*:

> After *Wall Street Journal* reporter Daniel Pearl was kidnapped and murdered in Pakistan in 2002, news companies began to take security much more seriously. In Baghdad (2003–present) most major American news organizations contract with private security firms. Big guys with thick necks meet you at the airport and give you a bulletproof vest before they even shake your hand. The company that CNN contracts with provides former British Special Forces soldiers—tough professional men who've done things you can't imagine, in places you've never heard of. They don't talk much about where they've been, but they'll tell you right away: Baghdad's the worst they've seen.[12]

The use of security guards and other safety measures aren't welcomed by all conflict journalists. Correspondents in Iraq, Afghanistan, and other trouble spots talk of a lack of access and an inability to do their jobs well. News organizations will justify such measures by publicly stating their concern for the welfare of their employees, but privately management expresses concern over liability issues. A legitimate fear is that lawsuits will be filed against media companies when family members are killed or seriously wounded while covering stories in unsafe environments. A related question is whether journalists will sue their employers for compensation due to mental health diagnoses such as PTSD? And are journalists who admit they have been emotionally affected by their stories at risk of being categorized unfairly as "damaged goods" and deemed incapable of returning to front-line reporting—even when they request these assignments?

Such issues have resulted in a growing emphasis by news organizations, trade groups, and professional associations on the psychological effects of trauma journalism coverage on victims, their families and loved ones, their communities, and on the journalists themselves. Since the early 1990s, an international movement has been underway to reform the news media through education, intervention, and advocacy. Some supporters refer to instilling a culture of caring within the journalistic community. Critics, however, claim that news media staff and management who are prudent, dutiful, and ethical reflect the enduring tenets of responsible journalism. And new attitudes and empathetic approaches are unnecessary.

While the subject of emotional trauma has long been the purview of the medical-psychiatric profession (e.g., *Diagnostic and Statistical Manual of Mental Disorders, DSM-IV*), the collaborative examination of mental health issues and journalism (e.g., the psychological impact of media coverage of violent and tragic stories) is arguably just two decades old.[13]

In 1991, Frank M. Ochberg, a noted psychiatrist, former state mental health director, and faculty member at Michigan State University (MSU), established a "Victims and the Media Program" for journalism students, faculty, working media, and mental health professionals. Subsequently, Ochberg's efforts resulted in the creation of the Dart Center for Journalism & Trauma at the University of Washington (UW) a decade later. In 2009, the Dart Center's headquarters, moved to New York, where it is defined formally as "a project of the Columbia University Graduate School of Journalism." Dart Center West, the organization's academic programs arm, remained at UW. The Dart Center conducts research on trauma science and its application to the field of journalism and serves as a multifaceted resource for news media worldwide.

In addition to the Dart Center for Journalism & Trauma, two leading international advocacy organizations in this reform effort are the Committee to Protect Journalists (CPJ) and the International News Safety Institute (INSI). The CPJ, founded in 1981, is an independent, nonprofit organization that promotes press freedom worldwide by defending the rights of journalists to report the news without fear of reprisal. The CPJ, based in New York, works in more than 120 countries, many of which suffer under repressive regimes, debilitating civil war, or other problems that harm press freedom and democracy. An article in the winter 2009 Neiman Reports publication ("Trauma in the Aftermath: Voice, Story, Character and Journalism") reported that in 2001, CPJ created a Journalist Assistance Program to aid news gatherers in peril, who were in hiding or in exile to escape death threats. In the last decade, some 374 journalists from 50 countries have received more than half a million dollars in CPJ payments.[14]

According to its website (www.newssafety.org), INSI is a unique coalition of news organizations, journalist support groups, and individuals exclusively dedicated to the safety of news media staff working in dangerous environments. This not-for-profit association is supported entirely by membership contributions that are channeled back into programs and services. INSI's purpose is to create a global safety network of advice and assistance to journalists and others who may face danger covering the news on international assignment or in their own countries. It was founded on World Press Freedom Day (established by the UN General Assembly on

May 3, 2003) in response to the rising death toll of among journalists and other news media workers.[15]

INSI publishes guidelines on safety principles and practices and advocates with governments, military organizations, and other groups worldwide. Honorary officers and advisory board members include Chris Cramer, INSI cofounder and president, global editor, multimedia, Thomson Reuters and Tom Curley, INSI vice president, president and CEO of the Associated Press (AP). Executive board members also include former journalists and academicians, notably Professor Judith Matloff, Columbia University. According to executive director Rodney Pinder, INSI is committed to providing hostile-environment training and other services to journalists who could not otherwise afford such programs.

Similarly, the CPJ recognizes that reporters who are often most at risk are local (indigenous) journalists who cannot afford protective equipment, much less hostile-environment training. Both journalist advocacy groups urge news media organizations to properly equip, train, and insure all journalists in conflict zones (including freelancers, stringers, drivers, and "fixers").

Honorary CPJ cochairman and former AP Chief Middle East Correspondent Terry Anderson speaks plainly and directly to journalists in hazardous situations: "Always, constantly, constantly, every minute, weigh the benefits against the risks. And as soon as you come to the point where you feel uncomfortable with that equation, get out, go, leave it. It's not worth it. There is no story worth getting killed for."[16]

Trends and Resources

A significant body of research has been produced in the last two decades (see Chapter 5: Traumatic Stress Studies) on the effects of trauma journalism. In the early twenty-first century, reporting on war, terrorism, and other tragic events worldwide has altered perceptions and perspectives of the news media regarding the impact of such stressful coverage. Further, the challenging economic climate currently affecting media corporations has heightened attention to issues such as newsroom stress, staff-management tension, and career burnout. Increasingly, journalism educators are responding to these emerging trends through trauma-related coursework.

The University of Central Oklahoma (UCO) offers an upper-level class called "Victims in the Media." Kenna Griffin, a doctoral student at the University of Oklahoma, is a graduate of the innovative course that helps prepare future journalists for issues likely to accompany coverage of tragedy and trauma (e.g., "emotions reporters are trained not to have or show"). In an April 4, 2009, article ("Preparing Journalists for Emotions") posted on the dartcenter.org website, Griffin noted that it wasn't just large-scale events, such as the coverage of 9/11, that affected reporters' emotional states. Having to write an obituary or cover a local violent crime, for example, could make a young reporter sick to her stomach, she wrote. Griffin is part of a growing cadre of authors and researchers investigating the secondary victimization of journalists.[17]

The Dart Center for Journalism & Trauma states: "Reporting responsibly and credibly on violence and traumatic events—on crime, family violence, natural disasters and accidents, war and genocide—are among the greatest challenges facing contemporary journalism."[18] The Dart Center, the Poynter Center, the INSI, the CPJ, CNN, the BBC, the AP, and Thomson Reuters are among several major news and advocacy organizations engaged in efforts to raise journalists' awareness of stress and trauma issues and the role of timely, targeted postcoverage intervention (e.g., counseling). In addition, the Nieman Foundation for Journalism, the Society of Professional Journalists (SPJ), the American Society of Newspaper Editors (ASNE), Military Reporters and Editors, and Investigative Reporters and Editors (IRE) have all included material on trauma journalism issues in organization publications and at professional conferences.

As a writer, I specialize in immersive narratives on societal issues. I have studied the trauma journalism reform movement since 2005. My research has featured interviews with US and international print and broadcast journalists and trauma experts, including many involved with tragedies such as the Oklahoma City bombing, Columbine (Colorado) school shootings, September 11, 2001, the Iraq War, the 2004 South Asian tsunami, Hurricane Katrina, the Amish school murders in Lancaster, Pennsylvania, the 2007 mass killings at Virginia Tech University (VTU), the Valentine's Day 2008 shootings at Northern Illinois University, and the 2010 Haitian earthquake.

Among the most important books on the topic is *Covering Violence: A Guide to Ethical Reporting about Victims and Trauma*, authored by former journalists and academics Roger Simpson and William Coté.[19] Their book combines research on trauma, Post-Traumatic Stress Disorder (PTSD), and secondary (vicarious) traumatic stress with recommendations for enhanced newsgathering and writing. It also includes extended anecdotes and detailed accounts from journalists who covered large-scale events such as 9/11 and the Oklahoma City bombing. The text features several chapters on journalistic practices (e.g., interviewing) and sections on the reporting on violence, rape, and children. It concludes with guidelines for journalists and resources on trauma journalism.

Jim Willis draws on his reporting career in the *Human Journalist*, describing news media work as an evolving craft and profession.[20] He challenges the tradition that says journalists must remain detached from human emotions when covering stories, especially when affected by personal trauma. He says reporting is inseparable from interpretation if the journalist is to be a credible and convincing witness to events. Willis cites research on traumatic stress among reporters, editors, and photographers in advocating for enhanced education and training to humanize newsroom culture.

The emotions and experiences of war correspondents are the focus of *Journalists under Fire: The Psychological Hazards of Covering War* by Dr. Anthony Feinstein, a Canadian psychiatrist.[21] The 2006 text describes the physical and psychological hazards facing these journalists, the damage to their personal and professional lives, and how this negative impact is often overlooked or minimized by supervisors, peers, and colleagues, or assumed to be an integral part of journalism's norms, attitudes, and values (e.g., bravado and denial). Subjects covered include what motivates risk-taking behavior, the stresses facing reporters in the field, and the inadequate support systems typically in place for those who encounter trauma on the job.

In a 2003 work of journalism history, *War Stories: Reporting in the Time of Conflict from the Crimea*, Harold Evans discusses the role of news organizations past and present in covering wars and other conflicts.[22] The book features accounts of journalists discussing the dangers they face in trying to "get the story" and the effects of such crisis reporting. It also reveals the ultimate price paid for such commitment: the hundreds of lives lost by reporters, photojournalists, camera crews, and media professionals in covering conflicts in the Middle East, Eastern Europe, Africa, and other locales since the 1990s.

George Sullivan also focuses on the challenges confronting war correspondents at the front lines in his 2006 book, *Journalists at Risk: Reporting America's Wars.*[23] He cites the risks faced by journalists, such as the legendary Ernie Pyle, a popular correspondent in World War II who was killed in 1945, the victim of enemy machine-gun fire. Among the book's emblematic quotes is one from distinguished international correspondent Christiane Amanpour: "Most of us feel we have a duty, a mission for this kind of work."

Award-winning CBS and ABC News foreign correspondent John Laurence reviews the impact of his years reporting on the Vietnam War in a detailed 2002 autobiography, *The Cat from Hué*, that documents his enduring personal struggles resulting from coverage of tragedy and trauma.[24]

In his 2002 autobiography, *Ambushed: A War Reporter's Life on the Line*, Ian Stewart describes a reporter's experiences in "hot spots" such as Kashmir and Kabul, including details on how he survived a near-fatal shooting, and how his life and views on war coverage changed.[25]

Widely traveled war correspondent Scott Anderson, who observed deadly conflicts in Beirut, Chechnya, Sri Lanka, and Uganda, reveals the personal toll of covering traumatic events in his extended narrative, "Prisoners of

War: The Lure of Gunfire and the Enemy Within," in a January 1997 *Harper's Magazine* article:

> I finally understood that I was not merely an observer of war and never had been. I had always been a participant—by my very presence I had been a participant—and war will always find a way to punish those who come to know it. I had watched people die. I had walked through killing fields and felt human bones break beneath my feet. I had picked up the skulls of murdered children and rearranged them with an eye to photographic composition. I had cajoled or intimidated or charmed scores of people into revealing their most intimate horrors, and then I had thanked them perfunctorily and walked away. If I was to be punished—and there were charms in my pocket to forestall this, there was an ocean behind my head to hasten this—it would be because I deserved it. God knows I deserved to be punished for the things I'd seen.[26]

Another vivid first-person account was published in 2006 by female war correspondent and *Washington Post* staff writer Jackie Spinner. In her book, *Tell Them I Didn't Cry: A Young Journalist's Story of Joy, Loss, and Survival in Iraq*, Spinner discusses her nine months of reporting from Baghdad, Fallujah, Kurdistan, and Abu Ghraib. She describes the daily challenges of life in a war zone, including the effects of living with violence over an extended time period. She addresses the emotional toll on her, her colleagues, and family.[27]

A 2002 collection of articles by the US and international journalists and editors titled *Journalism after September 11*, explores the impact on the media and the broader society "when trauma shapes the news."[28] One chapter in the text examines the physical safety and emotional welfare of journalists and attempts to answer the question of why journalists are willing to subject themselves to physical and psychological hazards and harm.

The narratives of young journalists who covered the 9/11 attack in New York City are contained in *At Ground Zero: 25 Stories from Young Reporters Who Were There*.[29] It features emotional stories of contributors, many of whom were at the scene of the collapse of the World Trade Center towers, describing the anger, excitement, terror, and depression that accompanied their reporting.

Profiles of reporters engaged in crisis coverage are an integral part of Ann S. Utterback's *Broadcasting through Crisis*.[30] The text provides working journalists with strategies and techniques to deal with stress and trauma. Utterback targets the physical and emotional health of individuals and their coping mechanisms.

The authors (Rogers, Leydesdorff, and Dawson) of *Trauma and Life Stories* assess the lifelong impact of traumatic experience through the narratives of survivors of crime, conflict, and tragedy.[31] A seminal text published in 1992, *Trauma and Recovery*, by Judith Herman, a psychiatrist at Harvard Medical School and director of training at the Victims of Violence program at Cambridge Hospital, provides insight into trauma and the healing process.[32]

Although my research on the subject of trauma journalism has been extensive, and I acknowledge the contributions of many individuals and organizations, my book is not intended to be an encyclopedia. It is difficult to chronicle even a fraction of the poignant personal stories of journalists who have covered and continue to cover conflict, tragedy, and trauma worldwide. But I have included contemporary representative profiles (see "Faces of Trauma Journalism"—eight in-depth accounts of international and domestic reporting from print and broadcast journalists whom I interviewed in 2010 and 2011). Similarly, I have chronicled media and academic innovations and exemplars (see Chapter 6: Media Training and Intervention and Chapter 7: News Reform 101), while admitting I have certainly not contacted every major news media organization or advocacy group.

I have written this book as an unfolding multilayered drama with complications, developments, points of insight, and resolutions. The subject of psychological trauma has been of interest since my graduate studies at the University of Oregon. In 1994, I wrote *FRONTLINE*, a ten-chapter narrative nonfiction account of a nontraditional community crisis intervention team. The subject matter (e.g., suicide hotline, mental health issues, and domestic violence counseling) was dramatic; however, my focus was not on the clients but on the professional and personal lives of the counterculture counselors who comprised the crisis team. I learned what drove these unique individuals was an overriding desire to heal others while they helped heal themselves from past traumas such as war, gang violence, drug abuse, and prostitution.[33]

A decade later in 2005, a colleague at Ball State University (BSU), Professor Scott Reinardy, shared his early research on newsroom burnout.[34] Among his references were studies by Dr. Anthony Feinstein and representatives of the Dart Center for Journalism & Trauma. By immersing myself in the field's literature, I became much more aware of the risks and impact of crisis reporting and on the vulnerabilities of news media workers to both primary and secondary trauma effects.

A most startling realization is the extent of journalist deaths. The Journalists Memorial, located in the Newseum in Washington, DC, honors reporters, photographers, and broadcasters who have died reporting the news in the twentieth and twenty-first centuries. According to the Freedom Forum's website, www.freedomforum.org, the names of 2,007 individuals worldwide are etched on the glass panels of the two-story commemorative structure. The memorial is rededicated annually to add the names of journalists who have lost their lives on the job in the preceding year. The Newseum compiles lists of journalist fatalities from information circulated by the CPJ, the International Press Institute, the International Freedom of Expression Clearing House, Reporters sans frontières (Reporters Without Borders), the International Federation of Journalists, the Inter American Press Association, news stories and other sources. Adjoining the memorial are photographs of hundreds of those journalists, and electronic kiosks containing data on every honoree. The Freedom Forum lists journalist fatalities from conflicts and crises, including World War I (2), World War II (68), Korean War (17), Vietnam War (66), Argentina (98), and Central America (89).[35]

The CPJ maintains data on journalists killed on duty in other twenti-eth- and twenty-first-century conflicts: Afghanistan (2001–04: 9), Algeria (1993–96: 58), Balkans (1991–95: 36), Colombia (1986–present: 54), Gulf War (1991: 4), Kosovo (1999–2001: 7), Philippines (1983–87: 36), Sierra Leone (1997–2000: 15), Somalia (1993–95: 9), Tajikistan (1992–96: 16), and Turkey (1984–99: 22). CPJ's statistical profile of journalists killed in the Iraq War (from March 2003 to October 2009, when "CPJ concluded its regular updates as media deaths and abductions subsided") totaled 140, with another 51 media worker (e.g., drivers, interpreters, fixers, and guards) fatalities during that time period. More than 80 percent of journal-ists killed in the war were Iraqi, and in excess of two-thirds of all fatali-ties were listed as murder and not cross fire or other acts of war. In other words, journalists were targeted for death in Iraq. But this is no surprise to officials at the CPJ and INSI, who readily state that most of news media victims are local or indigenous journalists and support staff who have been murdered at the hands of military, paramilitary, or police squads in their native countries.[36]

The most egregious example of the intentional killing of journalists occurred in November 2009 in the Philippines, where at least twenty jour-nalists were among the dead at the hands of gunmen representing warring factions in the volatile southern provinces of the country. In a November 25, 2009, *New York Times* story by Carlos Conde, Reporters Without Borders denounced the massacre in a written statement: "Never in the his-tory of journalism have the news media suffered such a heavy loss of life in one day."[37]

In another highly publicized incident, the website WikiLeaks.org released a graphic video in April 2010 showing an American helicopter shooting and killing a Reuters photographer and driver in a July 2007 attack in Baghdad. The April 5, 2010, *New York Times* story by Elisabeth Bumiller quoted David Schlesinger, the editor-in-chief of Reuters news, who called the deaths "tragic and emblematic of the extreme dangers that exist in covering war zones. We continue to work for journalist safety and call on all involved parties to recognize the important work that journalists do and the extreme danger that photographers and video journalists face in particular."[38]

In its March 2007 report, *Killing the Messenger: Report of the Global Inquiry by the International News Safety Institute into the Protection of Journalists*, INSI officials stated:

> The deliberate targeting of journalists by U.S. forces would indeed be a matter of huge controversy, and there remains no convincing evidence to suggest that there is such a policy. In its statement to the INSI inquiry, the CPJ concurred, noting that "there is no evidence to conclude that the U.S. military has deliberately targeted the press in Iraq, but the record does show that U.S. forces do not take adequate precautions to ensure that journalists can work safely. And when journalists are killed, the U.S. military is often unwilling to launch an adequate investigation or take steps to mitigate risk."[39]

Beyond such controversial accusations, the INSI report emphasized a fundamental truism for contemporary war correspondents: "The main danger today facing journalists and other news media personnel in conflict zones is the loss of what used to be seen as press neutrality. News media personnel are being targeted as never before, perceived by one side or another as being part of the enemy."[40]

The report also discussed the stark choices faced by correspondents who covered the Iraq War in "an increasingly insecure work environment in which the alternative to operating embedded among western and Iraqi government forces is to gamble on operating independently in a hostile environment where deliberate attacks and kidnappings by insurgents and criminal groups can occur with relative impunity and in which there is considerable risk of being caught up in the violence between the belligerents."[41]

Journalists covering war and conflict have always been at risk. But in areas of ethnic, tribal, or rebel violence, such as in Bosnia or Africa in the late twentieth century, where there were few if any front lines, correspondents suffered significant losses. In 2000, the deaths of veteran journalists Kurt Schork, a Reuters correspondent, and Miguel Gil Moreno, an award-winning videographer for Associated Press Television News (APTN), in the same ambush in Sierra Leone (Africa), not only shocked colleagues around the world but also led to industry activism concerning the safety of news media workers.

In "Deadly Competition" published in *Brill's Content* in September 2000, Peter Maass states that the deaths of Schork and Moreno "should give pause to the rest of us who take for granted the stories and pictures we see on the news." But he also questions if Moreno, like other journalists caught up in conflict zone competition for stories, may have taken unwise

risks. Maass writes: "No one knows exactly what Gil Moreno was thinking when he headed down that road with his friends from Reuters, but
many journalists, particularly at The Associated Press, fear that it was the
pressure of competition that led to his death."[42]

The CPJ lists the three most common news beats covered by victims of
violence as politics, war, and corruption.[43] Although large-scale conflict
garners the headlines and poses serious risks for war correspondents, individual reporters covering injustices on a local level also face threats to their
lives and livelihoods. Natalya Estemirova, a 50-year-old award-winning
Russian human rights activist and journalist, was murdered on July 15,
2009, in Grozny, Chechnya, where she lived and worked. Christiane
Amanpour eulogized Estemirova in *TIME* magazine's "Person of the Year
2009" issue on December 16, 2009:

> Like the murdered Russian journalist Anna Politkovskaya before her,
> Natalya Estemirova—who was killed in July by four bullets fired at
> point-blank range—documented the gross violations of human dignity
> in Chechnya. Repelled by both Chechen and Russian nationalism, she
> worked in a shell-scarred building in Grozny that had no electricity or
> running water. She filed stories of rockets slamming into hospitals, of
> kids being killed as they stood with their mothers collecting water from
> outdoor pumps. . . . She tried to force the media to report these crimes,
> and prosecutors to investigate them. I did not know her personally, but
> I know what drove her. She was a woman who struggled for justice,
> a mother who was forced to balance love for her daughter with the
> dangerous duty she shouldered.[44]

The intimate account of a murdered journalist in Sri Lanka, written by his
investigative reporter wife who was also threatened with death, was published in the winter 2009 issue of *Nieman Reports*. Sonali Samarasinghe
Wickrematunge worked with her late husband, Lasantha, for more than
a decade before fleeing Sri Lanka after his murder. The two reported on
widespread corruption, unsolved killings, the plight of the poor and des-
titute, and the "300,000 men, women and children of the war interned
still in Sri Lankan concentration camps." The Wickrematunges had been
married only two months before Lasantha's car was "ambushed in a
commando-style operation by eight men on four motorcycles, according
to witnesses."

The widowed wife, Sonali, contemplates the pain of her loss in the article "When They Come for Us":

> So how does a journalist deal with trauma? I don't know. I only know
> this. When it strikes you personally, when you are afraid to sleep in your
> own bed, when thugs on motorcycles kill your husband then come back

for you, when you are compelled to leave your home and family, your work, your country, and your life as you knew it, that's when you realize you cannot give up. You have to do more, you have to speak louder, write bolder. And now, it's personal. . . . Suddenly, I am not telling the story. I am living it.[45]

On August 11, 2007, the *Washington Post* published an editorial titled "A Journalist's Death," commemorating the life of reporter Chauncey Bailey, who was "murdered while performing an essential task of democracy." Bailey was investigating the activities of Your Black Muslim Bakery, an establishment operated by Yusuf Bey, a controversial figure in the Oakland community:

Having become editor of the Oakland Post, a small weekly newspaper focused on the African American community, Mr. Bailey probed the baker's murky finances—until the morning of Aug. 2, when a masked man approached and fired a shotgun at his head. According to police, a 19-year-old employee of the bakery has confessed to the murder, saying he carried it out because of Mr. Bailey's reporting. . . . Job-related murders of journalists are extremely rare in the United States: The last one took place in 1993, and there have been only 13 since 1976 (including Mr. Bailey's), according to the Committee to Protect Journalists. Yet this murder is a reminder of the need for reporting by professional journalists, even in an era when amateur video of war zones can be had at the click of a mouse. Aggressive journalism is still a vital part of every community's defenses against corruption and crime. It can save lives. Chauncey Bailey died doing his duty as a reporter. That duty is not only indispensable in a democratic society; it's also risky.[46]

As with my study of an Oregon crisis intervention team in the early 1990s, I remain profoundly interested in the motivation of individuals who confront trauma, the effects of such involvement, and the success or failure of coping techniques by practitioners. The psychology of high-risk journalism is the focus of this book.

As a writer and teacher of literary nonfiction, I have been struck by how often the work of trauma journalists meets the criteria for dramatic narrative, including complication and conflict (both *external*, such as war, terrorism, crime, and natural disaster, and *internal*, such as resultant psychological effects), colorful characterization (ordinary individuals facing extraordinary circumstances), and a story arc (how the journalists are affected and changed as a result of their coverage).

Writing about tragedy and trauma has been integral to the history of literary nonfiction or literary journalism, illustrated by noted practitioners including John Hersey, Ernest Hemingway, Truman Capote, Ted Conover, Joan Didion, Hunter Thompson, and Michael Herr. As Norm Sims cites in his 2007 book, *True Stories: A Century of Literary Journalism*, writers such as Michael Herr, Joan Didion, and Hunter Thompson were "sending back reports from the front lines; they ended up on the psychological barricades whether they were in Vietnam [as Herr was] or not, and their breakdowns tended to happen on the pages of their journalism."[47]

In 1967, Thompson published his harrowing ethnographic account of riding a motorcycle with the pathological gang known as Hell's Angels.[48] In the 1980s, Didion chronicled her struggles reporting on the tragic civil war in El Salvador.[49] Sims describes the impact on Didion of reporting from a "land of prolonged violent revolution and repression in the eighties where thousands had died and even more had simply 'disappeared.'"[50]

Didion recounted how after a visit to a morgue where victims' bodies ended up, threatening uniformed agents of the military trapped her in her car: "I did not forget the sensation of having been in a single instant demoralized, undone, humiliated by fear, which is what I meant when I said that I came to understand El Salvador the mechanism of terror."[51] About fifteen years earlier, Didion had admitted to having been evaluated at a psychiatric clinic as a person who "feels deeply that all human effort is foredoomed to failure, a conviction which seems to push her further into a dependent, passive withdrawal."[52]

Perhaps Michael Herr's self-revelatory writing in his impressionistic book on the Vietnam War, *Dispatches*, provides the best insight into the impact of trauma on the immersion journalist. Sims quotes Herr in *True Stories*: "I was pretty crazy when I came back. For a long time I was, in fact, very crazy."[53] Herr returned from Vietnam in 1969 with plans to write his book. Then he ran into several problems, "not the least of which was the famous post-Vietnam syndrome." Although he had completed about two-thirds of his book when he returned, it took him until 1977 to complete the work of literary journalism. During this time, Herr endured "paralysis, a 'massive collapse,' and depression." He required psychoanalysis to deal with his PTSD.[54]

Herr was somewhat unique in pursuing therapy to deal with his trauma. As author Eric James Schroeder (*Vietnam, We've All Been There: Interviews with American Writers*), notes: Few people talked about war correspondents (such as Herr) suffering from the psychological disability known as PTSD.[55]

One of the most famous literary journalists to suffer long-term disabling effects of covering tragedy and trauma was Truman Capote, author of the best-selling 1965 book *In Cold Blood*.[56] For six years, Capote was intimately connected to and immersed in the lives of convicted murderers Dick Hickock and Perry Smith. In biographies by Gerald Clarke and George Plimpton, friends and associates speak of the damage the writing of the book took on the health and well-being of Capote. In his 1988 biography of Capote, Gerald Clarke claims: "After *In Cold Blood* he was no longer able to summon the energy to perform that magic act (i.e., using his imagination to manufacture his happiness). Nostalgia descended into sorrow, and to those who knew him well he seemed to be in perpetual mourning, overwhelmed by a sense of loss that was no less keen because he could not say precisely what it was that had been taken from him."[57] Capote's friend Phyllis Cerf told biographer Clarke quite simply: "He never really recovered from that book."

In Norm Sims' *True Stories*, literary journalist Madeleine Blais writes:

> Capote said somewhere that he felt writing the book, or more precisely, living with the details of that story so intimately for so long, catapulted him into ill health and led to the insomnia and substance abuse that dogged him during his final years. . . . In the end, the author (Capote) may have driven himself nearly insane with the question: what purpose is served by making art out of something so vile?[58]

Journalism historian Sims concludes: "Capote, Herr and Didion all suffered difficult personal and psychological reactions as a result of such intense involvement with the people and the cultures they were reporting on. As they researched their stories, they were not separate from the worlds they were researching: they were participants."[59]

Although it isn't definitive whether these and other narrative nonfiction authors suffered psychological setbacks because of their empathy, emotional involvement, psychological transference, or any combination of these factors, their accounts serve as cautionary tales for all journalists.

A goal of this book is to discuss noteworthy developments in the field of trauma journalism since the 1990s and to cite media issues, effects, and practices that are not regularly discussed in journalism classrooms or newsrooms. As Professor Jim MacMillan of the University of Missouri and a Dart Center Ochberg Fellow observes, the media reform movement, known by some as the "culture of caring," has three key components: (1) the psychological challenges facing journalists, (2) the obligations to victims and survivors of traumatic events, and (3) the media's responsibility concerning the potential effects reporting on tragedy and trauma may have on communities of news consumers.[60]

This book includes extended sections of narrative nonfiction, such as in the emblematic story of journalist Joe Hight and the early years of the trauma journalism movement (see Chapter 2: Transformer). Firsthand accounts of journalists and representative profiles of people willing to discuss their experiences are also featured along with excerpts of published oral histories (see Chapter 3: Frontline Reporting). These chronicles offer additional documentation about the impact of dangerous and stressful reporting on journalists. But *Trauma Journalism: On Deadline in Harm's Way* is not intended to be merely a collection of tales of woe. For, as discussed in Chapters 4 through 8, there are significant advocacy, education, and reform efforts underway for trauma journalists in the turbulent twenty-first century.

Faces of Trauma Journalism:
Terry Anderson

Photo courtesy of the University of Kentucky

On a pleasant Saturday morning, April 10, 2010, in the University of Kentucky (UoK) Student Center's Worsham Theater, Journalism Professor Terry Anderson joins in a heated discussion on the role of embedded journalists in wartime. Terry, 62, a Vietnam veteran and former Marine Combat Correspondent, responds to a panel of young vets who have recently served in Iraq and Afghanistan. At about 10:30, Nate Noble, one of the panelists (all wearing dark sport coats and serious expressions), discusses the problem when a "new in-country journalist" is assigned to a platoon of troops. Often these reporters don't understand standard operating procedures and haven't received hostile-environment training, thus jeopardizing the success and safety of combat missions.

"The operational security issue that concerns me most is anything that puts soldiers at risk," says John Hearse, another panelist.

Terry Anderson, former Chief Middle East Correspondent for the AP, and hostage in Lebanon from 1985 to 1991, is organizer of this international conference on war, journalism, and history ("Covering Conflicts in the Modern World"). Terry is a burly, bull-necked, and mustachioed man who bears a striking resemblance to Teddy Roosevelt. He wears a gray tweed suit and white shirt (sans tie) and limps slightly. This man, who was imprisoned by Shiite Hezbollah partisans for 2,454 days, is now a lecturer in the UoK School of Journalism and Telecommunications. This morning he speaks in a strong, gruff voice. He grasps the microphone in his thick fingers and challenges the panel:

> I just want you to know that we in journalism are concerned about preparedness for combat situations. . . . The guys and women who are with you now quite often have no military experience, have very little training, and very little understanding of how the military operates. And we're trying to collectively figure out ways to get them better prepared to deal with the military. But your command structure has to help in that effort, too. . . . How does a small, highly trained combat unit operate, and where can you [as a journalist] fit in with the least amount of damage? This is something the military ought to be talking about.

When one of the vets replies critically, Terry holds his ground:

> You've got to accept this [embedded journalists] just as we accept that you don't like having somebody dropped in on your highly trained team when lives are at stake. But you've also got to accept that this is a decision that your command structure has decided is the way it's going to be.

In his Thursday night keynote address, Tom Curley, president and CEO of the AP, cited Terry Anderson's lifetime devotion to international and conflict reporting. Curley called Terry an enduring inspiration and discussed the vital role of war correspondents:

> But the fact is that war coverage by a free and independent media with reasonable access to the battlefield forces policy makers and strategists to deal with the reality of what is happening on the ground instead of what they want the public—or even Washington—to think. Nowhere is truth more at risk—or more elusive—than in today's wars.[61]

Curley noted how journalists face the same risks as the military (e.g., attacks by gunfire, rockets, mortars, IEDs and mines, kidnappings, and ambushes). "In this new era of warfare, journalists are targets, too," he said. "This relentless risk of harm separates war coverage from all other journalism we pursue every day."[62]

The UoK conference attracted news media from the United States and around the world, including Curley and Robert Fisk, venerable British journalist and Middle East correspondent of the (London) *Independent*, plus representatives of the BBC, the CPJ, McClatchy Newspapers, Middle Eastern press, the US Military Academy at West Point, Louisiana State University, the University of Edinburgh (Scotland), as well as documentary filmmakers, freelance journalists, and retired military personnel, including Dale Dye, a former Marine captain who served in Vietnam (where he was Terry Anderson's commanding officer) and Beirut. Dye is now an actor and military adviser on war films like *Platoon*, *Saving Private Ryan*, and, most recently, *The Pacific*.

Terry Anderson had hoped the UoK conference would encourage open and cordial dialogue. When he senses the mood in the auditorium has grown tense this Saturday morning, he draws laughter with a brief self-deprecating comment about his age. Minutes later as the first morning session ends, Terry stands at attention near the stage in the cool, starkly lit hall, his hands clasped behind his back.

The panel discussion and lively Q&A have set the tone for the rest of the day's events, featuring an impassioned afternoon presentation by Terry's friend and colleague of almost thirty years, author Robert Fisk, who has covered the Middle East since the mid-1970s. Terry introduces the 63-year-old Fisk by describing how they had traveled together in the 1980s to many strange and dangerous places. In his best-selling memoir, *Den of Lions*, Terry wrote of Fisk's "brilliant analytical mind and cold, critical look at everything that passed before him":

> I often wondered where Fisky put the pain. I know he felt it, had seen him wince, seen the anger in his eyes as we watched the bodies pile up at the scene of some bombing or pointless firefight. He had done it for so long. That's where his profound neutrality came from. He had seen them all do it, counted the bodies on everyone's side, until there could be no sides for him. What was left was just rage at everybody who misused power, low or high.[63]

In his book, Terry had commented on the adrenaline rush and self-deception that drove so many trauma journalists:

> Despite the horrors, the bodies, the blood and despair that surrounded us, the fascination never faded. And mixed with it was the awful, heady rush of danger. We covered that war almost as if it were a horror movie, feeling ourselves exempt from death, our eyes and ears wide, hearts thumping wildly, careening from sporadic encounters with wild-eyed gunmen to terrifying, stretched-out minutes huddling under shells and bombs or cowering from snipers, only to return to the Commodore Hotel, climb on a bar stool, and blandly trade the day's war stories with our colleagues over a giant gin and tonic. The pose of observer, the veteran immune to the pain of others, was just that, though—a pose, and a protection. No one, not the most cynical, blasé correspondent, got through that summer in Beirut without pain of his or her own.[64]

Toward the end of *Den of Lions*, Terry discussed how he had battled years of physical and psychological abuse as a hostage. He also dwelt on the impact of his media career:

> About journalism, I could see now what it had done to me and so many of my friends and colleagues. So much violence to take in as daily fare, so much of other people's pain, and nowhere to put it except in a few pages of copy or a couple minutes of film. No wonder I knew no more than two or three journalists still on their first marriage,* and so many who were semialcoholic, or bitter and cynical, or just plain weird. I know now I could never really go back to that. I couldn't stand any more violence . . . . (* Terry's first marriage ended after sixteen years. He has two daughters—Gabrielle, from his first marriage, and Sulome, from second wife, Madeline.)[65]

Terry Anderson says he healed from his personal trauma of two decades ago thanks to months of therapy, his renewed Catholic faith, and the support of family and friends. Today, he is working to establish an educational center at UoK to study how crises are covered by the news media.

About a week after the UoK conference had ended, Terry talked in depth about trauma journalism. He noted that our phone conversation was on April 19, 2010, the fifteenth anniversary of the horrific Oklahoma City bombing, which had claimed 168 lives.

He quoted from his poem "High Wire": "You cannot go on bathing in the world's violence unscathed, touch so many people's pain and grief, and not be burned." He discussed how twenty-some years ago while imprisoned, he had thought often about how his work, though successful on many fronts, had contributed to him being "pretty arrogant and very aggressive and probably pretty hard to get along with."

Terry then highlighted some of his accomplishments since the start of his "new life"—December 4, 1991 (the day of his release from captivity). He cofounded the Vietnam Children's Fund, which has built schools in that Southeast Asian country, attended by more than 12,000 students. He created the Father Lawrence Jenco Foundation (named for one of his fellow hostages) with an endowment to honor and support charitable and community service projects in Appalachia. Terry also serves as honorary chairperson of the CPJ, the international advocacy organization dedicated to ensuring the safety and welfare of journalists. For decades he has pushed for trauma counseling and awareness of issues such as PTSD and the need for hostile-environment training for journalists exposed to war, violence, and tragedy. He is concerned that the industry's economic problems may intimidate journalists from disclosing the emotional effects of their coverage.

Terry Anderson is an inspirational figure to many in the news business. I found this transplanted Kentuckian, who loves raising horses, to be a self-effacing man with a contagious sense of humor. He admits he "stumbled into journalism," credits many mentors and colleagues along the way, and appreciates the respect of his peers. Though well aware of the risks of being a reporter, he is convinced that:

> Most good journalists are idealistic. Their primary motivation is not curiosity or adventure. It's really a need to take the world by the lapel and shake them and say: "You need to pay attention. This is important. I need to tell you this. You need to know this."

But Terry also cautions his students to think seriously about their career choice and commitment to the field of journalism:

> It's a profession that exacts its costs from you personally and psychologically. You're probably not going to make a whole lot of money. So if you're not passionate about it, if you don't feel strongly about it, then you really shouldn't be doing it.

CHAPTER TWO

Transformer*

Oklahoman Joe Hight is a throwback to a time when most men parted their Brylcreem-glistening hair, when only Elvis had sideburns, and when you kept your suit coat on and necktie taut until quitting time. The stocky 49-year-old journalist with the high-pitched laugh may strike some as too ordinary a fellow to be a reformer. Others may correctly note that Hight didn't launch the movement to humanize newsroom culture and transform media coverage of tragedy and trauma. He was preceded by advocates in the United States and overseas. But Joe Hight learned the lessons firsthand and found a cause when terrorism struck his community, forever changing his life and those of so many others.

He was in the newsroom of the *Oklahoman* a dozen years ago, when at 9:02 a.m. on April 19, 1995, the Murrah Federal Building exploded, shaking the earth 6 miles away and sending a mushroom cloud over Oklahoma City. On that fateful day, Hight was the assignment editor at the Gaylord family-owned *Oklahoman* newspaper. Hours later he was serving as Victims Team leader, assembling a corps of reporters from varied beats, including community, business, sports, and features, and directing coverage of the men, women, and children killed and injured in the bombing. He would oversee the writing of 168 "Profiles of Life" vignettes to honor the import of those individuals lost in a senseless, savage act. There would also be stories on some of the more than 850 wounded, including inspirational tales of the youngest survivors, such as "miracle" babies found alive in the rubble.

---

* An abridged version of "Transformer" appeared in the fall 2009 issue of *River Teeth: A Journal of Nonfiction Narrative*, published by Ashland University (Ohio). However, the initial research and reporting for this extended account of Joe Hight and the trauma journalism reform movement occurred in 2006–07, the final year of Hight's term as president of the Dart Center for Journalism & Trauma.

As an experienced journalist, Hight was no stranger to death and destruction. He had reported on grisly oil field accidents, deadly natural disasters, and shocking murders. On August 20, 1986, he had supervised initial coverage of the Edmond (Oklahoma) Post Office massacre that left fifteen dead and launched the ominous phrase "going postal" into the American lexicon.

But Hight and the 150-person *Oklahoman* newsroom were in an uncharted territory in April 1995. How to report accurately and compassionately on the devastating news day after day? How to cope with the emotional impact of such a tragedy on the families of victims, on injured survivors, on a traumatized community? How to help journalists covering these stories take care of themselves?

Hight and his boss, then-managing editor Ed Kelley, watched reporters in tears as they filed their stories. Others coped as best as they could, denying their feelings, clamping down on emotions as they had been taught, driven by their work ethic, deadlines, and the belief that journalists were supposed to "just deal with it" and not bring their own "stuff" into the newsroom.

"Most of us aren't very good at admitting we have a problem," says reporter Ann DeFrange, a fixture in the newsroom since 1969. Another veteran staffer Clytie Bunyan agrees with that assessment, noting that in 1995: "Some people chose to stay stuck rather than talk about it." Bunyan, the newspaper's business editor, had been in downtown Oklahoma City on April 19 when the 4,800 pounds of explosives (jet fuel and ammonium nitrate) packed into a yellow Ryder rental truck ignited, shearing the face off the federal building, killing and maiming a thousand people and damaging some 300 structures across several city blocks.

The *Oklahoman*'s page-one headline on April 20, 1995, read: "Morning of Terror: City Struggles with Shock of Deadly Bombing." What made covering this tragic story so daunting was its scope and personal connection to the Greater Oklahoma City community. The victims were ordinary people whose children attended the same schools as reporters' kids, whose families worshipped at the same churches, and who shopped in the same stores. The local media and their families lived with this sad narrative long after the stories had been filed.

"I remember going to funerals all the time in '95," says Nan Hight, Joe's wife.

Newspaper staff (including clerks, copy messengers, secretaries, and production crews) worked overtime for weeks following the bombing. Many reporters ate meals at their desks and had to be told by supervisors to leave and get some rest. Editors like Hight didn't get home most nights until after midnight, and they were at their desks early the next morning.

Some *Oklahoman* reporters such as Penny (Owen) Cockerell and Bryan Painter found it cathartic to write their stories, especially those about the youngest survivors, including 3-year-old Brandon and 2-year-old Rebecca Denny. It helped them to process feelings by putting words to page. Both reporters had spent long hours at the bombing site and even longer days talking to relatives and friends of victims. They each spoke of the lasting effects of covering the tragedy.

Painter, a tall, imposing presence whose appearance is softened by his sad dark eyes and folksy charm, arrived at the bombing site within minutes of the blast. He recalled the surrealistic scene as "a bad Sunday night movie"—the air filled with the nauseous odor of sulfur, swirling clouds of dust, and streams of gray and blackened smoke from smoldering car fires. The cacophony of noise was deafening: police and fire sirens, building and car alarms. Stunned and wounded people walked about like zombies, covered with broken glass and blood. Medical personnel set up triage in the middle of downtown streets. Painter came home very late on April 19 with a bloodstained button-down shirt. He didn't say much to his wife, Teri, that night, and he wouldn't talk about his feelings about the bombing until months later.

"I kept myself away in 1995," he recalls. "But you take in that much emotion, and you end up staring at the ceiling tiles."

Four years later at 35, when he was named by Hight to head another Victims Team to cover a string of Oklahoma tornadoes that killed forty-four people, Painter admitted to team members that he should have sought counseling after the 1995 bombing. He encouraged his coworkers to talk about what they were experiencing, to debrief about their reactions and emotions. Many of the stories they covered were heart-wrenching, such as "Mother Sacrifices Life for Son," which ran on page 15 on May 8, 1999. *Oklahoman* reporters Mark A. Hutchinson and Ron Jackson wrote:

> As a tornado sucked Kathleen Walton from beneath an H.E. Bailey Turnpike overpass Monday near Newcastle, she quoted scripture to her 11-year-old son, said, "I love you," and let go of his hand. Levi Walton never saw his mother alive again.[2]

A year after the killer tornadoes struck Oklahoma, Painter covered the death of a popular 17-year-old bronco rider named Tyler Blount. Painter had been at the rodeo when the pale chestnut horse kicked Blount as he dangled like a rag doll, his boot caught in a stirrup. Painter rushed to the Edmond hospital, where he would console the boy's mother and father.

"I just put my notebook down," Painter says. "You try to cover victims and their families with common sense and compassion."

That night at the hospital, Pat Blount, Tyler's father, gave Painter the boy's blood-soaked shirt and vest, which he took home to his wife to dispose of. Within weeks of Blount's passing, Painter talked to his editor about a change of assignments. The 1987 Oklahoma State University

(OSU) graduate, who had first worked at an Amarillo, Texas, daily, started his career with the *Oklahoman* in 1991 on the police beat, covering car crashes, domestic violence, petty crimes, and murders. Then came the bombing in 1995, the tornadoes in 1999, and Tyler Blount's passing in 2000. By then, Painter was "tired of death." He became the features editor and eventually a columnist for the paper.

"Sometimes you wade through life the hard way," he says.

In April 1995, 26-year-old Penny (Owen) Cockerell was assigned to the newspaper's Law Enforcement Team. For months, she wrote front-page stories about the bombing and subsequent investigation. In her three years with the newspaper, the wispy, amiable UCO grad, had gravitated toward the "tough" stories, the ones that got reporters noticed but also took their toll. According to Joe Hight, himself an alumnus of UCO (then: Central State University), Cockerell was the "go-to-reporter" for crisis-related news for years. She explains that the stories she covered years ago were simply "the more interesting ones."

During the aftermath of the 1995 bombing, Cockerell says she knew counseling was available and appreciated management's responsiveness, but she didn't feel that was the right option for her. She didn't want to call attention to herself as warranting pity. What she really needed during those demanding days and nights, according to her account in a 2004 trauma journalism guide coauthored by Joe Hight, was "down time with fellow journalists . . . to talk through all the things that happened." But she added, "By the time we slowed down, everyone was so tired of the bombing that we never really got [to] have that big hashing out session."

When interviewed in July 2006, Ed Kelley, the 53-year-old editor of the *Oklahoman*, recalled a spike in absences and sick days about six months after the intense period of bombing-related news coverage. Other reporters noted that marriages and relationships ended, and emotional problems ensued among employees within a year of the bombing. Some of those who had written stories on PTSD in April 1995 were manifesting symptoms months later—recurring intrusive recollections, emotional numbing, and feelings of fear and anxiety.

Cockerell continued to cover the follow-up stories to the bombing, including the trials of the defendants in 1997 and the execution of Timothy McVeigh in 2001. She admits that her debriefings in those days would follow the time-honored journalist's tradition of meeting colleagues for drinks and after-hours commiseration. But that didn't fill the emptiness Cockerell was feeling after years of emotionally taxing news coverage. In 1999, she moved to Dallas to head the small *Oklahoman* bureau there. She married a Dallas attorney in August 1999. Since 2000, when she received a national journalism fellowship to attend a week of intensive trauma training, Cockerell has worked to educate fellow journalists on the psychological effects of victim-based reporting.

Although Cockerell and Painter never sought counseling or a formal intervention in 1995, there were reporters at the newspaper willing to talk about their emotions surrounding the most devastating and deadly act of domestic terrorism in the US history (until September 11, 2001). Some of these journalists wanted to debrief with a professional. They appreciated when editors Kelley and Hight said a counselor was available on site. Coworkers, in particular, praised Hight, noting his sensitivity, credibility, and loyalty: "He established a sense of family here." "He was very conscientious about how his staff was doing." "Joe will stand by you."

Trauma's Impact on Journalists

Charlotte Lankard, an Oklahoma City family and marriage therapist, met with newspaper reporters on the day of the bombing. The empathetic preacher's daughter would return regularly in future weeks and months to counsel staff members. More than a decade later, many would still call her a friend.

Lankard, a buoyant 67-year-old with more than a passing resemblance to the late-actress Donna Reed, was raised to conceal her emotions and to be unflappable in the face of crisis. Her upbringing gave her insights into the journalistic code of detachment—of denying personal feelings and masking emotional problems when on the job. But the dramatic events in April 1995 challenged such newsroom codes, myths, and misperceptions.

On the afternoon of April 19, Lankard was called to the *Oklahoman* to conduct a crisis intervention with a reporter. "I remember just holding her hand and listening," she says years later. The reporter had been three blocks away from the Murrah Federal Building when the explosion rocked the downtown. Within minutes, she was watching firefighters carry the dead and wounded, including infants, from the scene. Despite being shaken, she phoned in details to the newsroom. But when she tried to write her story hours later, she experienced what some described as a "meltdown" as sadness, shock, and guilt washed over her. Here she was working on the biggest story of her career while so many people were suffering. No one had prepared her for what she saw or experienced. Could anyone have been expected to?

Lankard tried to help the panic-stricken reporter and about a dozen others make sense of the senseless. She met one-on-one and in group therapy sessions. In these voluntary meetings, Lankard tried to prepare employees for possible emotional setbacks, triggered by memories and sensory recall for those who had been at the site in the hours and days after the bombing. Several women reporters met weekly with Lankard for more than a year. They still gather with her annually for a reunion of sorts.

The *Oklahoman* newspaper's efforts would attract the attention of international trauma expert Dr. Frank Ochberg, a Michigan-based psychiatrist and former associate director of the National Institute of Mental Health. In 1991, Ochberg had established a "Victims and the Media" program for MSU students, faculty, media, and mental health professionals. He had pioneered the study of PTSD in the 1970s and 1980s, noting that symptoms included recurring intrusive memories of the traumatic experience (e.g., where the person experienced a life-threatening situation, a violent assault, or other serious incident), a feeling of detachment and estrangement or psychological numbing, and a heightened sense of anxiety or a lowering of the "fear threshold." According to Ochberg, these symptoms required at least a month's duration before they could meet the criteria for PTSD, which was often accompanied by related problems such as depression, substance abuse, and other physical and mental health issues.[4]

In Ochberg's career, he had advised the FBI, Secret Service, and Scotland Yard on hostage negotiations. He also reportedly had coined the phrase "Stockholm Syndrome," describing the potential for hostages to become emotionally attached to their captors. But Ochberg's enduring legacy would be to explore the application of trauma science to journalistic coverage of conflict and tragedy. He and a small cadre of researchers and psychotherapists would discover that the impact of traumatic stories on journalists was similar in intensity to that experienced by frontline first responders, including soldiers, police officers, and firefighters.

In a November 2001 article in *American Journalism Review* ("After the Adrenaline"), Ochberg described the "heroic phase" for journalists when disaster strikes:

> At first, there is a tendency to work intensely, adrenaline flowing with a sense of purpose that is crystal clear. This phase kicks in quickly and, depending on the scope of the crisis, can last for days, weeks, even a month or two. Then comes a period of mental exhaustion and burnout, of physical fatigue and a tendency to feel confused and depressed.[5]

Ochberg noted that the potential for health and emotional problems for journalists engaged in traumatic news coverage mirrored those suffered by people in high-risk professions, including alcoholism or drug abuse, high blood pressure and heart attacks, eating disorders and depression, even PTSD and suicide. The Michigan-based psychiatrist's passion for the subject would result in the founding of an advocacy organization known as the Dart Center for Journalism & Trauma, headquartered initially at MSU and later at the UW. Funding for the organization was provided by a charitable foundation of the Dart Corporation, a Mason, Michigan, manufacturer and distributor of disposable cups.

In 1997, Frank Ochberg, 57, and Joe Hight, 39, would meet for the first time. Hight had recommended the *Oklahoman* sponsor a national workshop on coverage of disasters and tragedies, using the $10,000 award the newspaper had earned in 1996 when it received the Dart Foundation Award for Excellence in Reporting on Victims of Violence. The annual award, for sensitive, responsive news coverage of those affected by tragedy and trauma, had been established by Ochberg two years earlier as a vehicle to raise visibility of the Dart Center. Although the *Oklahoman* would not win the Pulitzer, as many at the newspaper expected for its coverage of the 1995 tragedy, there were honors from the National Press Foundation and SPJ, as well as the Dart Foundation.

Ochberg and Hight, two overachievers, would present an interesting study in comparison and contrast as their lives, philosophies, and operating styles intersected for the next dozen years. Native New Yorker Ochberg, son of a shopkeeper, had graduated with honors from Harvard College and, later, the Johns Hopkins University School of Medicine. He quickly distinguished himself in the mental health field. Known worldwide for his vision, compassion, and humor, Ochberg is fondly called the "indigenous rabbi" of the trauma journalism reform movement. With his distinctive mottled gray beard and ready smile, he is a charming, charismatic spirit. In terms of temperament and leadership techniques, the emotional Frank Ochberg is a foil to the more reserved Joe Hight.

Hight was raised as one of seven children of German-Irish-Cherokee heritage by a strict ex-Marine drill instructor father and a nurturing, protective mother in Guthrie, Oklahoma. (The state's original territorial capital and location for some memorable moments in the movie *Rain Man*.) Hight has deep-set, piercing blue-gray eyes, a wide fleshy face, and a full head of chocolate-brown hair. The one-time lanky high school tennis player has morphed into a thickly built man, who lists when he walks because of a chronic bad back. His personality is light and dark. He has a warm, caring nature, sparked by contagious bouts of cackling laughter and endearing colloquialisms ("funnest," "dang," "frickin'"). But Hight's smile can dissolve into a tight-lipped scowl, accentuated by an intense gaze. Although colleagues praise his patience, he does not suffer fools gladly, relying on a jab of sarcasm to keep people in check. A devout Roman Catholic, he draws on his faith and spirituality to bolster him on his dual missions: to reform journalistic practices and to raise awareness of mental health issues.

The Newsroom's Macho Myth

The *Oklahoman*'s progressive attempts to cover tragedy and trauma were cited in a major article, "Confronting the Horror," published in the January/February 1999 issue of *American Journalism Review* (*AJR*). Author Sherry Ricchiardi, a senior writer at *AJR*, professor at Indiana University–Purdue University Indianapolis (IUPUI), and years later a Dart Center consultant, examined the psychological stresses encountered by journalists covering war, crime, and disasters and their traditional responses.

"We're taught in journalism school that this is a macho business, that you check your feelings at the door, that your personal emotions have nothing to do with it," *Oklahoman* editor Ed Kelley said in the article. "Unlike anybody else in this society, we're supposed to shut it out. It's a myth. We can't do it."

Kelley was credited with recommending counseling services for his newsroom on the day of the Oklahoma City bombing and for the next year. A tall, polished man with patrician good looks (imagine a bespectacled Jeff Daniels or Ed Begley Jr.), Kelley knows all-too-well the impact that extended crisis coverage can have on journalists.

His words were reinforced in the *AJR* article by Martin Cohen, a Tampa, Florida, clinical psychologist, who has worked with law enforcement officers, firefighters, medical personnel, and journalists at the Poynter Institute for Media Studies: "You're not just an objective journalist doing your job, but a human being who has been exposed to something awful. To whatever degree the compassionate heart still works, there are going to be consequences for seeing someone else's suffering."

The therapeutic community uses the term transference to describe the potential for a counselor to absorb a client's emotional pain. This same potential exists for the journalist covering a tragic or traumatic story. Joe Hight refers to the "wall of grief"—the emotional effect journalists face when interviewing trauma victims. Hight hit that wall as a young reporter in July 1985 when he spent 17 straight hours covering the killing of three people in an IGA store robbery. The story had a personal connection for Hight because he knew one of the victims, a local graduate student. The next morning his managing editor, Ed Kelley, called him at home, asking Hight to go to the courthouse to write a follow-up story.

"If it's OK with you, I'd rather not," Hight recalls saying. It was an unusual exchange between a reporter and an editor. In other newsrooms, it could have led to an ultimatum. But Kelley recognized that Hight was not shirking his responsibility. He was exhausted. He was asking for a brief reprieve, a chance to regroup before returning to his job. A decade later, both men would be confronted with similar reactions from reporters covering the tragedy in Oklahoma City.

Psychologist Cohen said that when covering horrific events, journalists are injected with a kind of "poison" that can injure people without an antidote, such as debriefing about experiences and feelings.

The *Oklahoman*'s Penny (Owen) Cockerell admitted to author Sherry Ricchiardi that she "almost fell apart [on] the first anniversary [of the OKC bombing]. I'm pretty tough; I'm not the whiny or emotional type, but this blindsided me."[9]

Ricchiardi's 1999 *AJR* article discussed how "the standard newsroom script calls for stoicism" and the movement to reform journalistic practices "collides with the detached, dispassionate demeanor on which the profession prides itself."[10] She garnered commentary from journalists on concerns about being perceived by peers as too sensitive or empathetic. Chris Cramer, then-president of CNN's international news division, noted: "They fear being exiled as some kind of wimp."

In the same article, Rick Bragg, Pulitzer Prize-winning *New York Times* reporter, acknowledged that the impact of chronicling human suffering is "one of the things I always dreaded talking about." Bragg, who went from covering the Oklahoma City bombing to a multiple murder in New Orleans, and later the March 1998 murders of nine children by two classmates in Jonesboro, Arkansas, said: "I never felt it was appropriate to whine. . . . I don't feel I have a right to call myself a victim."[11]

If Bragg's comments reflect the prevailing journalistic demeanor about being emotionally affected ("We can't act like it, or we can't get the job done."), then Cramer's represent those in the profession who are trying to enlighten attitudes and operations. Ricchiardi's article stated that Cramer, "while head of the newsgathering for the British Broadcasting Corp. (BBC) in London, helped launch debriefing programs for journalists handling high-risk assignments." These assignments included coverage of war-torn Bosnia and Afghanistan. The BBC's efforts and those of other international news organizations, such as Reuters and CNN, reflected innovative approaches toward trauma journalism.[12]

Author and BBC correspondent David Loyn freely discusses the role of psychological intervention for trauma journalists. He sought brief crisis counseling following harrowing assignments in Kosovo in 1998 and after being embedded with the Taliban during its takeover of Afghanistan at the end of the twentieth century. When a thief arrested for stealing his videographer's camera was executed before his eyes (despite Loyn's pleas to spare his life), the BBC correspondent and his cameraman knew they had to escape. Loyn made it home safely but told newsroom management he needed a break from conflict reporting. And he met with Royal Air Force psychiatrists to help expel disturbing memories.

"I had to puke on the carpet," he says metaphorically and matter-of-factly.

Most reporters aren't as forthcoming as Loyn. For centuries, journalists have witnessed war, violence, and chaos, the unspeakable, and unimaginable. Covering such stories is part of their duty and responsibility, they will proclaim.

"You're supposed to 'cowboy up'," says Dave Forstate, a Pittsburgh-based news videographer whose camera has captured tragic events for almost thirty years. His first major traumatic story was the Kansas City Hyatt Hotel Skywalk collapse in July 1981, where more than one hundred people died. Forstate says it never occurred to him that he could have benefited from a debriefing after spending hours filming death and destruction.

Other journalists like Jim Wooten, former ABC-TV News correspondent, speak of months of emotional "downtime" between trying assignments. Wooten's "armpits," as he calls them, included the following: the 1973 Yom Kippur War, the conflict in Bosnia and Kosovo, Operations Desert Storm and Iraqi Freedom, Afghanistan, Beirut, Chechnya, the Congo, El Salvador, Ethiopia, Eritrea, Granada, Haiti, Interfada I and Interfada II (West Bank and Gaza), Nicaragua, Northern Ireland, Northern Iraq, Rwanda, Somalia, and Uganda.

In November 2006, Wooten recalls how he was driven by the exciting nature of war and conflict stories, but he admits that for years he would "click off emotionally and just do my job." Now retired, the 69-year-old says he would probably have been better served if he had sought counseling along the way. However, taking that step would have required significant "consciousness raising."

Ron Steinman, a contemporary of Wooten's, who was NBC-TV's bureau chief in Saigon during the Vietnam War, wrote in an October 2005 online article, "Trauma: Journalism's Hidden Malady," that in his long broadcast journalism career he saw "breakdowns, near breakdowns and suffering by the men and women who covered these events for periods lasting just a few weeks to many years."[13]

Steinman's words were reminiscent of those of famed World War II correspondent Ernie Pyle, who was killed in April 1945. Before he died, Pyle wrote: "I've been immersed in it too long. My spirit is wobbly and my mind is confused. The hurt has become too great."[14]

In calling for twenty-first-century reform, Steinman, who acknowledged the advocacy work of the Poynter Institute ("when assessing the possibility of stress-induced trauma") said: "Every news organization should make trauma control part of the way it treats its staff. We in the media and the public will be better for it."[15]

Covering Community-Based Violence

On April 20, 1999, four years and one day after the Oklahoma City bombing, a new tragedy would dominate national headlines—the murders and suicides at Columbine High School in Littleton, Colorado. The horrifying event would generate renewed interest among the media about the psychological impact of reporting such traumatic stories.

In *Covering Violence: A Guide to Ethical Reporting about Victims and Trauma*, photojournalist David Handschuh admitted the Columbine tragedy had a lasting effect, haunting him for months: "I cried at Columbine. A lot of photographers stood outside the church that day and did a lot of self-reflection. We asked ourselves why we do what we do and how we do it."[16]

Two years later, Handschuh would be seriously injured by falling debris while photographing the 9/11 terrorist attacks in New York City. An adjunct professor of photojournalism at New York University (NYU) since 1995, Handschuh has been a Poynter Institute Media Ethics Fellow, a Dart Center Ochberg Fellow, and a researcher studying the effects of trauma on visual journalists. In 1994, he coauthored the *National Media Guide for Emergency and Disaster Incidents*. He currently serves on the board of directors of News Coverage Unlimited, an international organization that provides support for journalists exposed to tragedy and trauma in their work.

"Newsgathering can be hazardous to your emotional health," Handschuh says. "My hope is that we become more aware and more helpful to others as journalists."

During the last decade, Handschuh has joined Hight, Ochberg, Cockerell, and a network of activists engaged in media reform. Other communication professionals have become actively involved. Case in point: Barb Monseu, president of the National Center for Critical Incident Analysis (NCCIA), which studies political violence, pandemic threats, and crises involving law enforcement and the media.

In April 1999, Monseu was an assistant superintendent in Jefferson County, Colorado, responsible for three school districts, including the one overseeing Columbine High School. Monseu implemented crisis management and media relations programs after the shootings. Her involvement in the Colorado tragedy would lead to her participation with the Dart Center for Journalism & Trauma.

In fall 2001, she and Dr. Elana Newman, a University of Tulsa psychology professor and Dart Center research director, would direct a six-month effort to assist journalists covering 9/11 at Dart Center-Ground Zero (DCGZ) in lower Manhattan. Two years later, Monseu would serve as vice president on the international Dart Center's executive committee.

"Journalists are the public's surrogates as witnesses to grief, suffering, and tragedy," Monseu says.

Trauma Journalism Research

By the end of the twentieth century, researchers had started investigating the effects of traumatic journalism coverage. In 1999, Professor Roger Simpson and doctoral student James Boggs published an insightful article about emotional stress, based on the reactions of 131 reporters, photographers, and editors from Michigan and Washington State.[17] Nearly half of those surveyed said they were not prepared for their first "deadly" assignments, such as automobile crashes. The results suggested that the youngest reporters were frequently sent to bloody scenes, whose images and memories were the hardest to process. This study concluded that the longer respondents were exposed to trauma, the more likely the prevalence of avoidance tendencies and intrusive thoughts, and the more difficult it was to deal with those emotions unless there was some formal support.

In a *Seattle Times* story, published just months after 9/11, Simpson discussed how journalists covering traumatic stories are subject to the transfer of feelings and emotions from other first responders, victims, and survivors:

> If you are an observer, it doesn't matter how hard you try to be objective— you talk to survivors, police and rescuers; this begins to take a toll on your own emotional well-being. You are sharing everybody's else's pain without a chance to address your own.[18]

But Simpson and Coté in their 2006 book, *Covering Violence: A Guide to Ethical Reporting about Victims and Trauma,* also acknowledged: "While some journalists are reporting on violence with extraordinary sensitivity, others do continue to treat victims as props for stories about human cruelty but props without a chance to affect the way the stories are told. It isn't surprising that the public and the people in the stories complain about insensitive, callous and excessive coverage."[19]

In January 2000, the Dart Center for Journalism & Trauma was formally recognized by the UW Department of Communication, funded with an initial grant of $200,000.[20] Simpson was named executive director of the advocacy organization, a position he would hold for six years until replaced by former East Coast investigative reporter Bruce Shapiro. By that point, the organization's annual operating budget had grown to $1.4 million.

Tragedy Strikes Again

Joe Hight was promoted in 1999 to become one of two managing editors at the *Oklahoman*, overseeing features, research, and development (e.g., external relations). That same year he recruited Charlotte Lankard to write a weekly column for the newspaper. Readers would draw comfort from the words of the then-60-year-old therapist who had known her share of pain and loss. At

40, she had almost died in a rock-climbing accident. At 50, she was divorced after thirty years of marriage. Since 1996, she had been grieving the death of her second husband and former high school sweetheart, who had died unexpectedly of pancreatic cancer after just three years of marriage.

In her 2007 memoir, *It's Called Life*, Lankard explained her spiritual journey to healing:

> I discovered my faith held me fast, anchored me, sustained me, and gave me hope when all I had was despair. . . . I discovered a strength and courage within me that would not allow me to give up. I discovered that I am a woman who simply refused to wallow in self pity for very long, not because I am noble, but because I soon tire of it and find it boring.[21]

Lankard and Hight, native Oklahomans, appear cut from the same sturdy cloth. Both have been buffeted by personal tragedies. And each has responded with a resilient spirit and gritty resolve. The same could be said for the Greater Oklahoma City community, which in April 2000 witnessed the dedication of its national memorial, an inspiring monument of towering black stone and soothing pools of water. The centerpiece is the outdoor amphitheater arrangement of 168 metallic chair sculptures (including dozens of smaller chairs for the children who perished in the bombing) lining a grassy knoll where the federal building once stood.

For Joe Hight, the year 2000 would end with painful memories of yet another victim of violence. His oldest brother, Paul, a former Catholic priest and diagnosed paranoid schizophrenic, would be killed on a snowy night on December 14 in a confrontation at his apartment complex with Oklahoma City police. He would be the twelfth person suffering from mental illness to be shot by the police and the fifth killed in Oklahoma City in 2000.[22]

Joe Hight didn't seek grief counseling after Paul's death. Instead he said he channeled his emotions into advocacy for mental health reform in Oklahoma City and throughout the state. Six months after Paul Hight's shooting, the Oklahoma Legislature voted to give the state's Mental Health Department a $12 million increase in funding, including money to be used for a mobile crisis intervention team in Oklahoma County. In December 2001, the *Oklahoman* reported that state and local officials were taking steps to avoid deadly encounters, such as had occurred a year earlier when Paul Hight was killed. A new program was being launched to train up to 100 officers of the Oklahoma City Police Department in how to defuse situations involving people with mental illness.[23]

The Crisis Intervention Team (CIT) police model had been pioneered in Memphis, Tennessee, a decade earlier. It provided police with alternative approaches to help stabilize mentally ill people in a crisis. In addition, CIT police officers were equipped with less lethal weapons, such as Tasers, to help immobilize people needing to be subdued.

For several years since Paul's death, Joe Hight has served on the Oklahoma Governor's and Attorney General's Blue Ribbon Task Force on Mental Health, Substance Abuse and Domestic Violence. He sits on the task force with police officials, representatives of the mental health community, ministers, educators, and legislators who are trying to address the "escalating health and public policy crisis" in Oklahoma.

"What happened to my brother taught me that you have to fight stigmas in life, and overcoming those stigmas is a challenge worth pursuing," he says.

Born to Lead

Joe Hight's systematic efforts after Paul's death demonstrated a steely resolve that had been instilled in him as a boy by his father, Wilber. When Joe tackled his next major issue—trauma journalism—he knew he would have to fight once again for what he believed in despite the consequences. Hight was no Hamlet. He knew what was expected of him. It was how he had been raised.

He had been groomed for leadership since childhood in the modest, red-brick ranch-style home on the outskirts of Guthrie, a town of about 10,000. His larger-than-life father, Wilber, who had fought at Guadalcanal in World War II, dominated the Hight household. A neighbor recalls: "That Mr. Hight, he didn't mess around. And you didn't mess around with him."

The former Marine drill sergeant would deliver sermons to young Joe and his other siblings before Sunday Mass. This iron-jawed Oklahoman, who had left home at 16 and won all-state honors in high school football, wanted his six children to learn early and well that the world wasn't for the weak of heart. (A seventh child, a daughter, had drowned as a 2-year-old.)

You were born to be a leader, Wilber would say, pacing in front of his attentive audience. He expected the Hight kids to step up and be accountable. *You have to pay the fiddler if you want to dance.* Wilber's point was clear: The earlier Joe and his siblings learned those lessons, the better off they'd be.

Joe Hight remembers his parents as "amazingly resilient." His father worked the 4 p.m.-to-midnight shift in the logistics (supply) center at Tinker Air Force Base. Then from dawn until early afternoon, he tended to the 5-acre "garden" adjacent to their house. Joe's mother, Pauline, was a slight woman who was "the emotional foundation" of the Hight home. She also worked long hours in the garden, which provided the family of eight with much of their food. The garden was the "envy of the town," according to Joe, who with his parents and siblings raised corn, okra, potatoes, tomatoes, squash, cantaloupes, and watermelon, as well as apples and grapes.

To earn spending money, Joe sold tomatoes to area restaurants. He also sold golf balls he would retrieve from the private golf course across the road from his house. The Hights were frugal folks who stayed close to home.

"My travels as a boy consisted of going to Wichita Falls, Texas, for glasses," Joe Hight recalls.

Like many Oklahomans, Hight rooted for the St. Louis Cardinals baseball team (Lou Brock was his favorite). He also painted, wrote poetry, performed in high school plays, and had a stint as a teenage disc jockey on a local radio station. The slender youngest son was considered too small to follow in his father's footsteps on the gridiron. But he would join his dad as a diehard fan for University of Oklahoma football. To this day, Joe Hight bleeds Sooner crimson every autumn.

Although he describes his youth as happy, there was little time for dawdling or daydreaming. *Get off your duff*, was one of Wilber Hight's favorite expressions. He led by example as well as by his intimidating presence ("My father was powerful in his physical strength and in his ability to deliver a message."). When he wasn't working at the air force base or in the 5-acre garden, Wilber was building furniture in the two-story barn he had erected behind the house. In later years, the elder Hight also taught woodworking and shop skills at the Guthrie Job Corps. For a couple summers, Joe coached softball and basketball in the corps' recreation division. He recalls being challenged by tough inner-city youth from New York City, Philadelphia, St. Louis, Dallas, and other urban areas. But Joe, a teenager himself, never backed down, earning the respect of his players.

Hight had confronted racial issues at Guthrie High School, where whites barely outnumbered blacks. He tried to stay out of trouble, but he remembers getting into shoving matches and being on the receiving end of sucker punches.

For a man who would make journalism his career, one would envision the younger Hight as having had a newspaper route or penning stories for his high school paper. Neither was the case. At 16, he worked briefly in the circulation department of the Guthrie newspaper. But he wasn't drawn to the profession. In fact, he was somewhat adrift after graduating from high school in 1975. But that didn't last long, not with Wilber Hight on the case.

"My father sat me down one day and said: 'You have a choice. You can either go into the Army, Navy, or Marines. Or you can go to college.'" Wilber delivered the ultimatum from his rocking chair (which Joe still has today) while his attentive son sat on a nearby couch.

He recalls that it took about a minute to decide he was going to college. He speaks respectfully about that living room dialogue, his voice rising as he accents the recollection with noticeable pauses.

I think he was saying that if I wanted to further my life, I had to make some decisions about doing that. He thought the military would be good for discipline. I thought college would be a better place for me.

Joe Hight chose Central State University (later named—University of Central Oklahoma), where he went to work at the student newspaper (*The Vista*) only at the urging of a classmate who told him it would boost his grade in a required communication course. But soon he was hooked. He started as a sportswriter and quickly became sports editor. By his senior year, the journalism major became newspaper editor and, he says, "one of the most powerful students on campus." When Hight graduated in June 1980, he was named "outstanding senior male student" and "outstanding journalism graduate." (Dr. Terry Clark, current chair of UCO's mass communication department, describes Joe Hight as a "career-driven person of high standards and incredible loyalty.")

Over the next four and a half years, Hight was a sports editor at the *Guthrie Daily Leader* and then promoted to managing editor. Hight became an area reporter at the *Shawnee News-Star*, rising to city editor. He was a general assignment/wire editor at the *Lawton Constitution*. He was editor of an Edmond paper for two weeks before it folded. Hight then freelanced primarily for the *Oklahoman* but also for other publications including *USA Today*. In February 1985, the *Oklahoman* hired him as a metro section reporter.

In his free time, the 6-foot, 200-pound Hight enjoyed weight lifting, tennis matches, and playing video games with his pals, challenging the image of the dashing, hard-drinking, devil-may-care reporter. He dated regularly but was never very serious about romance. In his late twenties, he was active in the young adult program at St. John's Catholic Church in Edmond, near where he was living north of Oklahoma City. One evening at church, he met Nan, a trim athletic woman with a ready smile. Nan says she pursued Joe, asking him to a Sadie Hawkins dance on Valentine's Day 1986. He says he "doesn't remember it that way." They both agree that they "clicked immediately." Less than a month after their first date, he proposed on March 10. Her caring nature reminded him of his mother, who had passed away just three months earlier at age 65. She was attracted by his "good heart and gentleness" and impressed with his strong work ethic.

On September 20, 1986, Joe, 28, and Nan, 26, were married in a large wedding (375 invitations) at St. John's. Joe wrote a poem for the ceremony, and his father, widower Wilber Hight, wept in the church. The "giddy" married couple honeymooned in Eureka Springs, Arkansas.

Before and after their daughters were born (Elena in 1989 and Elyse in 1992), Joe and Nan enjoyed vacations through the western United States. On one memorable road trip, they invited seventy-something Wilber along. Nan recalls how he would "roust" everybody before dawn, load up the car, and insist on driving at least 3 hours before stopping for breakfast. No one would dare complain, at least not to his face.

As a young girl, Elena Hight recalled her grandfather as "rough." Joe is quick to step in and explain that for many of those years, Wilber was being treated for prostrate cancer and was just a little cantankerous. In December 1999, Wilber Hight lost his long battle with cancer at age 83.

When Hight talks of his values, he often refers to his father and the lessons he imparted. Those lessons and his hardscrabble upbringing keep Joe pragmatic as the trauma journalism movement encounters entrenched attitudes, skepticism, and the status quo in perhaps the most cynical of professions. He knows that the same mind-set that enables a reporter to ferret out information, to sort through the facts, and to write an accurate story on deadline may also prevent that same reporter from reflecting on the damage such coverage may be having on him and others. Hight also realizes that the average reader or viewer of the news doesn't necessarily reflect on the lives of journalists presenting these stories, just as the typical diner isn't interested in the personal side of waiters or waitresses. Just bring me what I ordered. Take care of yourself on your own time.

More Mourning

A month after Joe's brother Paul died, Hight and others at the *Oklahoman* mourned again when, on January 27, 2001, a plane carrying the OSU basketball team and university officials crashed, killing all aboard. According to sportswriter Berry Tramel, the OSU plane crash affected him more emotionally than any other newsroom tragedy he had covered. He had written in-depth stories of firefighters during April 1995 in Oklahoma City. He had covered the deadly 1999 tornadoes. But the OSU plane crash struck him the hardest because of the personal connection he had with players, coaches, and others on that plane.

"That story wiped me out physically and emotionally," says Tramel. Joe Hight considers Tramel one of his newsroom "champions," a reporter who is both popular and respected. He is someone Joe relies on to talk to fellow reporters about the value of debriefing or crisis counseling, if the situation warrants such action. Tramel, himself, had talked with Charlotte Lankard to sort out his emotions after covering the tragic 1995 bombing.

The *Oklahoman*'s experiences with community-based trauma would be shared with newsrooms on the East Coast after September 11, 2001. Nine days following the destruction of the World Trade Center's twin towers, 20 miles due south of White Plains, New York, Henry Freeman, editor and vice president/news of the *Journal News* newspaper, spoke with Ed Kelley, Joe Hight and other editors. Freeman was concerned about the impact of stress on his newsroom.

"The call to the *Oklahoman* was invaluable," Freeman says, sharing how he was advised to consider his news coverage as a marathon not a sprint, despite the frantic pace of reporting in the aftermath of the tragedy. In the days and weeks to come, the newspaper would cover more than 200 funerals, and reporters and photographers would speak of "fatigue factor" and "heartbreaking memories." Freeman had learned of the role counseling played at the *Oklahoman*. Within days, group-debriefing sessions were held at the *Journal News*. Perhaps more importantly, Henry Freeman used self-disclosure to connect with his newsroom, sending out e-mails in which he talked about his own emotions and the effect of the tragedy on the southern Westchester County community. He urged reporters to treat victims' families with dignity, and he encouraged his staff to take care of themselves.

Elaine Silvestrini, who had received a 2000 Dart Center Ochberg (trauma journalism) Fellowship (along with Penny Cockerell of the *Oklahoman*), was working as a reporter at the *Asbury Park Press* (New Jersey) on 9/11. She was also an internal ombudsman at the paper, conveying concerns and requests from staff to management. One of her first tasks was to secure pizza for those who were working long hours after the terrorist attacks. A simple enough request, it seems. But Silvestrini remembers that some in upper management groused about spending money for newsroom meals. She said that less than a week after September 11, one editor commented: *I think people should be back to normal by now.*

Silvestrini, who later worked at the *Tampa Tribune*, knew better. She had been sensitized through her interactions with the Dart Center to realize the "cumulative effects of covering sad stories." She e-mailed Joe Hight for his advice on validating the emotions of fellow stressed-out staffers.

"He was extremely helpful," Silvestrini says about Hight. "It was like talking with a minister. He 'walks the walk.'"

The unparalleled events of 9/11 raised awareness of traumatic news issues among media advocates and researchers. Three days after the collapse of the World Trade Center towers, Al Tompkins of the Poynter Institute for Media Studies, posted the following statement on the *Poynteronline* website:

> Journalists' symptoms of traumatic stress are remarkably similar to those of police officers and firefighters who work in the immediate aftermath of tragedy, yet journalists typically receive little support after they file their stories. While public-safety workers are offered debriefings and counseling after a trauma, journalists are merely assigned another story.[24]

Canadian psychiatrist Anthony Feinstein observed: "Domestic journalists of all types post-September 11 had significantly more PTSD symptoms than

domestic journalists pre-September 11." The levels of PTSD among these journalists now approached those of war correspondents.[25]

Author Jim Willis, who had covered the 1995 Oklahoma City bombing, acknowledges the psychological effects of traumatic news coverage. He references researchers like Feinstein and others who have studied PTSD. But he also refers to the personal growth that is possible during trying times. In other words, not everyone who is engaged in dangerous or stressful news-gathering is negatively affected. The vast majority of individuals recover from exposure to trauma, and journalists are arguably sturdier emotionally than others. As Willis wrote in *The Human Journalist*, citing an earlier study of American newspaper editors: "Many individuals flourish under stress, and if they have control, they are highly productive and enjoy the challenge."[26]

Trauma Journalism Ambassadors

During the last decade, newsrooms in the United States and abroad turned to international trauma journalism "ambassadors" Joe Hight and Frank Ochberg for counsel in response to tragedies such as Columbine, 9/11, the 2004 South Asian tsunami, Hurricanes Katrina and Rita, the Nickel Mines, Pennsylvania (Amish) school shootings, and the 2007 Virginia Tech tragedy. Their target audiences were crisis journalists. Their message: promoting the ethical coverage of trauma and the ethical treatment of those affected by tragedy. The two men addressed the press in areas of conflict (Northern Ireland) and tragedy, such as Port Arthur (Tanzania), Australia, where a man named Martin Bryant went on a rampage and killed thirty-five people in 1996.

Hight, who met with journalist groups on a two-week trip to Australia in 2006 on the tenth anniversary of the Bryant massacre, speaks of how the victims of tragedies (and their families) have touched his life and those of other reporters. "That's the blessing," he says, "not the tragedy itself but the people who trust you to share their stories.

Joe Hight's final year as president of the Dart Center began at an evening reception on November 4, 2006, for the new class of Ochberg Fellows at the Renaissance Hollywood (California) Hotel. Hight was dressed crisply in a navy suit, white shirt, and gray and blue checked tie. Per usual, his black tassel loafers were polished. He sat at a small round table sipping a glass of red wine and chatting with executive committee members who passed by, such as Penny Cockerell, president of the Dart Society, Elana Newman, Dart Center research director, and Cait McMahon, director, Dart Centre Australasia.

Cockerell was representing the "spin-off" group of 60-plus former Ochberg Fellows (chosen since 1999). Known as the Dart Society, this nonprofit organization of journalists work to advance the compassionate and ethical coverage of trauma, conflict, and social injustice. In 2005–06, group volunteers had worked with reporters from hurricane-stricken Louisiana and Mississippi. Their efforts would subsequently be chronicled in a documentary ("Breaking News, Breaking Down"), written and produced by Dart Society board member and broadcast journalist Mike Walter.

At the November 2006 Dart Center reception, Hight was content to observe the goings on, while an ebullient Frank Ochberg worked the room, and executive director Bruce Shapiro shepherded the nine new Ochberg Fellows. The group included Sharon Schmickle, a reporter for the *Minneapolis Star Tribune*, who had covered conflict in Iraq and Afghanistan, the aftermath of the South Asian tsunami, and school shootings in Red Lake and Rocori high schools in Minnesota.

Her *Star Tribune* colleague Paul McEnroe, a 2005 Ochberg Fellow, addressed a panel session the next day on war coverage at the annual conference of the International Society for Traumatic Stress Studies (ISTSS). McEnroe talked about his time in Iraq and his concerns for young journalists who may be ill equipped for war reporting and thus at risk physically and emotionally. He urged young reporters to be extremely cautious and to "suss it out," a term the BBC correspondents used, referring to taking minimal risks when on assignment in a conflict zone. McEnroe became emotional when advising his fellow journalists to "have the courage to talk honestly about your vulnerabilities."

Several members of the Dart Center's executive committee were at the November 4 Los Angeles hotel reception, including Edwin (Ed) Chen, formerly of the *Los Angeles Times* and later a White House correspondent with Bloomberg News Service. Chen had first coined the term "modern journalist" to refer to the type of empathetic reporting advocated by the Dart Center. Joe Hight subsequently worked on defining the criteria, which he used in almost all of his seminars with media audiences. In Hight's estimation, the modern journalist: understands that you can be aggressive, tough, and sensitive at the same time; knows how to treat victims of violence and tragedy; knows how to be ethical during tragedies; learns how to take care of him or herself; knows that every newsroom role, from reporter to assignment editor to copy editor to designer to photographer to artist, is important in the coverage of tragedy; understands the effect of the coverage; realizes that mistakes in the short term can cause detrimental long-term effects; holds him or herself to the highest standards during disasters, rather than lowering them for the sake of being first.

Another familiar Dart Center executive committee member in Los Angeles in November 2006 was Mark Brayne, director, Dart Centre Europe. A British broadcast news correspondent for decades, Brayne became a therapist in the 1990s, working on innovative media training programs for the

BBC and other news organizations across Europe, Scandinavia, the Middle East, and Russia. A couple months earlier, Brayne had come to the United States for a series of Dart Center seminars on traumatic news coverage, codirected with colleagues Joe Hight and Bruce Shapiro, with staff of the *Times-Picayune* (*T-P*) (New Orleans) newspaper. These sessions followed earlier post-Katrina workshops in Biloxi and New Orleans, cosponsored with the Poynter Institute.

In December 2006, Joe Hight and former Dart Center vice president, Barb Monseu, codirected a seminar in Lancaster, Pennsylvania, with area media who had covered the shooting of ten girls in a one-room school house in the Amish community of Nickel Mines. The day-long session ("Trauma: Covering and Recovering. How to Report on Tragedy and Stay Healthy in the Process") was held December 9, in the cozy downtown Lancaster Pressroom restaurant, framed by lit Christmas wreaths and garlands and dozens of poinsettias. In addition to the approximately fifty local and regional journalists, two Pennsylvania state troopers and two Amish couples were in attendance, including the grandparents of one of the five murdered Amish girls.

The Amish ("these gentle people") told those listening aptly in the room that they were "weary of the media and don't want to answer questions anymore. It's time to move on and leave the families alone. Give them time to grieve."

Joe Hight would later write in an online story ("Local Tragedy, National Spotlight"), posted December 26, 2006, on the Dart Center website, that the Amish community and the local journalists were upset by the actions of the national media who descended on their community, disrupting long-honored customs and displaying the type of rude, insulting, and insensitive behavior that angers and disgusts the general public.[27]

In his remarks at the seminar, the dark-suited Hight was equal parts preacher and professor as he spoke for some 90 minutes without notes. He moved about the cluster of round tables, telling the gathered journalists to empathize with victims, that it's OK to say they're sorry, and to follow the Golden Rule (e.g., NEVER ask: How do you feel?). At times, Hight's voice cracked as he shared poignant accounts of loss from Oklahoma City and from his own life—when his brother Paul was killed. But Hight also injected doses of levity and self-deprecating wit, such as his failed "Okie" attempts to correctly pronounce "Lan-CAS-ter."

After lunch, Barb Monseu was an engaging speaker who looked as if she would be as confident addressing a boardroom audience as this dining room gathering. The comely bespectacled brunette used PowerPoint slides to discuss media—community relations: "We need to find better ways to better understand the challenges of each other's jobs and resolve . . . misconceptions about each other's interests and motives." She and Hight then adroitly handled several minutes of Q&A, displaying their expertise, mutual respect, and friendship.

Linda Espenshade, a reporter with Lancaster Newspapers, and co-coordinator of the seminar, had introduced Joe Hight as a "man with a passion." In contrast, she admitted she had been surprised that many of her fellow reporters who covered the Amish school shootings said the story didn't really affect them. For them, these accounts had no more emotional impact than any other story. But Espenshade noted that these "unaffected" reporters were typically young and had no children. That wasn't the case with Espenshade, a parent who, after spending hours in the Amish community following the crime, returned home with "a sickening sense of having been way too close to tragedy. Way too close to the reality that I don't know if I will be alive tomorrow, or if I will see my children again when they go off to school. I came away with an overwhelming sense of how fragile our lives are."

That crisp December evening after the seminar, Joe Hight returned to his Lancaster hotel room. He called home and spoke to his wife, Nan, and his two spirited auburn-haired teenage daughters, Elena and Elyse. They were squabbling over something silly. Joe had to play peacemaker. At the end of the call, he was tired but glad everyone back in Oklahoma was safe and sound.

Time of Transition

In early 2007, president Joe Hight had listed three primary concerns for the Dart Center in the months ahead: (1) selecting his successor and electing an executive committee (EC) vice president and secretary, (2) deciding on the potential relocation of the Dart Center from the UW, where it had been headquartered since 2000, and (3) hiring a consultant to conduct an audit of the Dart Center's governance, management structure, operating principles and processes, and its long-term planning needs. This audit would affect issues such as the role of executive director Bruce Shapiro, a possible reorganization of the Center's staff, and its operations worldwide, including expansion into Latin America, Africa, and Asia.

"They couldn't make this easy on me, could they?" Hight jokes months later, but his laughter is short lived as he evaluates the key tasks facing him and the executive committee before his second two-year term ends. He wants to ensure a proper structure to enhance future growth, but he's also committed to preserving the Dart Center's mission of being accessible to the "frontline journalist."

On a warm July 2007 morning, Hight sips cups of hot apple cider (never tea or coffee), as he works at his desk still wearing his suit coat. He routinely multitasks, checking phone messages and e-mail while working his Blackberry. His two-room office overlooks the entrance to the sleek twelve-story dark metallic and tinted glass headquarters building ("the tower") that dominates the adjoining low-rise commercial property on the outskirts of Oklahoma City. His office walls are lined by framed landscape photos of his native state, including beautiful sunsets and a decorated downtown Guthrie at Christmas. The most eye-catching photo is of a grizzled cowboy in leather chaps and a purple shirt at some rundown Western storefront, accompanied by his trusty white horse. Nearby sits an old blue-and-red Pepsi machine.

Joe is like a burr, a sticker, Frank Ochberg says, noting Hight's persistent, detail-driven operating style. Hight doesn't argue with that characterization. In fact, he gets a kick out of being called "a burr." Although his years as president of the Dart Center have been "gratifying," he says it has also been "exhausting" balancing that responsibility, his managing editor job at the *Oklahoman*, and his family life.

During the next few months, Hight would rely primarily on his weekly conference calls with Ochberg, Shapiro, and Beth Frerking, the vice president who had replaced Barb Monseu on the executive committee in 2006, to advance the Dart Center agenda. On average, Hight had been on the road a few days a month for four years, performing his presidential duties, delivering speeches, and conducting training seminars. But in the spring of 2007, he was thankful to have more time to spend at home with his family, attending his daughters' musical recitals, poetry readings, and athletic events.

He was also deeply involved in a major design overhaul at the *Oklahoman* that would affect not only the future look of the newspaper and its multiplatform presence, but also how stories are written in print and online (e.g., greater use of narrative leads in print and standardizing the inverted pyramid story structure online). These were substantive changes that Hight and others believed were vital to retaining readership and advertising dollars and maintaining the newspaper's leadership position as an information source in the Oklahoma City metro area.

But Joe Hight also knew that tragedy and trauma followed no schedule. Unexpected horror, sorrow, and loss could strike a community without warning or reason. So it was on April 16, 2007, when a gunman (named Seung-Hui Cho) killed thirty-two students and professors, then himself at VTU. As Hight noted in an e-mail two days later, the campus killing spree would become the worst mass murder in US history (by a single gunman) and second only to the 1996 Port Arthur (Tasmania), Australia, massacre in recent world history. He wrote that journalists covering the latest tragedy should remember that their reporting affects the families of victims, the survivors, and the community: "Finally, journalists must realize that the stories which will have the most effect will be those about the victims' lives, instead of the ones of how they died."

On Sunday May 20, 2007, Hight was moderator at a closing session of the National Writers Workshop (NWW), cosponsored by the *Wichita Eagle* newspaper and the Poynter Institute, in Wichita, Kansas. An estimated two hundred fifty people came to hear Robert (Bobby) Bowman, the clean-cut, enthusiastic 21-year-old managing editor of the *Collegiate Times* (*CT*) student newspaper at Virginia Tech. The young journalist, majoring in industrial systems engineering, impressed Hight and others as he recounted the drama on campus and in the newsroom during the hours and days after the shootings. Bowman noted that he, his editor-in-chief, Amie Steele, and other *CT* staff depended on instinct, their attachment to the Virginia Tech community, and guidance from their faculty adviser. Kelly Furnas had given the student journalists an impromptu 30-minute workshop on how to approach family members and gather material before they wrote and published a special ten-page section containing the thirty-two vignettes on the victims' lives. Print and web editions of the *CT*, which received millions of hits, were produced in the aftermath of the tragedy, despite the constant calls from national and international media and the fact that student reporters were leaving because classes had been canceled, and parents wanted their children home.

"We did a good job of covering it not only for the victims but especially for their families," said Bowman. "It was close to all of us."[28]

At the NWW session, Joe Hight spoke of the reporting challenges facing journalists who live in and love a community that has been assailed by violence. After the event, Hight continued to receive e-mails from Bowman for several weeks. He told him he would come to Virginia Tech, if Bowman and the *CT* student journalists ever needed visits from him or other Dart Center officials. Hight believed that Bowman, despite never covering a violent incident before April 2007, did several things to take care of himself during and after the crisis, including debriefing with fellow staff members and the newspaper adviser, and by getting away and spending time with family when the term ended.

But Hight emphasized that colleges need to think seriously about what situations they're sending their inexperienced student journalists into when covering violence, tragedy, or trauma. "I think it is becoming increasingly important that college journalism programs incorporate trauma training into their curricula as standard for anyone receiving a degree," Hight said, noting that nationally only the UW, MSU, and UCO offered trauma journalism courses. One encouraging sign, however, was that dozens of journalism educators from across the country had attended two Dart Center-sponsored weekend seminars at Louisiana State University and the University of Oklahoma in spring 2007.

On June 2, 2007, Hight spoke to the Bluegrass chapter of SPJ in Lexington, Kentucky, site of a fatal plane crash in 2006.

Seminar attendants included print and broadcast reporters and journalism students from the University of Kentucky and Eastern Kentucky University. He reminded those in the audience that unintended generalizations in news stories, such as "the community is still grieving," could actually offend victims and their families by perpetuating coverage of the tragedy.

On June 14, in a conference call vote by the fourteen executive committee members, Joe Hight's successor as Dart Center president was vetted and accepted in a unanimous vote. Deb Nelson, a Pulitzer Prize-winning investigative journalist, former president of IRE (Investigative Reporters and Editors), and a faculty member at the University of Maryland, would officially assume her two-year term at the November meeting in Washington, DC. Hight was pleased with Nelson's selection, citing her credentials and leadership ability.

In late July 2007, Hight was on the road again—this time by car 5 hours north to Kansas City. He traveled with soft-spoken eldest daughter, Elena, who would be attending college in the fall. Joe enjoyed the company of family on business trips whenever possible, and he seemed like the average dad with a sweet tooth as he drove his maroon 2007 Dodge Charger up the interstate, sipping his strawberry "slushy" and nibbling Werther's caramel candies. Along the way, the Hights stopped for Mexican food and wrangled over air conditioning settings. The atmosphere was largely convivial, until the car hit violent evening thunderstorms on the outskirts of Kansas City. The normally calm and collected Joe Hight became flustered as he tried to find his exit and follow directions to the hotel in a torrential downpour, barking out questions ("Where am I going? Turn here? Where?") like a drill sergeant.

The next morning, he seemed back on an even keel, with just a bit of grousing about the high cost of the room service breakfast. About 1:30 p.m., Hight (surprisingly without his trademark dark suit and wearing navy slacks and a short-sleeved blue and yellow windowpane shirt) addressed ten print and broadcast reporters participating in the Midwest Health Journalism Fellowships Program, sponsored by the Association of Health Care Journalists. A half-dozen other media types and association officials were in attendance.

For 2 hours Hight reviewed crisis protocol and procedures for dealing with short- and long-term press coverage affecting victims, communities, and journalists. He used a community crisis role-play scenario, "What If?" The exercise described the explosion of two "dirty bombs" in Overland Park, Kansas, during a holiday event with a crowd of more than one thousand people. He organized the room into three teams, broadcast, major metro, and hometown press, and challenged each group to develop crisis coverage strategies. Later, after receiving their critiques, the reporters thanked Hight for his presentation and readily collected Dart Center booklets, articles, and other materials on covering tragedy and trauma. One sheepish individual lingered, a senior writer/editor with the Kansas Health Institute. An experienced reporter before entering the health communications field, the man discussed how he got "burned out" after years on the police beat. He had found it especially stressful in later years to cover murder trials and executions.

At the end of the Kansas City seminar when asked about his experiences with reporters seeking counseling, Hight referred to it as people "exposing their deepest fears in life on the couch." Two days later back in Oklahoma, he admitted he had never been in a formal counseling session. Did he think that managers might have greater credibility with staff if they themselves participated in counseling and acknowledged that experience during times of crisis? Hight looked uncomfortable when discussing such feelings. His face reddened and his gaze intensified. He cocked his head to one side and with a steely stare, replied, choosing his words carefully: "It's not like because I'm walking naked, you have to walk naked." He disputed the efficacy of "baring your soul," especially to "journalists who are very skeptical about other journalists." He said what matters is how leaders are perceived before a crisis—are they caring, credible, and empathetic? Hight then eased back in his chair and said calmly, "Managers have a responsibility to take care of themselves while encouraging others to do so." He said that type of leadership has proven effective in his newsroom, where he has shared with reporters some of the things he does to manage stress, such as exercising (Hight still enjoys lifting weights), confiding in his wife, Nan, coaching children's sports, and attending his daughters' extracurricular events.

Charlotte Lankard says that Joe Hight will call her on occasion to discuss matters on the job or at home, but the two have not participated in a formal therapy session. Not everyone needs that kind of intervention, Lankard says, noting how impressed she has been for a dozen years with Hight's "equilibrium," his sense of humor, and steadiness under pressure. She believes his strong family life centers him, as does his devout religious faith.

A couple days before Joe Hight traveled to Kansas City, Bryan Painter was somber as he toured the Oklahoma City National Memorial and Museum, after interviewing Memorial officials. Painter had never visited the museum, with its extensive artifacts on the 1995 bombing, including photos, video, and audiotape of the disaster and personal mementoes of the 168 victims. He walked reverently through the floors of exhibits. It took him several minutes to regain his characteristic wit en route back to the *Oklahoman* offices.

The next day, he headed to Guthrie to meet with Vickie Blount, the mother of Tyler, the young man who had died in the rodeo accident in 2000. Tyler's father, Pat, was on a business trip to New York. The Blounts and Painter participated in a conference call from the family's investment company offices in Guthrie—also the site of the Tyler Blount Memorial Foundation ("promoting outreach and training for tomorrow's leaders whose focus is on agriculture, tourism and economic growth"). Seven years after Tyler's death, the Blounts consider Bryan Painter a good friend. Their lives have been connected by grief and loss. On this particular visit, the reporter and Tyler's parents uncovered new insights wrapped in painful memories.

Vickie Blount, a petite red-haired woman with striking blue eyes was dwarfed by the dark-haired, mustachioed 6-foot-2 Painter, who bowed from the waist as he shook her tiny hand. As they sat at a long wooden conference table, topped with an 8-by-10 black and white photo of a 3-year-old Tyler, wearing a cowboy hat and riding a pale rocking horse, Vickie and Painter, together with Pat (via the speakerphone) reconstructed the events of that horrible June night in 2000. Pat Blount and Bryan Painter were already at the hospital when Vickie arrived. Before Vickie would see Pat, his shirt covered in his son's blood, she met Painter, who averted his eyes.

"That look on your face told me that Ty was dead even before I saw him in the hospital room," Vickie said, trying to comfort Painter, who apologized for causing the grieving mother any unnecessary pain that night. "That look on your face," she continued, "made me feel as sorry for you as anyone."

On the ride back to the office, Painter talked of the Blounts' friendship. He then bragged about his baseball-star son, Cody, a high school senior, and his freshman daughter, Keilee. He had never mentioned to the Blounts that in April 2001 he had received a statewide AP award for spot sports reporting for his coverage of Tyler's death. Some awards, he felt, were better left on the shelf.

Minneapolis Bridge Collapse

On Wednesday, August 1, 2007, during the Minneapolis evening rush hour, the I-35 W. bridge collapsed, plunging cars into the Mississippi River, killing thirteen people. The next day, Joe Hight checked in with Brenda Rotherham, news recruiting and training manager, *Minneapolis Star Tribune*. He had first met her when he was chairman of the Mid-America Press Institute. Subsequently, the Dart Center had run training sessions at the *Star Tribune* offices. Now, Rotherham was asking Hight if he had any advice about how the staff could take care of itself while covering such a difficult community-based story.

We need to react so the newsroom can be prepared, she told Hight. On Friday, August 3, Hight responded with two lengthy e-mails, containing recommendations on crisis coaching: (1) have a calm sense of energy, (2) establish priorities, (3) be compassionate and understanding, (4) set good examples, and (5) communicate constantly (through one-on-one conversations, through e-mails, through memos). He recommended that management post notices about available (phone, e-mail, and on-site) counseling. But Hight advised against EAP (Employee Assistance Program) counselors because "newsroom staff members are usually very skeptical of them, unless the person is trusted within the newsroom." He wrote: "Sometimes, even the offer of a counselor can be calming to staff members, even if they don't use the person. Again, it shows that management cares about their welfare." He also contacted Frank Ochberg, who agreed to provide three days of free phone counseling to *Star Tribune* staff.

In addition, Hight recommended that management offer hats, sunscreen lotion, and bottled water for those going to the accident scene. And he suggested "healthy food and snacks" be provided at least through the weekend for the newsroom. Hight concluded his e-mail by telling Rotherham that the *Oklahoman* newsroom was collecting "stress-related fun items (e.g., squeeze balls) and comfort food," to send by the next week. "It's our way of saying we're thinking of you and know what you're going through."

The *Oklahoman*'s generous spirit would be mentioned on Tuesday, August 7, 2007, in an online article by Joe Strupp, senior editor, *Editor & Publisher.* He wrote that in the wake of the bridge collapse tragedy, editors at the *Roanoke Times* (Virginia) had sent boxes "filled with Moon Pies, pork rinds, and other treats, . . . likely meant more as a sign of sympathy than just a snack pack" to the *St. Paul Pioneer Press* and the *Star Tribune* in Minneapolis. As Strupp noted, in the wake of the Virginia Tech tragedy in April, "The Roanoke paper had received its own care package then— from the Oklahoma paper that lived through the trauma of the Timothy McVeigh Terror bombing." According to Carole Tarrant, the editor in Roanoke:

> A few days after the Virginia Tech shootings, a large box arrived in our newsroom. Inside was a note and lots of stress-relieving junk food. The note was from Joe Hight, managing editor of the *Oklahoman*. Hight wrote that similar boxes arrived in his newsroom after the McVeigh bombings. He recalled what that gesture meant to his staff, which had been worn down to a nub covering the catastrophic community event. She said that Hight concluded by writing: "Please consider this a journalistic chain letter of sorts, one that you'll pass on when the next bulletin breaks in a newsroom somewhere·in America."[29]

As fall arrived, Joe Hight and Frank Ochberg made plans to collaborate again, this time for a professionals-in-residence presentation on trauma journalism at BSU in Muncie, Indiana. It would be the first time the two of them had been copresenters in many years, and the site would be about an hour northeast of Indianapolis, where Joe Hight gave his first speech on the topic back in 1996. But Hight and Ochberg wouldn't appear on stage together on Wednesday, September 26 because Hight had been called to serve on federal jury duty in Oklahoma City. He had petitioned to be excused for just a couple of days. But the judge refused. So Hight sent a PowerPoint presentation on "Covering Tragedy and Trauma," which was delivered by a BSU professor moderating the panel. He then talked briefly to the audience of students and faculty via a speakerphone and answered a few questions until the connection was interrupted. Ochberg was glad to carry the load the rest of the evening, engaging the students with a primer on PTSD, handling the Q&A on traumatic news reporting, and urging BSU journalism program officials to incorporate more crisis coverage techniques in their reporting and media ethics courses.

A few weeks before the fall 2007 BSU presentation, a research study (by professors Dworznik and Grubb) "Preparing for the Worst: Making a Case for Trauma Training in the Journalism Classroom" was published in *Journalism & Mass Communication Educator*, a leading academic journal for college journalism instructors. The article discussed the work of researchers like Feinstein, McMahon, Newman, and Handschuh. It spoke of the "psychological hazards of journalism." Echoing the words of Hight, Ochberg, and a host of trauma journalism reform advocates, the article concluded: "More investigation into this area may shed light on another avenue that can be used to ensure that future journalists not only have the reporting skills necessary to compete in the high-pressure world of news, but they also have the emotional and psychological skills needed in order to survive it."[30]

In early November 2007, Joe Hight was en route to Washington, DC, where he would spend a couple days with daughter Elena, a freshman at Georgetown University. They would visit the J. M. W. Turner art exhibit at the National Gallery. (Joe Hight is a lifelong art lover; an extensive and eclectic collection of paintings adorns the walls of his 4,000-square-foot handsome brick home in Edmond, Oklahoma.) Hight and his daughter would also engage in some window-shopping at boutiques in Georgetown. A devotee of estate sales and auctions, Hight says he avoids store shopping at all costs.

Earlier in the day on November 10, Hight addressed a mental health advocacy group on the Georgetown campus. Later that afternoon and evening, he would preside over his last executive committee (EC) meeting as president of the Dart Center for Journalism & Trauma. Days before the annual meeting, Hight had wondered aloud if the committee had "taken on too much" as his presidency came to a close. He sounded aggravated that several actionable items were either "mired in debate" or delayed. He said some committee members seemed "shaky and wary" about what would occur in DC. "It's all colliding," Hight said, referring to the October 30 release of the consultant's report and upcoming decisions on relocating the Dart Center from the UW when the school's five-year contract ended in September 2008.

The Last Meeting

At 3:30 p.m. on November 10, Hight looks calm and presidential in his dark suit, white shirt, and red and white striped tie. As he waits for the rest of the committee to arrive at the 80-year-old Hotel Tabard Inn on quiet, tree-lined N Street NW, he speaks eagerly about his successful presentation to the "Active Minds" group at Georgetown University earlier this afternoon. He discussed trauma and mental health issues and talked about the death of his brother Paul. Afterward, he met a colleague of the late *Wall Street Journal* (*WSJ*) reporter Daniel Pearl. The woman was touched by Hight's remarks and interested in learning more about his advocacy.

The Dart Center's EC meeting is in room 26 at the top of the Tabard's Inn sagging, creaking stairs (lined by portraits of George Washington and former Soviet premiere Mikhail Gorbachev). This quaint historic (some would just say "old") hotel is located in a nineteenth-century row house. Room 26 is suitably Victorian with its cranberry-colored walls, eggshell blue ceiling, accentuated by white wooden cross beams, a wide mantle and large ornate mirror, antique loveseat, three multicolored oriental rugs, and an upright piano in one corner. Dinner will be served at 7 p.m. at the long dark wooden table where the dozen executive committee members and staff now gather.

Before the meeting begins at 4:30 p.m., there is laughter, chatter, and hugs all around. A spirit of bonhomie warms the drafty high-ceiling room on this mid-November eve. Yes, there are serious matters to attend to tonight but also several people to honor. Four committee members are leaving the board: Joe Hight, Elana Newman, Penny Cockerell (who is unable to attend the event), and Mark Brayne, the former British journalist-turned-therapist who had headed the Dart Center's European operations for several years.

"Tomorrow, you'll be in charge, and I'll be relieved," Hight says at one end of the table to incoming president Deb Nelson, who sits to his immediate left. If Hight reflects a corporate style of dress and demeanor, Nelson resembles an academic, at home in Cambridge, Evanston, or Berkeley. She wears gray stretch slacks, black boots, a black jacket over a tan top. Her straight brown hair falls to her shoulders. She is slender and of medium height. Her long face appears serious, even austere, accentuated by dark-framed glasses. But when she laughs along with Hight and others in the room, her appearance brightens.

For the next 90 minutes, the group listens to a presentation by New Hampshire-based consultant David Brown, who has hobbled in on crutches and a surgical shoe. He had planned a PowerPoint presentation, but there is a snafu with the computer projection system. No bells and whistles this time, just highlights of the nineteen-page operational audit for the Dart Center.

Though the report is well received, it appears the executive committee is still coming to terms with the Dart Center's evolution and organizational development from its early entrepreneurial history, when Frank Ochberg, chairman emeritus, was both founder and administrator. (A week later, Hight will e-mail the committee, expressing his hope that the Dart Center retains its personalized and strategic outreach. "Frank taught me that, and I think it's worked tremendously through our formative years and will into the future. Throughout the strategic planning process, I think it's important to identify values and traditions that have generated success thus far and treasure them throughout the process.")

In room 26 at 6:35 p.m., a somewhat heated discussion about Dart Center publications and other agenda items ensues, and the mood grows more intense. Ochberg, who sits at the opposite end of the table from Hight, appears glum, as some of his comments seem to have fallen on deaf ears. Just then, the tall wooden double doors open, and a frazzled Bruce Shapiro bounds in, apologizing for being late (due to delays at LaGuardia). Rumpled in his tweed sport coat, the compact, erudite Shapiro still looks and acts like a reporter with his tousled brown hair, somewhat frenetic style, and rapid-fire delivery.

"Chill out," Australian Cait McMahon says cheerfully at the table as executive director Shapiro hurries to his seat next to Ochberg. "We're fine."

The last item on the agenda for today's meeting is an attempt to edit the language for the annual Dart Center award. The group spends several minutes debating whether to use "covering" or "coverage of" tragedy and trauma. Hight has been moving the agenda along fairly well until this delay. But now he laughs aloud, breaking the tension in the room. Any vote on this matter and the presentation of Shapiro's report can wait until tomorrow when Deb Nelson will officiate the meeting. The group shifts gears, settles back, and prepares to dine on Dijon-crusted rack of lamb and roasted salmon filet, accompanied by free-flowing red and white wine. After dessert (caramelized apple crisp with dulce de leche ice cream), appropriately sweet tributes are made to the four honorees.

Joe Hight recognizes the efforts of many around the table. He thanks Bruce Shapiro for his energy and management ability. He acknowledges the invaluable support of Frank Ochberg. He jokes with Seamus Kelters, a fellow Catholic about how they attended Mass together in Northern Ireland years ago after a fairly heavy night of drinking pints of Guinness stout. (The next day, he and Kelters will attend 7 a.m. Mass at St. Matthew's Cathedral, a few blocks away, where President John F. Kennedy lay in state on November 25, 1963.) Then, it's time to pass the wooden gavel to Deb Nelson, whom Hight praises for her ability to listen and to be assertive when needed. "I know the Dart Center is good hands."

Nelson replies that she has "learned from your patience and wisdom." Others chime in around the table. Hight is called a "workhorse, pioneer, and trailblazer." Ochberg stands and delivers an eloquent, emotional tribute, citing Hight's devotion to his presidency and his fairness. "You always knew where Joe stood on issues," Ochberg says, acknowledging that through the years they have had "heated disagreements," but they were always able to work through their differences and maintain mutual respect and a close friendship. "We are indebted to Joe for raising our standards and meeting our goals."

After the tributes, Hight says he is honored by the words and gifts, including two black cast-iron typewriter bookend/paperweights. Hight sits ramrod straight, his hands clasped in his lap as Ochberg announces there is one more presentation for the evening. The doors to room 26 again open. In strides a smiling Dr. Terry Clark from the UCO. Hight is momentarily surprised by the unexpected appearance of his old friend Professor Clark. He jumps up, and the two men embrace as laughter and applause fill the room. Terry Clark announces that the Dart Center has established a $10,000 endowment in Hight's name at UCO. The Joe Hight Award will be given each year to a junior or first-semester senior student showing outstanding promise in ethical journalism. Applicants will come from two journalism classes: "Media Ethics" and the "Victims and the Media" course. Hight listens, remaining dry-eyed at attention in his chair. He will later say how surprised and honored he was with the UCO endowment. Eldest daughter and Georgetown freshman, Elena, who attended the November 10 ceremony, will call home and tell mother, Nan, and younger sister, Elyse, about the honors bestowed on her father this evening.

Coming to Terms at Starbucks

The next morning, the Dart Center executive committee meeting continues in a conference room at the more modern and stylish Topaz Hotel two doors down from the Tabard Inn. Hight attends most of the 3-hour meeting as a courtesy, but he leaves at 12:30 p.m.

"I had to get out of there," he says, rushing out to the sidewalk, "before it got too emotional. I didn't want to be in the room when the meeting adjourned." With Elena by his side, Hight walks briskly up N Street toward Connecticut Avenue. On this sunny but cool Sunday afternoon, a nearby Starbucks looks inviting. Elena orders hot chocolate; her father gets hot cider without whipped cream.

Hight begins by summarizing some of the actions at the morning meeting. He is very complimentary of Deb Nelson's first steps as president, citing her "terrific job today." He then relives some of the events of previous night. After four years as president of the Dart Center, he seems a bit uncertain of his future role. "What do I do if someone contacts me because they still see my name as president on the website?" he asks, unable to answer his own question. He says that Ochberg and Shapiro are encouraging him to lead the Center's twenty-five-member advisory council of representatives from journalism and trauma fields. But Hight isn't making any commitments just yet. He has more pressing matters to attend to.

Elena quietly sips her hot chocolate, studying her father as his voice drops and his pale eyes glisten.

"It cost me," Joe Hight says, referring to his years as president of the Dart Center. "But there's always a price to pay." He seems unaware that he is channeling the words of his late father, Wilber.

Hight explains he has recently learned he will be changing jobs at the *Oklahoman*. As of November 19, he will no longer be a managing editor, a title he has held since 1999. Now, he will have the twenty-first-century moniker: director of information and development. Hight says that because of his significant time commitment with Dart Center-related activities (on average, about 20 hours a week over the past four years), he admits he wasn't able to have the "vision" regarding emerging developments at the *Oklahoman*. Because he was so tied up with his trauma journalism advocacy, he never told his superiors about his interest in pursuing the executive editor position at the newspaper. (Now a moot point because the position has been eliminated in the 2007 management reorganization.) For the first time in decades, Hight won't report to Ed Kelley, and he acknowledges he has had no recent conversations with Kelley about the job change.

"You have to be adaptable in this business," Hight says a month later as he is packing up his two-room office and moving to a smaller ninth-floor location on the northeast corner of "the tower."

Ironically for Hight, the more he advocated for a "higher sense of what journalists should be," the more distanced he became from certain members of the *Oklahoman*'s (now) 200-person newsroom. Some would label Hight as "soft" and "detached." Others would say they were unaware of his international media leadership. Even longtime friend and admirer Charlotte Lankard had confided in summer 2007 that she believed Joe Hight and Ed Kelley were striving to effect change, to raise standards, and to enlighten attitudes and behavior at the *Oklahoman*. "But they may not be doing as well as they think they are," she said.

However, a legacy is unpredictable. For example, 20,000 copies of the 40-page Dart Center booklet *Tragedies & Journalists* that Hight coauthored in 2004 with Frank Smyth, freelancer and Washington (DC) representative of the CPJ, have been distributed worldwide. Reporters speak of carrying the booklet to war zones in Iraq and Afghanistan.

Perhaps the best evidence of a cause well lived lies in the testimony of friends and colleagues. Upon Joe Hight's retirement as president of the Dart Center for Journalism & Trauma in November 2007, remarks arrived via e-mail before and after the annual meeting in Washington, DC.

Bruce Shapiro wrote about "how much I will miss you as a leader and collaborator." He added that Hight's friendship had sustained and inspired him.

"I treasure your integrity, your wisdom and deep commitments."

Penny Cockerell said she was looking back on her work with the Dart Center as one of the "greatest experiences of my career—and you play no small part in that. Over the years, I've watched you put Dart and the *Oklahoman* on the map in a most meaningful way and I am extremely proud to be associated with this profound and growing movement. I hope you feel a tremendous sense of accomplishment—you should. You have my applause."

Joe Hight's favorite scene in the film *Castaway* is not when Tom Hanks is rescued, or when he reunites with his former girlfriend. Hight prefers the image of Hanks at the end of the movie, standing literally and figuratively at the crossroads of life. After some thirty years, the one-time hustling reporter finds himself at that place—in transition.

He admits that as a younger ("hot-headed") man, he may have reacted differently to his job change. But now his first concern isn't about himself or his career; it's about those he loves. "How does it affect my family?" he asks. That's how he makes his decisions these days. He's also pragmatic: "I'm at a latter part of my career but not the latter part of my life." Hight says now that his service to the Dart Center has ended, he can begin thinking about other plans he has had to postpone for years, such as writing a book about his brother Paul and crafting short stories.

Just days before Christmas 2007, Joe Hight sounds upbeat, "relieved that I have this new initiative." He's having fun as director of information and development, something he hadn't expected. But toward the end of the phone call, his tone shifts as he reflects on all the years dealing with tragedy and trauma. "I saw a lot of pain, and it really wears on you. These sad stories are never ending." A few moments pass before Hight perks up once more. He is gracious and grateful for his opportunities to make a difference. "The amazing thing is the connections, those people you've helped along the way. That's worth everything."

Faces of Trauma Journalism: Molly Bingham

Photo by Ralph Alswang

Photojournalist and documentary filmmaker Molly Bingham is a gutsy 42-year-old brunette with a husky voice, salty tongue, and contagious laugh. She calls to mind actress Debra Winger. One can easily picture Molly holding her own drinking and smoking with a group of male war correspondents. But Molly Bingham is more than an independent, strong-minded woman. She is driven by her family's (newspaper publishing) history to do meaningful quality journalism. She believes that storytelling can make a difference and effect change in the world. Pretty heady stuff for a woman born of privilege (in Louisville, Kentucky), who once aspired to be an actress and admitted to being scared at the outset of her news career.

Molly overcame those fears to become a respected female journalist who has covered conflict, violence, and tragedy across Africa, Afghanistan, Iraq, and the Middle East for nearly two decades. She joined a "rarified group of people" who risk their lives to tell dangerous stories that otherwise wouldn't be told. In the process, she has been detained, imprisoned, and threatened ("shot at is more accurate") by both enemy and "friendly" armed forces.

In late March 2003, just days before the US invasion of Iraq, Molly was working as a freelance photojournalist when she and three other Western journalists were arrested by Saddam Hussein's security forces and taken to the infamous Abu Ghraib prison, where she feared she would be tortured, raped, and/or killed. She spent eight "terrifying" days as a prisoner, interrogated and accused of being a US spy.

The 2004 "A&E" Television Network documentary *Bearing Witness* chronicled the experiences of five women war correspondents during one year (2003) in Iraq.[31] Molly Bingham described how she had come as an independent journalist to Baghdad to cover what happened to civilians in the war. That's what she told her interrogators. She tried to reassure herself while in prison, maintaining the attitude: "Be calm, be centered, believe in what you do." She tried to remain positive, but she admitted to herself that: "If I die, I died believing in something. If I get out, I can continue working."

While she freely admits she and her fellow journalists were treated humanely by their Iraqi prison guards, she could hear the screams of other prisoners being beaten. Clear threats by her interrogators that she would be killed for being a US spy didn't require much imagination on her part. She would later learn of Kurdish prisoners across the hallway who were executed after she was released.

In an interview with Barbara Walters on ABC News *20/20* in April 2003, just days after her release, Molly Bingham said that Iraqi officials never explained why she and her colleagues were arrested or set free.[32]

To this day, she thanks her parents, sister, friends, and colleagues for their "overwhelming support" in helping to secure her release from prison and for caring about her health and welfare upon her brief return to the United States. Surprisingly, she didn't undergo any formal counseling in 2003. As she considered returning to Iraq, she spoke by telephone to a therapist, whom Molly had met with earlier in her life. The counselor said that she sounded as if she knew what she was doing and was fully capable of making a decision.

Molly returned to Baghdad just seventeen days after she had been freed. For weeks she experienced what she describes as "pretty minor PTSD." She had uncontrollable shaking whenever she talked about her imprisonment. And certain locations and sensory details triggered bouts of anxiety. She says that it was crucial for her to "relay, rewire, and overlay" her experiences in Abu Ghraib, which she did by revisiting the prison at least ten times:

I could re-experience the place I was in a way that I had control. If I hadn't gone back, it would have been a boogey man for me. It would have been terrible.[33]

Molly's readjustment included specific rituals such as "driving over the bridge leaving Jaddriya hundreds of times—the same bridge I'd been driven over that night I was arrested." Her healing also required the repetition of daily life in Iraq that she had previously associated with her imprisonment ("allowing certain details, smells, sand storms, colors to provoke a memory, recognize it and let it go"). Upon her return to Baghdad, she met a wide array of Iraqis and realized "a more complex, sophisticated, and nuanced experience of the country and its people."

She also wrote about her arrest and detainment at Abu Ghraib. "The writing wasn't a conscious way of dealing with my PTSD but simply a way of recording what I knew I would forget," Molly says.

Later, she would learn that such an articulation process (e.g., writing recollections) is a "classic treatment for PTSD—to begin to 'own' your narrative of a harrowing experience."

Molly Bingham's dangerous encounters—first when she was imprisoned early in 2003 and months later while she was filming a documentary on the Iraqi forces fighting American troops (*Meeting Resistance*)—have been shared by other trauma journalists in the Middle East and around the world during the last decade. The CPJ noted the rise in journalist kidnappings (usually for political reasons) and murders. The targeting of US and other Western journalists, symbolized by the 2002 abduction and execution of American reporter Daniel Pearl, heightened the news media's sense of risk. According to the March 2007 INSI report, *Killing the Messenger*:

> The result, for the media working in Iraq, has been an increasingly insecure working environment in which the alternative to operating embedded among western and Iraqi government forces is to gamble on operating independently in a hostile environment where deliberate attacks and kidnappings by insurgents and criminal groups can occur with relative impunity and in which there is a considerable risk of being caught up in violence between the belligerents.
>
> The main danger facing journalists and other news media personnel in conflict zones is the loss of what used to be seen as press neutrality. News media personnel are being targeted as never before, perceived by one side or another as being part of the enemy.[34]

Although proud of her work in Iraq and other hostile environments during her career, Molly Bingham is frank about covering war and dismisses its exciting image:

> It isn't macho and glamorous to cover war, and anyone who tells you otherwise is lying. It is gut wrenching, exhausting, and sometimes incredibly terrifying. . . . Being terrified is a very natural, healthy human response to danger, and if you don't feel scared, then in some ways you're not awake—and that's a different kind of danger.

She speaks of the challenge of managing the "constant low level of anxiety" in dangerous environments, the ongoing questions, assessments, and evaluations regarding personal safety. For example: "Am I making smart choices? Is this story worth the risks I'm taking?" In 2001, Molly completed a week of hostile-environment training, a regimen embraced by most major news organizations for their Western full-time journalists covering war and other violent stories. (Freelance and indigenous journalists have not typically been afforded access to such services.)

Molly says journalists in conflict zones are "never truly safe." As a freelancer, she won't hire armed security guards nor ask the US military for protection, preferring to work "as an unarmed, 'unprotected' person in the community." She explains that is "part of why I haven't been back to Iraq because operating independently, without security, became too dangerous."

She says a journalist's resilience in covering difficult stories is as much about the person's physical and emotional states as it is about professional craft attitudes:

> When you get isolated and you're tired, working in this kind of environment, and your brain is in overdrive to process what you're experiencing, that's when it's easy to feel extremely done. . . . People who break or have a particularly rough time, in my opinion, have pushed themselves past where they were doing OK. That means you should leave a story when you are too tired or too overwhelmed to continue.

However, she also emphasizes the importance of a sense of mission in keeping a journalist motivated and capable of enduring the stress of extended coverage. In her case, she acknowledges her "belief in the importance and possibility of journalism to shape society and our perceptions of ourselves as human beings."

To be successful as a trauma journalist, Molly says you have to both understand and feel the emotional impact of what you're seeing while continuing to work. Like others who speak of the need for empathy while reporting, she notes:

> You have to be there. You have to witness it, and you have to feel it. But you cannot let those feelings overwhelm you.

In July 2004, *Vanity Fair* magazine published an extended article by Molly Bingham titled "Ordinary Warriors," featuring several representative profiles of individuals participating in the Iraqi resistance (insurgency) to the US military occupation.[35] Subsequently, the documentary *Meeting Resistance* that Molly and her colleague Steve Connors released in theaters in 2007 included several of these same Iraqis and other Middle Eastern fighters, who were considered the enemy by most Americans. She said the film attempted to portray "their vision of themselves" as members of a violent movement.

On May 9, 2005, Molly's hometown newspaper, the *Courier-Journal* (Louisville, Kentucky), published an article adapted from a speech she had given at Western Kentucky University a month earlier. In the story, "Home from Iraq: Journalist Urges Americans to Search for Truth, Freedom," Molly wrote that her "sense of human values transcend frontiers and ethnicity." She said it was difficult to set her "American self" and perspective aside and "listen open-mindedly to a group of people whose foundation of belief is significantly different from mine, and one I found I often strongly disagreed with." As a journalist, Molly explained that in seeking out those resisting the presence of foreign (American) troops, she was trying to enlighten audiences on what was behind significant (and underreported) aspects of the ongoing conflict in Iraq. "How could you understand the full context of what was unfolding if what motivates the 'other side' of the conflict is not understood, or even discussed?" she wrote. She concluded by citing the role of American journalism as helping to promote and ensure the "highest form of patriotism—expecting our country to live up to the promises it makes and the values it purports to hold."[36]

After the 2005 speech excerpts were published, Molly was criticized (and "vilified" in right-wing blogs) by people who perceived her ideas as being somehow supportive of those who were fighting against the US and allied troops. When I talk with Molly five years after the controversy, she says with a laugh that, "Some of the kefuffle over that speech was more stressful than being in Baghdad!" It's evident that her sense of humor and inner toughness have enabled her to endure a host of challenges and crises in her life.

I find her most engaging when discussing her seven-year relationship with professional and personal partner, Steve Connors, a tall, dashing British photojournalist, veteran soldier, and experienced war correspondent. Connors' portfolio extends from the days of the "Troubles" in Northern Ireland to the Balkans, from Rwanda and Sri Lanka to Iraq and Afghanistan.

Molly says she and Steve believe in the same journalistic code, which was invaluable when making joint decisions and dealing with the dangers in Iraq while reporting and filming their documentary on the Iraqi resistance. At times, they felt as if they were in as much danger from American troops (being followed, arrested, subject to attack or bombing during interviews with people the US military viewed as "targets") as they were from the resistance members (being followed, kidnapped for ransom, or suspected of being spies or informants and, subsequently, injured or killed) they were profiling.

Molly Bingham openly shares her opinions about the movement in journalism to discuss the emotional effects of conflict coverage on sources and reporters. She emphasizes her career-long freelance status and financial independence. As a result, she says she doesn't feel qualified to address many newsroom issues. But she does believe it is a positive development that more journalists are willing to discuss the impact of reporting on tragedy and trauma. She closes her remarks by drawing a line in the imaginary sand of contemporary news media coverage:

> If the (journalistic) culture is: "Suck it up. Things are tough for everybody. Don't be a crybaby." That's not constructive for anybody. I'm a forthright, honest person who doesn't hide her feelings well, and I would die in an environment that expected me to deny being affected by what I've seen and done.

CHAPTER THREE

Frontline Reporting

For every noted trauma journalist, whether iconic like Ernie Pyle, Marguerite Higgins, and Robert Capa, or more recently renowned like Kurt Schork, Christiane Amanpour, and James Nachtwey, there are hundreds of thousands of reporters, photographers, and news media workers covering arduous stories. Most of these journalists take the risks, face the challenges, and endure the consequences of their jobs in relative anonymity.

In this chapter I explore the motivations of several individuals, identify their reporting techniques, and discuss how they cope with the physical and psychological effects of their work. Eight in-depth profiles ("Faces of Trauma Journalism") also accompany Chapters 1 through 8. The stories of these four men (Terry Anderson, Scott North, David Handschuh, and George Hoff) and four women (Molly Bingham, Amy Marcus, Judith Matloff, and Michelle Faul) include domestic (US) and international print and broadcast journalists (reporters and photographers). Some have earned their reputations from award-winning coverage of war, genocide, and terrorism. Others have covered crime, disaster, and tragic accidents primarily in their own communities. One of the "Faces of Trauma Journalism," Amy Marcus, has reported on conflict as a foreign correspondent, but in the last decade her work has focused on cancer and rare diseases. According to Amy, Pulitzer Prize-winning reporter for the *WSJ*, writing about life-threatening diseases, where the specter of death hovers, is as brutal as the longest war.

Many frontline journalists have chronicled their experiences in memoirs, such as John Laurence's *The Cat from Hué: A Vietnam War Story*, Chris Hedges' *War is a Force That Gives Us Meaning*, Jackie Spinner's *Tell Them I Didn't Cry: A Young Journalist's Story of Joy, Loss, and Survival in Iraq*, Chris Rose's *1 Dead in Attic: After Katrina*, and Anderson Cooper's *Dispatches from the Edge: A Memoir of War, Disasters, and Survival*. These accounts offer a window into the world of a profession that has been praised and criticized, and remains a source of fascination and frustration.

According to Bruce Shapiro, executive director of the Dart Center for Journalism & Trauma (headquartered at Columbia University in New York City since April 2009), trauma journalists often write "inside narratives," a term he notes was used by author Herman Melville in crafting his novel *Billy Budd*: "the attempt to grapple with evil and violence and sorrow and with the ineffable lingering suffering from terrible events that leave no one unscarred." In the winter 2009 issue of *Neiman Reports* ("Trauma in the Aftermath: Voice, Story, Character and Journalism"), Shapiro writes:

> Some journalists have lived inside narratives by being part of communities, families or neighborhoods where they've known intimately the lives and stories of the people they've reported on, whether their stories were about community catastrophes or intimate sorrows of tragedy that struck families in close-knit towns. Some have sought inside narratives after landing in a strange and complicated place where they have encountered acts of violence that demanded accountability or explanation.[1]

Covering War

Legendary CBS correspondent Edward R. Murrow became famous for his on-the-scene radio broadcasts during World War II in London during the blitz bombing campaigns and while accompanying American planes on combat missions over Germany. In *Killing the Messenger: Journalists at Risk in Modern Warfare*, Herbert N. Foerstel cites Murrow biographer Joseph Persico:

> He faced danger with stoicism, avoiding shelters, standing on roof tops, sketching word pictures of a man-made hell as it happened. . . . He never denied his fears. He particularly feared . . . being blinded by flying glass.[2]

What drove Murrow and continues to motivate today's war correspondents is a sense of craft and obligation: "In order to write or talk about danger, you must experience it," Murrow wrote. "The experience teaches you something about what happens to fighting men, and perhaps more important, it teaches you something about yourself."[3] Christiane Amanpour, who joined ABC-TV News in March 2010 after years of frontline reporting for CNN, has stated: "Most of us feel we have a duty, a mission for this kind of work."[4]

Retired ABC-TV News correspondent and longtime host of *Nightline*, Ted Koppel, covered the Vietnam War and other conflicts during his forty-plus-year career. According to his friend and colleague BSU Telecommunications Professor Emeritus Steve Bell, who reported from Southeast Asia with Koppel in the 1960s, after the excitement in the field passed, there would be melancholy periods Koppel described as "bell-blue funks." In *War Stories: Reporting in the Time of Conflict from the Crimea* by Harold Evans, Koppel commented on the "sense of invincibility" that accompanies many reporters: "As a young man, you feel you're not going to get hit, and I think that's the tragedy of what happens to a great many young men, both soldiers and journalists and others."[5]

The harsh reality is that war correspondents have always been vulnerable to attack, injury, and death. But in recent years, with conflict zones in Bosnia, Chechnya, Afghanistan, Iraq, and the Gaza Strip, among others, scores of journalists have been killed and wounded in unprecedented numbers. During the last 2 decades, the CPJ and INSI have recorded more than 300 deaths of reporters and photographers covering wars. Between 2003 and 2009, some 140 journalists died covering the Iraq War.[6]

Reporter Paul Watson, *Los Angeles Times*, praises fallen journalists in the summer 2001 issue ("Front Lines and Deadlines: Perspectives on War Reporting") of the *Media Studies Journal*, published by The Freedom Forum:

> I'm told time and time again, mostly by editors, no story is worth dying for. I beg to differ—there are stories worth dying for. Some of my colleagues have made that choice and have died in brutal ways. And they should be honored for having made the choice to get that story.[7]

Timothy J. Kenny, author of the *Media Studies Journal* article "In the Bleeding Fields," tells of war photographer Georgette "Dickey" Chapelle, the first female correspondent to die in Vietnam. Chapelle died from shrapnel wounds in Vietnam in 1965 while accompanying a Marine patrol. Kenny later discusses other deadly war coverage that, while quite memorable for journalists, is often overlooked by the layperson. The 1990s war in the Balkans was described as horrific by news media workers, who became indiscriminate targets for combatants. One such casualty was Egon Scotland, who, according to Timothy Kenny, was covering the war in Croatia in July 1991 for the German newspaper *Suddeutsche Zeitung*. When an inexperienced colleague went missing, Scotland drove a clearly marked press car to find him. Serb militiamen opened fire on the vehicle, killing the 43-year-old reporter with an exploding dumdum bullet.[8]

Another conflict overlooked by most nonjournalists was the civil war in Sierra Leone (western Africa) in 1999–2000. It was a "bleeding field" for reporters as a dozen lost their lives there, including Reuters correspondent

Kurt Schork and APTN cameraman Miguel Gil Moreno. Schork, who had left a career in corporate law to become a conflict journalist, was 53 when he died. The *Media Studies Journal* article cites Schork's haunting admonition to his fellow correspondents.

> "War reporting," Schork said, "is a job, is a craft—not a holy crusade. The thing is to work and not get hurt. When that is no longer possible, it is time to get out."[9]

Kenny writes: "Described by colleagues as the best war correspondent of his generation, Schork had covered fighting in Bosnia, Kurdistan, Chechnya, East Timor, Kosovo, and Sierra Leone. But all that experience was not enough to keep him alive."[10]

Still considered by many the preeminent war reporter, Ernie Pyle was killed during a battle in the Pacific in World War II. His life and death illustrate the risks facing all trauma journalists and the emotional toll that stressful (and life-threatening) stories can have on those who cover conflict and violence. In the weeks before his death at the hands of a sniper in April 1945, Pyle wrote:

> I've been immersed in it too long. My spirit is wobbly and my mind confused. The hurt has become too great.[11]

Sometimes the damage to those covering war and other tragedies appears far from the frontlines. Such was the case with a former Broadway actress-turned-photojournalist, Jana Schneider. In an article "A Fall from Grace," posted on the USNews.com website on May 9, 2004 (and published in the *U.S. News & World Report* print edition on May 17, 2004), author Kit R. Roane described the vibrant life and tragic decline of Schneider, who in the late 1980s and early 1990s achieved international recognition for her photos in Sri Lanka, Bosnia, Afghanistan, and Iraq, and for her work in global hot spots, including Northern Ireland, India, Pakistan, Cuba, Angola, and cities across the former Soviet Union.[12]

Schneider, who was nominated for a Tony Award in 1986 as "Best Featured Actress" (musical) for her performance in "The Mystery of Edwin Drood," made a dramatic life and career shift, reinventing herself as a combat photographer. "During the course of her journey, she toted her cameras to some of the world's darkest places, documenting pain, suffering, and death," Roane wrote. "But now she is in a cruel dark place of her own, the personal hell of mental illness." The article described how in December 2003, then 52-year-old Jana Schneider was homeless in Manhattan, taken by police to Bellevue Hospital Center for psychiatric evaluation.[13]

Fifteen years earlier, Schneider had secured assignments in dangerous places like Sri Lanka and Afghanistan, where she was among the few news media to document the retreat of Soviet forces. She also stayed in Baghdad during the First Gulf War in 1990, one of a handful of Western photographers to capture images of the bombing of Iraq. According to Richard Beeston, the diplomatic editor for *The Times* of London, Schneider was "one of those larger-than-life characters."[14]

Although many journalists respected her bravery and aggressiveness, others criticized her ambition and apparent disregard for personal safety, such as "wandering around in no-man's land with bricks flying" in a Northern Ireland riot in late 1989, according to *The Times* (London) writer Edward Gorman, as quoted in Roane's USNews.com article.[15]

In May 1992, Schneider arrived in Sarajevo, at the height of hostilities. Retired Maj. Gen. Lewis MacKenzie, the Canadian commander of the United Nations forces in the former Yugoslav city, told Roane: "Many journalists had been wounded or killed, so they began working in a 'pool,' where one team went out and shared its photos with others." But Schneider didn't participate in the pool arrangements, said MacKenzie. "She was after getting the story, not helping her colleagues."[16]

A month later, Schneider and a Slovenian journalist named Ivo Standeker crossed into one of the most dangerous parts of the city. The two correspondents made it past Serbian gunmen, who had been shooting at Bosnian civilians in their apartments. While pausing to take a photo, Schneider and Standeker were fired on by a Serbian tank. Standeker died from his wounds; Schneider almost lost a leg. She was flown back to the United States for treatment of shrapnel wounds to her leg and head.

The physical wounds could have hastened the onset of her emotional trauma. Or maybe the cumulative stress of years of risk-taking caught up with her. Perhaps Schneider's decline into mental illness was triggered long ago by life events prior to her work as a photographer. Before Schneider declined precipitously, she received national attention in the US newspaper and magazine stories and on Ed Bradley's former CBS-TV News program, *Street Stories*. She told Bradley that she relished staring into "the corridor of death" on her dangerous assignments. She admitted that in addition to her injuries, she had been raped more than once while covering war. During her convalescence, she started a fund for victims of the Bosnian conflict and returned to her native Wisconsin. According to Roane's article, she also starred in a Volvo commercial in 1994, touting the car as an asset to her work as a photojournalist.[17]

> But this was all illusion. Inside, Schneider was troubled. She returned to Wisconsin from Bosnia deeply depressed, according to her family and friends. Behind the bravado, she was haunted by her part in Standeker's death and her own close call.[18]

Her marriage ended in the early 1990s, and for the next several years Schneider began to "wander" across the country (Washington, DC, Fort

Myers, FL, Texas, Moose Pass, Alaska) and around the world (Slovakia, Austria, Germany, France, Spain, Italy). In 1999, she visited Slovenia and met with the mother of her former journalist colleague Standeker. When asked what she thought of Schneider's behavior, Darja Lebar said:

> A lot of people actually snapped after the war because they didn't deal with their issues. When I saw her, it was kind of like, I was always afraid that you go crazy after all of that. You go to sleep a normal person, then wake up crazy.[19]

At the end of Kit Roane's 2004 article, Bellevue Hospital was seeking to transfer Jana Schneider to a long-term psychiatric center in Rockland County, about 20 miles north of New York City. Her lawyer feared that she would be "lost in the bureaucracy . . . and become part of this system." The article generated significant reader feedback. People contacted *USNWR* asking what they could do to help. A *US News* Fund for Jana Schneider was established with the hope that money raised could be used to help in her transition to life outside the hospital. The fund was to be administered by Schneider's relatives. Six years later, according to an October 13, 2010, e-mail from Kit Roane, the healing process has been slow as now-58-year-old Jana Schneider reportedly continues having difficulty "navigating the outside world."

In *War Stories: Reporting in the Time of Conflict from the Crimea* by Harold Evans, freelance photographer James Nachtwey, who has covered conflicts in "every continent in countless countries" states: "Our own emotional well-being is one of the things that sometimes has to get sacrificed in order to fulfill our duties as journalists."[20]

In the article "Women War Correspondents: They are Different in So Many Ways," published in the winter 2009 issue of *Nieman Reports*, results of an extensive research study of 218 conflict journalists (164 male, 54 female) revealed the women respondents as:

> more likely to be single and better educated than their male colleagues, no more vulnerable to PTSD, depression or overall psychological distress, and keeping up with the men when it comes to drinking—suggests they are a highly select group. It is not by chance that these women have gravitated to the frontlines of war.[21]

Researchers Feinstein and Sinyor not only analyzed survey data; they read memoirs, interviews, and biographies of many female war journalists, culling anecdotes and opinions to supplement the quantitative data. "In their lives and outlook there seems to be woven an intrepid insouciance that overlays a seriousness of purpose driving and sustaining many of them," the authors wrote, citing an example of British war correspondent Marie Colvin (the *Sunday Times* of London), who lost an eye and almost her life while reporting on the deadly conflict involving the Tamil Tigers (rebels) in Sri Lanka. Colvin was upbeat and resilient despite the injury:

> I am not going to hang up my flak jacket as a result of this incident. . . . For my part, the next war I cover, I'll be more awed than ever by the quiet bravery of civilians who endure far more than I ever will. They must stay where they are; I can come home to London.[22]

Marie Colvin was one of five women journalists profiled in the 2004 A&E Television Networks documentary *Bearing Witness*. She said:

> When you're in a war, you're tested every single moment. Can I do this? How can I do this? You have to rely on your wits and on your ability to deal with people. And on your ability not to panic, not to be afraid that the shell that just came in is going to kill you.[23]

On screen, Colvin, who wears a black patch over her left eye, is shown on June 6, 2003, interviewing Iraqi men about the 11,000 corpses buried in mass graves. She is listed as senior foreign correspondent, the *Sunday Times* of London. In a later scene, Colvin is back in a newsroom setting. She looks weary and averts her gaze, saying: "I probably do get too involved, and I do have nightmares. . . . It still matters to me. When it stops mattering to me, I'll stop doing it."[24]

In *Bearing Witness*, Mary Rogers, camerawoman and editor for CNN, is shown standing amidst a crowd of angry Iraqis in Fallujha as her voiceover describes her world:

> Our lives are not routine. You can get a phone call anytime to go somewhere. But that's what I like about this. It's not routine. And we take cautious, calculated risks. Maybe when I just started out I did some foolish things. Now, no. I've had friends killed. I've had other friends who have been shot. . . . No, don't do foolish things.[25]

May Ying Walsh, an American-born producer for Al Jazeera Television, describes on camera how she returned to her parents' house in California after a series of harrowing incidents during the fall of Baghdad in 2003.

> And for an entire month and a half, I did absolutely nothing. I mean I was just like some kind of zombie. I think what happened was traumatic—even though I didn't admit that it was traumatic to me,

and I needed to kind of go into hibernation. And then I got a phone call from Al Jazeera asking if I would come back and work here (Baghdad). Even though I wasn't completely ready, I came back.[26]

Another journalist featured in the A&E documentary is Janine di Giovanni, who also writes for *The Times* of London. Her initial statements have been echoed by many other combat correspondents through the years: "It's a very addictive drug this kind of reporting. If you said to me now, 'This is your last chance to do something like this,' I would find that incredibly painful—because I really believe very strongly that as reporters we do have this obligation to bear witness."[27]

Giovanni, author of *Madness Visible: A Memoir of War,* says that during her fifteen years of conflict coverage, she learned that between trips, "you must decompress." She describes a couple years earlier when she went "from war to war to war to war" (Kosovo, East Timor, Chechnya, Sierra Leone, Liberia, the Ivory Coast). "It was literally move, move, move," she said. "I'd go back to my London flat, pay my bills, whoosh, jump on a plane. It's not good for you."[28]

Later in the documentary, Giovanni describes her dramatic escape from a city in Chechnya hours before a brutal assault. Giovanni's segment ends with her marrying French correspondent Bruno Girodon, then a final scene with her pregnant, awaiting the birth of her first child and contemplating how she will face her new life as wife, mother, and journalist.

Balancing personal and professional lives is a significant challenge confronting men and women war correspondents. The strain of the work, the time away from spouses and significant others, and the influence of drinking, drug use, and illicit affairs can combine to create unstable and unfulfilling existences for trauma journalists.

Some like Molly Bingham, the fifth woman profiled in the A&E documentary, establish exclusive relationships with fellow journalists, finding a level of understanding and camaraderie not always possible with those not in the news business. "The romance of working in a war zone together is a little bit of a far-fetched notion here," Bingham says with a hearty laugh, sitting next to photojournalist Steve Connors, with whom she later exchanged rings (though they're not married) in the summer of 2004 in Big Sur, California.[29]

Bingham and Connors worked as a team in 2003–04 to write and direct a film (*Meeting Resistance*) on those forces behind the emerging postwar violence in Iraq. Steve Connors, a 52-year-old former British soldier, has spent more than twenty-five years as a freelance photographer, selling to major newspapers, magazines, and photo syndicates in the United States, the United Kingdom, and internationally. In his career, Connors has often teamed with other photographers ("some of the best"). Although he says he valued their experience and companionship, he still preferred to work alone—with just "your own fears to deal with." He also notes the additional risks and burdens of being with people who were not cut out for dangerous assignments and shouldn't have been in the field.

As author Gary Knight wrote in the introduction to his article, "Up Close and Deadly," in the summer 2001 *Media Studies Journal*: "The unique dangers faced by photojournalists who cover war are best captured in the words of Robert Capa, the man who set the standard for modern war photography—and who was killed when he stepped on a land mine in Vietnam in 1954: 'If your pictures aren't good enough, you aren't close enough.'"[30]

Knight states that independent photojournalists like Steve Connors "rarely enjoy the support infrastructure that other members of the media have. In most cases this is because the vast majority of photojournalists who cover world conflict are free-lance contributors rather than staff members."[31]

Connors' colorful opinions tend to counter the research findings of a 2002 study published in the *American Journal of Psychiatry*, concluding that photographers (photojournalists and videographers) are more susceptible than other correspondents not only to physical injury but also to the negative emotional impact of conflict coverage (e.g., PTSD) because of their proximity to danger and also due to the reprocessing of troubling images during editing.[32]

One explanation of this higher potential for traumatic effects is that to capture their subjects in harrowing situations, photographers have to focus on getting "the shot" and not on the human instinct to assist people in danger, thus causing inner conflict. However, in his field experience, Connors says he observed more reporters than photographers upset by what they witnessed. And he theorizes that the reflection and writing stages required of reporters may be far more emotionally troubling than what photographers encounter. Connors, who served in Northern Ireland during the "Troubles," also believes that hostile-environment training may actually intimidate journalists and inhibit them from effectively doing their jobs. And, although he admits his preparation, stoic nature, honed instincts, and ability to "control his fear" have enabled him to be resilient through the years, Connors adds: "I'd also stop short of saying I've built up any sort of tolerance. I have felt, later on, that I was becoming more affected by what I saw, rather than less."

Georgian journalist Tengo Gogotishvili mirrors Connors' stubborn resiliency. Gogotishvili has spent almost twenty years covering tragedy and trauma in his Eastern European nation, in the Middle East, the Balkans, and Kurdistan. A print and broadcast reporter and public information specialist, he faced his greatest challenge during the summer of 2008 when Russian forces invaded his country:

> Jets were everywhere and bombarded every important region, including [the] capital Tbilisi, where my family lives. It was quite hard to stand—thinking about work and family [at the] same time. . . . And I can say it affects your reporting—it becomes much more personal and subjective. You are on one side, and all the academic talks about impartial journalism are nonsense.

The 39-year-old Gogotishvili says he had no formal education or training for covering conflict. Like Steve Connors, he had military experience (and is currently a lieutenant in the Georgian Army Reserve). He covered the 1991 civil war in Georgia as a student journalist. A year later, he reported on the war in Abkhazia and then became a press officer during the subsequent peacekeeping mission, dealing with refugees and other war victims. In 2004, he was wounded by a grenade in South Ossetia; he still has fragments in both legs. Despite his injury, he shrugs off any suggestion of posttraumatic effects—"no time for nightmares and stuff like that," he writes in a December 19, 2009, e-mail, adding that the most common problem of reporting in conflict zones is a lack of sleep. But he says the challenging working conditions are compensated by the motivation "to report about things that our country and the world should know. And perhaps a wish to help someone."

Gogotishvili, who is divorced with a 16-year-old son, takes a paternal attitude toward his news crew: "When you are a TV journalist you have a huge responsibility for your cameraman—and that's real trauma. . . . Because you are the boss in the situation, and it's you who decides where to go, what to film and how, and he depends on you—sometimes fatally."

The veteran "military" journalist says, with Russia as a neighbor, he keeps his armored vest handy and is "always ready to be deployed everywhere with a camera." He reflects somberly on the awesome responsibility a journalist has in Georgia:

> Again, when you work in your country's war, it's very hard to stay impartial, but you have to keep in mind that your audience is sometimes physically dependent on what you say and how you say [it]. For example, when they have to flee their homes just to survive—not to be killed or raped like it happened in Georgia in 2008 when we were late to inform people about the scale of aggression.

Steve Connors and Tengo Gogotishvili represent two contemporary journalists who have seemingly coped well with combat coverage. Similarly, two of their distinguished predecessors, Joseph Galloway and Kate Webb, who both retired as war correspondents after four-decade careers, are models of durability.

In May 2006, Galloway was honored upon his retirement by "more than 100 fellow war reporters, ex-soldiers, retired generals and other friends gathered at the National Press Club," according to an online article by Greg Mitchell (editorandpublisher.com). The article quotes Galloway as saying he considered himself "the luckiest guy in the world to have survived against the odds." The 2002 film *We Were Soldiers*, starred Mel Gibson as Lt. Gen. Hal Moore and Barry Pepper as the 24-year-old Galloway, who reported on the ground during the deadly la Drang Campaign, the first major clash between American and North Vietnamese regular troops in November 1965. The film was based on the 1992 book Galloway coauthored with Moore—*We Were Soldiers Once and Young*. The two men later coauthored a 2008 sequel, *We are Soldiers Still*.[33]

In May 1998, the US Army awarded Galloway a belated Bronze Star (with "V" for Valor) for rescuing a badly wounded soldier under heavy fire in the battle in the la Drang Valley in 1965. Commenting on his career, retired General H. Norman Schwarzkopf stated on the "We Were Soldiers" website: "Joe Galloway is the finest combat correspondent of our generation—a soldier's reporter and a soldier's friend." The website lists the Schwarzkopf quote along with other testimonials to the native Texan who joined United Press International (UPI) in 1961 and spent twenty-two years serving in and heading news bureaus in the United States, Asia, and Russia. He completed four tours as a war correspondent in Vietnam between 1965 and 1975. He also covered the 1971 India-Pakistan War and other regional conflicts during his years with UPI. In 1982, he became West Coast editor of *U.S. News & World Report*. In 1990–91, he returned to duty as a correspondent in the Gulf War. Subsequently, Galloway worked for *McClatchy* and *Knight Ridder* newspapers as senior military correspondent before his retirement.[34]

Commenting on the Iraq War in 2006, Galloway reflected on his experiences in an article by Steve Inskeep ("A Retiring War Correspondent Returns from Iraq"):

Look, I've been doing this for 41 years. I've been covering America's wars. And over and over and over I've had my heart broken. . . . You know in January I stood in a garbage-filled mud pit watching American troops tear apart the wreckage of a Kiowa Warrior helicopter that had been shot down minutes before and pulling the lifeless body of one of the pilots and the barely alive body of another out of the wreckage. They're pulling this wreckage apart with their bare hands. And I watched their faces as they were brought out and laid on stretchers and carefully and lovingly drug out of that mud pit. And I stood there and I wept, just as I wept when I saw the first face of a dead American in Vietnam 41 years before.[35]

New Zealander Kate Webb, who retired in 2001, had been UPI's Cambodia bureau chief during her ten years with the global news organization. She was later employed by Agence France-Presse (while based in Southeast Asia). Working with those media outlets and as a freelancer, she covered conflict and tragedy in India, Pakistan, Sri Lanka, Nepal, Bangladesh, Afghanistan, the Philippines, East Timor, and Indonesia. She had started her career as 23-year-old rookie correspondent in Vietnam in 1967.[36]

Her most harrowing experience was when she was captured in Cambodia by North Vietnamese troops in 1971 along with four other journalists and their driver. They were held captive for twenty-three days. In her account "Highpockets," published in the 2002 book *War Torn: Stories of War from the Women Reporters Who Covered Vietnam*, Webb writes of being interrogated for hours and marched often through hot humid jungle terrain. During her captivity, she "often vomited, shivered from fever, excreted blood in her stools, and walked for miles on pus-filled feet that she described as feeling like 'sacks of jelly.'"[37] On April 21, 1971, the missing UPI correspondent was reported dead in Cambodia by the *New York Times* and other news organizations.[38]

In an online article ("Being Where the Action is"), Webb spoke of the psychological toll of war coverage and the trauma of being a prisoner (both in Southeast Asia and briefly in Kabul, Afghanistan). And she addressed her endurance as a journalist:

> People always think I must be so tough to survive all this. But I'm a real softie. But maybe that's what it takes—you have to be soft to survive. Hard people shatter.[39]

Fellow Vietnam War-era reporters John Laurence and Robert Sam Anson serve as important reminders of how vulnerable even successful correspondents can be to the debilitating effects of conflict coverage. Anson, author of the 1989 memoir *War News*, reported on the Vietnam War for *TIME* magazine in the late 1960s and early 1970s. He covered major battles and small skirmishes. He discovered atrocities, and he was briefly held captive by Viet Cong troops.

Arguably, his most painful memory concerned a massacre that took place at Takeo, where dozens of innocent Vietnamese civilians were shot by Cambodian troops. Anson would confront a moral dilemma when he helped get a wounded 8-year-old boy to a French-run hospital. When Anson tried to enable more wounded to get medical attention, he was told by colleagues: "Look, you can't get involved in your story. . . . That's not your job."[40] Despite the emotional stress of such incidents, Anson continued to cover more war stories in Southeast Asia: "I'd become used to the action, addicted to it almost, and without my usual ration I was getting restless," he wrote in his book.[41]

Then, almost five years to the day that he was hired, Anson left *TIME* magazine. He described his years as a war correspondent as a kind of "romance." But eventually he fell out of love with war reporting. His first marriage ended, due, he says, in part to the strain of his extended time in Southeast Asia. He says he drifted through another marriage as his nightmares from his Cambodian years returned. He was diagnosed with PTSD in the late 1970s when he had a self-described "nervous breakdown." In 1985, he returned on a tour of Vietnam with some of his fellow correspondents from the war years. The visit helped Anson put in perspective the damage from his journalistic career.[42]

From 1965 to 1970, John Laurence, a correspondent with CBS News, was considered one of the leading television reporters of the Vietnam War. In his compelling memoir, *The Cat from Hué*, Laurence described the personal cost of covering tragic and traumatic stories that endured long after the war was over. For years, Laurence was embedded with the US soldiers and Marines in major battles (e.g., Hué, Khe Sanh, Danang, the Tet Offensive) across South Vietnam. He wrote of the "narrow separation between life and death in this place." As he noted in his book, "Reporters and photographers were killed and wounded in the same proportion as the frontline troops they accompanied."[43]

Laurence covered the war for a very specific reason: "I was determined to show people at home, especially families, what was happening to their young men, what the price was for having them here."[44] By immersing himself literally on the battlefield, Laurence was able to convey what it was like to be at war: "After days of nervous tension—hyperalert for snipers, rockets, ricochets, mortars, grenades, booby traps, friendly fire, loss of life, loss of face—after our long intimate proximity with death and the primitive instincts that go with it, suddenly the terror fell away."[45]

Laurence displayed no false bravado as a war correspondent—just the opposite. He acted as one trying to survive amid the dangers. He wrote of a near miss with a sniper that pushed him over the edge of self-control: "Every time a shell burst, I ducked for cover, even when no one else did."[46]

By sharing his emotions and experiences, Laurence could evocatively portray the conditions on the ground in Vietnam. In his memoir, he also revealed the camaraderie that journalists shared during trying times, often turning to alcohol and drugs to alleviate the tension, loneliness, and fear. "Journalists drank too, some as long and hard as anybody, numbing themselves from the calamity they were covering."[47]

According to Laurence, being a war correspondent was a "great adventure: fascinating, frightening, fulfilling—more high drama than I expected for a lifetime." He wrote that at 28 he thought he was tough-minded enough to take it, absorb it, and digest it. But he was naïve. "I had no idea that my involvement was far from over, that I would be going back again and again, repeatedly, indefinitely."[48]

Decades after he left Vietnam, Laurence experienced recurring nightmares, anxiety, and other emotional problems associated with his five years of war reporting. Writing about his experiences was painful, but it helped him process some of his feelings. However, the "trauma of past experience" returned to haunt Laurence throughout his journalistic career. He covered wars, revolutions, and violence around the world for years after he left Vietnam. "I continued to believe that getting shot at and being scared was part of the job that I could throw off when I got home. . . . The old emotions came back."[49] In the closing pages of his book, he wrote of people who "made it through the bad times (and the good), are stronger than they may think by having survived it, maybe also wise with the knowledge that nothing, ever, anywhere, would be as hard."[50]

In Judith Matloff's 2004 *Columbia Journalism Review* article, "Scathing Memory: Journalism Finally Faces Up to the Psychic Costs of War Reporting," John Laurence (then 64) is described as having sought therapeutic intervention off and on since 1966.

Counseling helped him cope with the psychological costs of his career. He describes his old self as a "mess"—heavy drinking, sleeplessness, paranoia, dependence on tranquilizers. At his lowest points, he says he would drop to the pavement at sharp noises. He was scared to leave his room, and had terrifying dreams of being trapped in a crashing cargo plane. Still, he went to Iraq last year [2003] (for Esquire and National Public Radio) and the familiar demons of depression scuttled back. "I have never felt cured," he says.[51]

Frank Smyth, a veteran war correspondent (Central and South America, Africa, the Middle East), is cited in Matloff's article as having wrestled with psychological issues after being a prisoner for eighteen days in Iraq in 1991. He had been traveling with Kurdish rebels after the first Gulf War as a freelancer.

While on assignment for CBS, Smyth drove straight into an ambush. For seventeen hours he hid in a ditch, listening as Iraqi soldiers executed a colleague who had been traveling with him. The soldiers eventually found Smyth and another colleague and locked them in a cellblock [in Abu Ghraib prison]. There, Smyth had a prime view of guards torturing prisoners with electroshock and hitting them with wooden boards. Engraved in his memory was a boy named Jaffer, who yelped like a dog while guards beat him with a rubber hose.[52]

Matloff quotes Smyth as she writes about the effects caused by extreme stress, such as guilt, insomnia, and depression:

Many mental health experts believe journalists should debrief as early as possible after the traumatic experience, so that disturbing thoughts don't fester. This could be with colleagues at the hotel bar, or a couple of sessions with a therapist. The important thing is to process it. "It's like carrying around a bowling ball if you don't deal with it," says Frank Smyth, the Washington, D.C., representative of the Committee to Protect Journalists.[53]

"The Chance to Cry," an essay published in the 2002 book *Sharing the Frontline and the Back Hills: Peacekeepers, Humanitarian Aid Workers and the Media in the Midst of Crisis*, describes how Smyth sublimated his memories of those events for years. "Trauma is often associated with memory loss," he wrote. But in time, sounds and smells triggered painful recollections of his imprisonment. He found himself reliving the trauma and experiencing PTSD-type symptoms (e.g., nightmares, anxiety, psychic numbing).

Journalists are people who, like almost everyone else who is exposed to pain, feel it whether it is theirs or not. Keeping it bottled up may lead to drinking, smoking, philandering, working, or doing something else in a compulsive way that provides a distraction, but not release. The need to articulate feelings after exposure to trauma is obvious, and it is more likely to happen sooner than later if a counselor who is paid to listen is on hand. Once I finally faced up to it, I paid for a counselor out of my pocket. I took the chance to cry.[54]

Smyth, whose work has appeared in the *Washington Post*, the *New York Times*, and *WSJ*, coauthored the 2004 Dart Center for Journalism & Trauma booklet *Tragedies & Journalists* with former executive committee president Joe Hight. Since 2000, Smyth, on behalf of the CPJ, has worked to enlighten news organizations and journalists about safety and insurance issues and the impact of covering tragedy and trauma, particularly for free-lancers and indigenous media workers. He is an advocate for articulation (e.g., writing, drawing, and painting), which may help channel emotions associated with a traumatic event, and the benefits of acupuncture treatments, yoga, and meditation.

In the foreword to Dr. Anthony Feinstein's book *Journalists under Fire: The Psychological Hazards of Covering War*, former *New York Times* foreign correspondent and author Chris Hedges speaks prophetically in apocalyptic verse about combat coverage:

War is a potent narcotic. Like any narcotic, it is highly addictive. In large doses, it can kill you. Once you sink into the weird subculture of war, it is hard to return home, where all seems banal and trivial. . . . And those who can control their fear go back to seek these experiences again, seek them in strange, twisted landscapes of human depravity.[55]

Hedges made three harrowing trips in the late 1980s to cover the civil war in El Salvador. "War's sickness had become mine." In 1995, Hedges covered ethnic battles in the Balkan city of Sarajevo, which "came close to Dante's inner circle of hell."[56]

He experienced traumatic scenes during his (Bosnian) war coverage:

The other reporters and I slipped and slid in their blood and entrails thrown out by the shell blasts, heard the groans of anguish, and were for our pains in the sights of Serb snipers, often just a few hundred yards away. The latest victims lay with gaping wounds untended in the corridors of hospitals that lacked antibiotics and painkillers. By that summer, after nearly four years of fighting, forty-five foreign reporters had been killed, scores wounded. I lived—sheltered in a side room in the Holiday Inn, its front smashed and battered by shellfire—in a world bent on self-destruction, a world where lives were snuffed out at random.[57]

Hedges is one of fifteen war correspondents featured in the PBS online series "Reporting America at War." In one of his two website videos titled "On How War Reporting Sanitizes War," he says:

If we really saw war as it is . . . we [the audience] would be horrified and disgusted. But we [the news media] sanitize war, and again that gets back to the fact that the lie of the coverage is the lie of omission. We never report war as it is because it would be too unpalatable.[58]

If the audience's view of war coverage is different than what the journalist observes, there is a significant disconnect regarding the reality of the situation, the scope of violence, and the impact on those who are providing the story. Because of this disconnect, the general public typically has only a vague idea of what the journalist encounters when covering violence. Consider the account of reporter Ben Lando in the February 8, 2010, *TIME* magazine titled "The Moment: 1/25/10 Baghdad." Lando is describing the aftereffects of two bombs that exploded near the Hamra Hotel compound where he lives and works: "Looking back, I'm gripped by the scent of oranges cutting through the smell of charred vehicles and flesh: tart, from fruit not yet ripe, shaken early from the trees by the blast and scattered amid the debris."[59] Such graphic sensory details are not part of the routine coverage provided to media audiences.

Chris Hedges, now in his mid-fifties, is married with three children. In *Journalists under Fire*, he reflects on his extensive Middle East reporting experience. He covered the first Gulf War in 1991 and later reported from Afghanistan and Iraq. He quotes researcher and psychiatrist Feinstein: "For many war journalists, particularly when young and starting out on their careers, it is not just the risk of novelty that drives them, but also the risk of danger." Feinstein states in his book that war correspondents like Hedges, whether they report symptoms of PTSD or not, share a belief that their work has changed them as individuals.[60]

Hedges' commentary is not merely an introduction to the topic of trauma journalism. Rather, it is a dire warning:

> But war perverts and destroys you. It pushes you closer and closer to your own annihilation—spiritual, emotional, and finally physical. And those who practice the trade of war reporting with a relentless intensity over many years flirt with their self-destruction. Greg Marinovich, Joao Silva, Ken Oosterbroek, and Kevin Carter were four South African photographers who chronicled the implosion of violence that swept across South Africa in the 1990s: "the rampaging mobs, the murder by stabbing or necklacing, the panic of crowds fired upon by the security police, the summary roadside execution of white supremacists by a black soldier." They were known as the "Bang Bang Club." By the time of South Africa's multi-racial election, Oosterbroek had been killed, Carter had committed suicide, and Marinovich had been shot. Their story is a microcosm of the cost. Weaning yourself from this addiction is difficult. It took me three years to return to a place where I could reconnect with those around me.[61]

> (Author's Note: Kevin Carter won the 1994 Pulitzer Prize for his haunting photo of a vulture watching a starving child in southern Sudan, March 1, 1993. Shortly after winning the Pulitzer, Carter committed suicide.)

In 2000, Feinstein interviewed then-34-year-old Anthony Loyd, war correspondent, *The Times* (London) and author of *My War Gone by. I Miss It So*. His profile is included in *Journalists under Fire* as an example of a reporter who, like Chris Hedges and many others, found it difficult to free himself from the addictive nature of war coverage.

Loyd's most shocking assignment was in Chechnya because "the violence was so intense and the war so encompassing." He says there was a "guarantee" that as a reporter you either saw people getting killed or people who had just been killed or terribly wounded. "Or you would have a near-death experience yourself." When Loyd was in the besieged city of Grozny in the winter of 1994, there was such an intense bombardment, journalists could find no safe haven from the violence.[62]

Several years later when he discussed his experiences with Feinstein, Loyd vividly recalled the memories of the shelling in Grozny: "there was this serum of an imprint. I still think of it very often. I certainly have not forgotten it."[63] Loyd tried to deal with the painful memories by "medicating" himself.

As Feinstein writes:

> Depression is but one of the conditions frequently found together with post-traumatic stress disorder. Substance abuse is another, as Anthony Loyd's memoir makes clear. *My War Gone by, I Miss It So* is an account of the Bosnian war unlike any other. Loyd goes far beyond revealing the brutality of that conflict and the hazards confronted by journalists trying to get their story out. He also dwells at length on his addiction to heroin and alcohol. The title itself reveals Loyd's addictive personality— the adrenaline rush of war fueled his deep-seated psychological need, akin to a biological craving, for excitement. Away from the front lines, the relative dullness of daily life was insufferable and relieved only by the seductive powers of heroin.[64]

Jackie Spinner and Sharon Schmickle both reported on the Iraq War for the *Washington Post* and the *Minneapolis Star Tribune*, respectively. Although they were each affected by the war coverage, they differed in terms of their preparation and training, and in the intensity of reactions to the violence they encountered. At the time of their immersion in the Middle East—Spinner was in her mid-thirties, Schmickle in her early sixties.

As Spinner explained in her 2006 memoir, *Tell Them I Didn't Cry: A Young Journalist's Story of Joy, Loss, and Survival in Iraq*, she spent more than nine months in 2004–05 as a war correspondent, having no prior experience as a reporter in a conflict zone. Also, because she was sent overseas with little notice, she did not take survival training offered to fellow journalists who were going to cover the Iraq War. She had made an initial visit in January 2004 and then returned in May 2004 when conditions in and around Baghdad had worsened. Although frightened by one harrowing incident outside Abu Ghraib prison, she wasn't ready to leave Iraq: "I did not want to go back to the newsroom defeated, to bide my time again unnoticed."[65]

The longer Spinner stayed in Iraq, the more savvy and determined she became. But she was also more aware of the risks she and fellow journalists were facing as the insurgency threats increased: "We were scared of being followed, scared of being ambushed, and ultimately, scared of our own fear." Medical checkups revealed that her blood pressure was twice its normal rate, and she was prescribed antianxiety medications, which she resisted taking.[66]

For a time, she was embedded with a regiment of Marines in Fallujah. At first, she was delighted to be out of Baghdad. However, after several weeks of "seeing the devastating injuries, of watching troops injured and killed, of watching insurgents blown to shreds, of seeing the city destroyed, of trying to capture all of it," Spinner was exhausted and "mostly numb to the fear."[67]

In February 2005, Spinner became interim bureau chief for the *Washington Post* in Iraq. Although she felt burned out from overwork, stress, and fear, she accepted the post for a few weeks. When she returned home later that spring, her editors urged her to take some time off. "But more important, in order to heal, I needed to hear their reassurance of purpose and direction for me."[68]

Spinner had returned home with postwar trauma:

I was going crazy, driven mad by the unknown of the future and the known dangers I had escaped in Iraq. . . . I did not want to talk about this with my colleagues who had been in Iraq because I feared their judgment of me as weak, feared the silence that might follow my question, "Is it just me?"[69]

Spinner found herself haunted by nightmares, "angry at everything," and guilty for the Iraqi staff she had left behind with no promises for the future. In the United States, she shunned her friends in favor of family "because they asked no questions and surrounded me in unconditional love."[70]

As chronicled in *Covering Violence: A Guide to Ethical Reporting about Victims and Trauma*, Sharon Schmickle was a grandmother and a 20-year veteran of the newsroom when she covered the invasion of Iraq in 2003. "It's a big story, and reporters always want to get to the big story. There was a bit of professional pride there," she recalled.[71]

She prepared for the assignment by training for a week in North Carolina with retired US Army Special Forces soldiers, learning first first-aid and how to handle herself in dangerous circumstances. Schmickle also thought about the emotional impact of her war coverage. She drew inspiration from people whose work brought them in regular contact with pain and trauma—firefighters, police, nurses, and doctors. She was driven by her belief that, "Our responsibility (as journalists) requires us to be there and see how our government conducts itself."[72]

Schmickle considered her reporting in Iraq as an embedded journalist similar to when she had written about domestic violence in the 1980s. She had worked closely then with police, social workers, and others dealing with trauma. Decades later, Schmickle commented on the long-term effects of such intimate reporting:

It never quite leaves you. When I talk about it, when I think about it, it always gives me a chill. It gives me this burst of passion, and I'll call it anger too, about how we human beings live our lives. I don't think I'll ever shake that.[73]

When she returned home after two months, her editors urged her and others who covered the war to seek counseling, but she declined. "I'm not going to say I didn't need it. I will say I'm adjusting in a pretty healthy fashion."[74]

Covering Violence

The career of Donatella Lorch illustrates the rigors of trauma reporting. She covered wars and conflicts in the Balkans, South Asia, the Middle East, Africa, and Europe for the *New York Times*, NBC News and *Newsweek*. She reported on Operation Desert Storm (Iraq) and the fall of Kabul to Afghan guerillas in 1992.[75]

But it was her work as East Africa bureau chief for the *New York Times* that resulted in her most painful memories. In *War Stories: Reporting in the Time of Conflict from the Crimea* by Harold Evans, she noted:

> Four of my friends were killed in Mogadishu (Somalia). I couldn't even react for the first week, but I was still crying a year later. Years after I left Africa, I still have terrible nightmares. I came out of Africa, and for six months there was this darkness in my soul that nothing could remove.[76]

Lorch documented her experiences ("Surviving the Five Ds: A Writer Struggles with the Emotional Aftermath of Covering Brutality in Africa") in the summer 2001 issue of the *Media Studies Journal*:

> In Africa my colleagues and I joked that we covered the five Ds: the Dead, the Dying, the Diseased, the Depressing and the Dangerous. In three years there (1993–96), I reported on six civil wars, genocide and massive refugee migrations. I walked over thousands of corpses. I was shot at, carjacked, arrested and contracted cerebral malaria. It was a roller coaster of intense emotions, an adrenaline high that included raw fear and anger and horror and pure, extreme fun. I loved it. I hated it.[77]

Like other journalists who spent years covering tragic stories, Lorch's memories were triggered by evocative sensory details. She wrote about visiting Nyarubuye in eastern Rwanda in 1994:

> The smell and the stillness were too overwhelming. I'd put Vicks VapoRub on my nose and a bandana over my mouth and tried hard to gulp little breaths. The rain had left scattered puddles, and bodies had rotted in them. It was impossible to escape that sickly, gagging stench.

This place, I knew, had witnessed true evil, an evil that I could see and smell. Yet it floated about, untouchable, and all I could do was take notes.[78]

Later in her article, Lorch discussed the impact of the emotional effects of viewing such horror. She talked about a close friend Michael Skoler, an award-winning Nairobi bureau chief for National Public Radio, who said: "There was no way to really share the experience, to put it into logical, analytic terms. So the feelings never got resolved, they just sort of sat."[79]

Lorch credited the *New York Times* for "turning the world of U.N. peacekeeping upside down to get me out of Rwanda" and for getting her treated for her malaria. She also stated that after she returned to the newspaper, a psychiatrist debriefed her.[80] The *New York Times* in the last decade has been considered one of the most progressive print news organizations in responding to journalists who have covered tragedy and trauma.

Lorch commented that back in the United States in the mid-1990s, editors "were often clueless about what we had witnessed or how it might have affected us." She closed her article with these haunting words: "I became intimately acquainted with fear, desperation, cynicism and total vulnerability. They remain my companions today."[81] On a more hopeful note, according to her website, Donatella Lorch married in 2003 and is a mother and stepmother.[82]

The impact of reporting on the horror in Africa in the 1990s was evident in the comments of BBC war correspondent Fergal Keane in *Journalists under Fire: The Psychological Hazards of Covering War*. By the time Keane went to Rwanda in 1994, he had already covered several African conflicts. But he was unprepared for the extent of the genocide he encountered in Rwanda. The violence was on a scale that made it difficult to describe much less comprehend:

> We lived out in the field. There was no hotel to go back to at the end of the day. So, we lived with them, the victims, in abandoned villages with the smell of the corpses around you. . . . The tensions were frightening, but this was a level beyond. There was a degree to which the whole moral order was gone, so killing was the right thing to do. There were no boundaries and everyone around you had this kind of blood frenzy . . . . We felt very threatened.[83]

Keane's first Rwandan visit lasted three weeks. When he returned to the country soon after the slaughter had abated, the "emotional residue of that first experience clung tenaciously." Keane said he felt guilty after filming a group of Tutsis who had seemingly survived the genocide. He would discover that these people were later taken and killed. On the last day of his second trip, he met a woman who had somehow escaped being killed. She had remembered Keane and his film crew. She said, "We thought you were with the militia because you did nothing to help us. We thought you must be with them." Keane apologized, telling her that he was too afraid at the time to help the people. "I mean it's hard to convey to you the level of fear in a situation like that," he told author and psychiatrist Anthony Feinstein.[84]

But Keane also described the stimulation of conflict coverage:

> What I got out of war was a buzz. You don't ever feel more alive. You know the shelling is going on and you are exposed to this intense experience and at the same time it seems like the most important thing in the world. It's just so addictive. So addictive.[85]

And in a melancholy moment, Keane, mourning the loss of a BBC colleague who was killed on assignment in South Africa, wrote:

> Journalists race around in search of civil war, secretly happiest when they sign off from some hellhole where the bodies are stacking up and the omens of apocalypse are most vivid. I am sick to the teeth of war stories, the flak jackets and all the attendant bullshit. Why did we do it all? Why do people like John and me and countless others race around townships and battle zones? I am still searching for the answer, but I know that pursuit of the truth is only one part of the equation.[86]

Ian Stewart, author of the 2002 book *Ambushed: A War Reporter's Life on the Line,* discussed similar themes and emotions as Fergal Keane in chronicling his experiences in Africa at the end of the twentieth century. In early 1998, Stewart became the AP's West Africa bureau chief, responsible for coordinating news coverage of twenty-three countries, including war torn Sierra Leone. In January 1999, he was shot in the head when the car he was riding in was machine-gunned by a rebel fighter.

As a war correspondent, the Canadian-born Stewart had long been familiar with high-risk assignments, such as his coverage of Afghanistan in 1995. He had been briefly held hostage in Kabul. But instead of being intimidated, Stewart was energized by the experience: "rather than scaring me away from reporting in dangerous places, [it] spurred me to seek them out."[87] When Stewart had been under fire in Kabul, he had felt invincible "with the excitement of someone who had cheated death." Not yet 30, Stewart had developed a "taste for the rush of adrenaline that comes in life-threatening situations. In the years to come, that taste would become insatiable, until it nearly killed me."[88]

Stewart says throughout his career, his longing for adventure had never waned. In 1997, he had traveled to Southeast Asia, where he came under fire in Cambodia. "I had become a war junkie—juiced as much on the thrill of combat as by the chase for a good story. It's not uncommon for photographers, but less typical of print journalists."[89]

By 2002, three years after Stewart was almost killed by gunfire in Freetown, Sierra Leone (West Africa), he had made significant physical recovery; however, there were serious long-term consequences (e.g., seizures). The one-time adventure-driven reporter said his past often returned to haunt him, such as when journalist Daniel Pearl was murdered in Pakistan.

> I am no longer the hard-drinking, chain-smoking war reporter who needed so desperately to be in the thick of combat to find purpose in life . . . . The craving for adrenaline has abated. Sadly, I had to almost lose everything to learn what I had. I suppose I had to stare into the heart of darkness to see through to the other side.[90]

CNN's Anderson Cooper was a young reporter in his mid-twenties, working for the media organization *Channel One* when he experienced the damaging effects of covering death and destruction on a large scale. He returned from covering the genocide in Rwanda. In his memoir, *Dispatches from the Edge*, Cooper told his boss: "My heart is too full."

> I didn't want to see any more death. I think he thought I wanted more money. The truth was I'd simply had enough.[91]

Covering Tragedy

Jim Willis, author of *The Human Journalist*, wrote:

> While war correspondents are clearly at risk, a reporter does not have to go into a war zone to be exposed to traumatic stress. Crime, highway accidents, and natural disasters all are staples of print and broadcast media. Covering violence and death is the rule rather than the exception for many journalists.[92]

Sometimes entire communities are traumatized by tragedy, whether from catastrophes, acts of terrorism, or violent crimes. In the winter 2009 issue of *Nieman Reports*, Don Corrigan, editor and copublisher of the *Webster-Kirkwood Times* and *South County Times* in suburban St. Louis, reveals the depth of pain and loss that occurs "When Murder Strikes a Small Community."[93]

Corrigan describes Kirkwood, Missouri, as a sort of Mayberry, "more accustomed to our upbeat stories," before February 7, 2008, when a disturbed community resident went on a shooting spree at city hall, killing two police officers, two city council members, the city engineer, and the mayor. One of the *Times'* reporters, who regularly covered city hall, was not physically injured, but she was directly behind the city engineer who was murdered execution-style. A reporter from another community publication also witnessed the carnage and was wounded in the attack.[94]

In the article that reads more like a memoir, Corrigan discusses his concern for his staff and for a community shaken by the terrifying crime. He also explains how his "own situation was compounded by the death of a close friend just days before the shootings, and then learning my dad was diagnosed with inoperable brain cancer days after the shootings." In the newsroom, staffers were offered counseling and time off. They were also advised to "come together to talk among ourselves about our feelings and how we were coping with conflicting emotions."[95]

While acknowledging the role of the Dart Center for Journalism & Trauma in educating him and others on the damaging emotional and psychological effects that may result from tragedies reporters often must cover, Corrigan raises questions appropriate for community journalists in places such as Oklahoma City, Littleton, Colorado, New Orleans, and Blacksburg, Virginia:

- What is a news organization's responsibility to its reporters who are eyewitnesses to murder? Can an editorial staff experience depression or long-term PTSD as a result of such exposure?

- What are the local news media's obligations to the national news media as requests for background information and interviews pile up? In the case of a community weekly, when do we say "no" and take care of our own coverage and our own needs?

- When the national dailies, TV networks, and the cable news channel operations finally go away, what should the continuing coverage of the local news media operation be like? Can the content of such coverage help with the healing of a community as a newspaper's own staff?[96]

In searching for answers, Corrigan says simply and compassionately: "In the time since the city hall massacre, it has been important to be human as we go about doing our work."[97]

Debra McKinney's profile in *Covering Violence: A Guide to Ethical Reporting about Victims and Trauma* chronicles how the *AnchorageDaily*

News (Alaska) reporter had written an evocative account of a Baptist preacher's family's attempts to recover from years of childhood sexual abuse. "They would live the rest of their lives without feeling whole," she says. "He had raped their souls." After writing the story, McKinney was emotionally drained. She says for a time she wanted a break from covering crime and violence. But then she met other adult incest survivors and documented their accounts.[98]

In order to secure the trust of her sources, McKinney offered them the chance to review the story for factual accuracy. The review courtesy was not about changing the material; it was about "easing the shock of seeing themselves in print." Her sources had assured her before they read the article that they were committed to being quoted and profiled. In commenting on her approach, McKinney says: "We felt a strong sense of responsibility to them for trusting us with their stories."[99]

Although she had never experienced the trauma of sexual assault in her life, McKinney approached the writing of her story with extensive knowledge of the subject. She had covered rape support groups and was familiar with a range of community resources: therapists, detectives, attorneys, and an administrator of a statewide sex-offender treatment program. She says that the strength to write about the aftermath of violence came from her sources. According to Migael Scherer, author of the McKinney profile:

> Like a reporter who follows soldiers in the field, exposed to combat and the trauma that follows, McKinney bravely follows those who have been wounded—some by the very adults who should have protected them. Carefully charting the course of recovery, she discovers the heroes.[100]

Florida International University Professor Fred Blevens became a journalist because he wanted to make a difference, and he believed media work was a "righteous" occupation. But like many former journalists, Blevens left the business decades later and entered academia. Since 1991, he has been a teacher and administrator at several universities in the United States. But for almost twenty years, Blevens worked as a reporter and editor at daily newspapers.

His last assignment was as state editor for the *Houston Chronicle*. He recalls coverage of a serial murder in Killeen, Texas, in 1991. After working on stories of this killing spree for more than a week, he recalls telling his wife, "I don't think I can do another of these."

Blevens says that what had first attracted him to the news business—the adrenaline rush of covering high-profile stories—eventually wore him down and drove him out of the news business. Like other journalists, he had often turned to drinking and smoking to deal with the stress on the job. He said his family and friends grew concerned over the years as his self-medicating became more frequent. Eventually, he pursued a second career as an educator. Today, he helps train young journalists about the challenging realities they will face.

In 1981, Tim Twyman was a 23-year-old cameraman who had been working at KNBC-TV in Kansas City for three years. On that fateful evening of July 17, he arrived at the Hyatt Hotel site about 20 minutes after the Skywalk collapse, which killed more than one hundred people. He described the scene as a "sea of blood." He says he fixed his eye on his viewfinder and began filming. Years later, he admits: "I don't know if I could shoot that story today. I'd want to put the camera down and help people."

Twyman, who has worked at the Kansas City NBC affiliate for more than thirty years, says he was "bummed out for quite a while" after the Hyatt Skywalk tragedy. He processed his emotions by talking with family, friends, and coworkers. He also drew on his religious faith to help him cope.

He says that journalists who cover tragedy and trauma need to find creative ways to balance their lives. On the subject of counseling, he believes that the threshold of most journalists to seek therapeutic intervention is very high compared with police officers, firefighter, and EMTs, adding that professional egos and newsroom peer pressure are key reasons why most journalists wouldn't consider counseling. But he cautions his fellow journalists: "You can't bottle those negative emotions up. There's a limit to how much you can take."

In the world of trauma journalism, a Kansas City (Missouri) videographer like Tim Twyman and a leading broadcast journalist like Peter Harvey from Australia are kindred spirits when it comes to discussing the effects of covering tragedy and recommending postevent intervention measures. Harvey, a commentator on the Nine Network's *60 Minutes* program, based in Sydney, is one of several journalists featured in *News Media & Trauma*, produced in 2008 by the Dart Centre for Journalism & Trauma, Australasia. The DVD is introduced as "produced by newspeople for newspeople" featuring journalists speaking "candidly about the stories that had the greatest impact on them, from car crashes to natural disasters."[101]

The first tragedy Harvey covered, then as a print journalist, was a fatal air crash in the early 1960s. At just 19, the young *Daily Telegraph* reporter Harvey was shown the mangled bodies of the dead airplane crew by a morgue attendant. "It was just a terrible, terrible sight," he says on camera. "It affected me very deeply for quite some time." Harvey admits he didn't realize that the way to relieve his anxiety about what he had seen was to "talk about it." His experiences as a rookie reporter being assigned to the crime beat are standard in newsrooms around the world. While some veterans reminisce about their grueling rites of passages, others acknowledge the effects of such coverage.[102]

In the Dart Centre video, the *Age* newspaper reporter Gary Tippet discusses the coping skills of cynicism and black humor that so often form a protective wall for young journalists, such as those working the police beat. He also describes the common assignment for young reporters—"death knocks" or "intrusions"—when next-of-kin are interviewed after a tragedy has claimed a loved one. In the rush to make deadlines and headlines, Tippet says, "We can forget that these human beings we're dealing with are suffering the worst trauma of their lives." He adds that if reporters can't be empathetic in these cases, they can't be effective storytellers.[103]

Australian Broadcasting Corporation (ABC) journalist Philip Williams talks of being emotionally affected by a tragic story, such as the one he covered involving a terrorist attack on a school that claimed children's lives. He says there was a delayed reaction on his psyche. Even a year later, he found himself anxious and angry with his own family. "We're just as vulnerable as any other member of the community," Williams says. "Otherwise, we're sort of setting ourselves apart, saying actually being a journalist somehow magically makes you bulletproof, and it doesn't."[104]

Jessica Adamson, a reporter with the Seven Network, was candid in discussing her troubled feelings regarding a tragedy that unfolded "right outside her newsroom" in Adelaide, Australia. A baby boy in a stroller had been abducted and was later pulled from the river—still strapped in the stroller. Adamson says she regretted acting first as a journalist, narrating at the scene as the mother "dragged her dead baby from the river." She felt guilty that she hadn't tried to help the mother, although she was the one to call for an ambulance as police worked to resuscitate the boy, while the mother watched in horror.[105]

Adamson continued working that day, filing her report on "every mother's worst nightmare." But she broke down at just after 6 p.m. when the news aired. For days afterward, she received vicious hate mail and e-mails, blaming her for her insensitivity.

"People have this conception that journalists don't have feelings," she says. "I'd have given anything not to have been there that day."[106]

Viewing the video, produced by Brett McLeod and Paul Webber, with the resources of Nine Network Australia, one is struck by the candor forthcoming from these journalists. A likely influence for such progressive behavior is the work of Dart Centre Australasia's director Cait McMahon, who has led trauma journalism research and reform efforts during the last decade. In his closing remarks, journalist Peter Harvey sums up the spirit of advocates for more enlightened newsrooms: "If you're dealing with something that is shocking, ghastly, heart-wrenching, don't leave it inside you."[107]

The Dart Center for Journalism & Trauma, headquartered at Columbia University in New York City, maintains an excellent website, dartcenter.org—a comprehensive repository of resources, including publications, educational materials, and articles on covering conflict, violence, and tragedy. One vivid example is "How Covering Jonesboro Changed a Reporter" by Audrey Lott Watkins, who reported on the tragic shootings on March 24,

1998, that claimed the lives of four young girls and teacher and wounded ten students.[108]

Watkins, who was a member of the *Jonesboro Sun* news team that was named a finalist in the 1999 Pulitzer Prize competition for its coverage, details the difficult process of interviewing victims (wounded students) and the families of the injured and the dead. In one case, she talked with the father of a young girl critically wounded in the shooting: "Once the interview started, he poured out his heart to me—a complete stranger—and I questioned what right I had to even be in his presence when his own daughter was struggling for her life in intensive care."[109]

As emotionally draining as the days surrounding the tragedy were, Watkins says it was a year later, when the newspaper and the community were marking the anniversary of the Westside Middle School shooting, that the cumulative effect of the trauma coverage caught up with her. She found it hard to concentrate, even with her own family. At times, she was bored and emotionally numb. At other times, she was angry. In retrospect, she writes: "During the entire year *The Jonesboro Sun* staff reported on the shooting and its aftermath, no one ever suggested that counseling could be beneficial for those covering the story. . . . I suppose we all knew we could ask for assistance if we needed it, but exposing such a weakness could result in being removed from the story and being passed over for difficult stories in the future."[110]

Watkins' concerns about disclosing emotional or psychological issues related to trauma journalism coverage are at the eye of the storm in contentious discussions about roadblocks to newsroom reform. And those concerns are heightened in the current recessionary economic climate affecting media worldwide. Yet, increasingly more journalists are asking questions like Watkins raises in her online article:

> Why was it that emergency responders such as police and paramedics were offered debriefing sessions and counseling to help them cope with the trauma they had witnessed but those who reported on the stories were not? Was it realistic to believe that a reporter or photographer could stand in a bloodstained school yard where innocent students and teachers had been ambushed and not be personally affected?[111]

After nearly ten years on the news staff at the *Jonesboro* newspaper, Watkins left to pursue a master's degree, hoping to shift her career focus to "help educate others in the profession about critical incident reporting and how they may be affected." In her article, she says she plans to continue her advocacy to enhance communications among journalists covering tragedy and trauma and to ensure that debriefing and counseling programs are available to those who may need such assistance, without fear of reprisal.[112]

Watkins' article about the deadly school shooting at an Arkansas middle school in 1998, may remind readers of the frequency of other tragic (secondary) school shootings in the last two decades in Scotland, Finland, and Germany, and across the United States (e.g., Alaska, Kentucky, Mississippi, and Oregon). In recent American history, the Jonesboro (Arkansas) tragedy was prelude to an even more horrific community crisis, foreshadowing the multiple murders just a year later at a Colorado High School now known infamously as Columbine.

Faces of Trauma Journalism: Scott North

Photo by Mark Mulligan, *The Daily Herald*

Scott North has spent most of his journalistic career in the northwest Washington (state) community of Everett, where he was raised as the second of nine children in a close-knit middle-class rural family. After a short stint as an environmental reporter, he was hired by the *Daily Herald* in 1987 to cover crime and courts, a beat he has worked for almost twenty-five years. Early on, he connected with local police and prosecutors, enhancing his interviewing by studying detectives' interrogation techniques. He credits a former editor, Joann Byrd, and the Dart Center for Journalism & Trauma with instilling in him a heightened sensitivity to the ethics of trauma coverage. In 2010, Scott completed his three-year term as president of the Dart Society, an organization of journalists from several countries who have earned Ochberg (Dart Center) Fellowships and have been introduced to progressive methods in the reporting of conflict, violence, and tragedy.

He recalls covering stories earlier in his career when he lacked empathy. Several years ago, Scott wrote about a 17-year-old girl who was murdered by a serial killer. As he discussed in *Covering Violence: A Guide to Ethical Reporting about Victims and Trauma*, his newspaper article portrayed the girl as a victim not as a person. A local advocate wrote him, describing how the girl's father was hurt by the story. Scott spoke with the man. As a result, he had to rethink the effects of his reporting on victims, their family members, and friends.[113]

Scott says his connection to victimization results from his upbringing, where he was taught to confront bullies, and his later encounters with secondary trauma. In 1994, he witnessed the hanging of a convicted murderer. He was unprepared for the emotional residue of observing that death. Yet, he didn't undergo any intervention after the execution, something that surprised Scott's sources on the local police force, who have mandatory debriefings after deaths in the line of fire. That same year (1994), a study was published in the *American Journal of Psychiatry* concerning the stressful psychological reactions of fifteen journalists who had witnessed an execution and had experienced dissociation, anxiety, and other symptoms—even in the absence of physical risk.[114]

After covering several murder trials ("ugly things") and being exposed to years of people's suffering, Scott felt as if he were "rubbing his soul against a cheese grater." He dealt with sleeplessness, flashbacks, anger, and emotional numbing—telltale signs of PTSD symptoms. When the strain of his job began to affect his home life (he has been married since 1982 and has an 18-year-old daughter), Scott, a solid 200-pounder with an intimidating glare, turned to budo (the study of Japanese martial arts) and outdoor pursuits—fly fishing, hiking, and rock climbing. He finds comfort and meaning in studying Eastern philosophy, including the writings of Yamamoto Tsunetomo. Scott's favorite quotation is: "The wisdom and courage that come from compassion are real wisdom and courage."[115]

In the *Daily Herald* newsroom, Scott has helped implement innovative approaches to crime reporting, such as establishing panels of community experts and residents for feedback and advice on high-profile tragic stories (e.g., the murder of young children). He says these efforts help treat people with compassion and honesty and generate trust with sources. His newsroom's heightened awareness of trauma journalism has focused attention on the impact of stressful stories on reporters. Scott says informal debriefings are encouraged with friends, colleagues, or peers. As an assistant city editor in charge of investigative reporting and crime coverage, Scott now looks "constantly for signs of trauma-related stress and burnout" among his staff. He evaluates assignments and tries to anticipate how they will affect people. He uses three-to-five-person team coverage for long criminal trials and extended stories of violence and tragedy. He emphasizes restorative breaks and directs reporters to leave work at a reasonable hour.

"I think that many of the trauma-related problems that afflict reporters in community news operations are the result of too much immersion over time," he says. Scott also promotes "renewal stories," those assignments that address local problems, such as underlying causes of violence, and identify ways to make a difference.

Having been reared in Everett, Washington, Scott North is proud to call himself a community reporter, someone who has "sunk his roots deep . . . and covered it hard." He says that when he drives through Everett, he sees the places that are connected to tragedy as both "a beautiful and terrible thing." Among his proudest accomplishments are stories about local tragic events that never make national headlines. One such article concerned two unsolved murders of young women some six years apart. Scott wrote about the relationship of mothers of the two victims:

> A common loss became fertile ground for friendship. Each found in the other someone willing to listen who didn't mind tears and who understood a mother's prayer asking God for justice for a murdered child.[116]

In Scott's portfolio, his most noteworthy and personal story concerns the death of a 19-year-old Native American man named Mylo Harvey, a member of the Tulalip Tribes from Snohomish County, Washington, who died in a struggle with police while under the influence of hallucinogenic mushrooms. "I spent five years on the story, writing the dailies that were obvious, but mostly living it and trying to make sense of what it was compelling me to say." Scott's eleven-part serial narrative, "A Truth Beyond," was published in August 2008.[117]

In chronicling the death of the charismatic young man, Scott explored his own roots (his maternal grandmother was a Mexican immigrant) and the connections to the strong women who shaped his life. He wrote the series using first-person point of view, a device he rarely employed but one well suited to this narrative. He also relied on painstaking research, reporting, and fact checking, practices he says are often foreign to the frantic pace of twenty-first-century social media coverage. The series honors the life of Mylo Harvey as it seeks to answer the troubling questions about how and why he died. It is also a journey to the heart of a hometown journalist committed to finding answers without causing more harm to those who had already lost so much.

Scott begins the story at the young man's grave—"a place of lost promise." He notes that when Mylo Harvey was buried in 2002, more than 600 people walked to this spot on the Tulalip Indian Reservation. But what inspires Scott's account are the actions of 3 women from Mylo's family— his mother, an aunt, and his grandmother—who pressed authorities for answers and refused to let Mylo die in vain.[118]

The writing in "A Truth Beyond" is deceptively simple and understated: "For years, Mylo's family brought me to his grave. They allowed a stranger to walk with them, to do what a journalist does—to listen, to watch, to ask questions, and, now, to tell a story." Scott is frank in discussing the challenges of writing such an in-depth narrative:

> The journey placed me at odds with another group of people, Everett police officers, whom I respect and who also have extended me great trust. It made me think hard about the role of a newspaper reporter, and the things that bind and divide each of us who now lives in Snohomish County. . . . One of the challenges of writing about my hometown is being close enough to see events from the perspective of those involved, while keeping enough distance to hear other truths.[119]

As the account unfolds, Scott is both narrator and educator. He reveals how crime reporters get to know victims well, and how these stories happen "up close, in living rooms with mothers and fathers whose trembling fingers flip through photo albums and brush away tears." He describes the special dread that comes from being assigned "death knocks": the rite-of-passage for young reporters who must literally knock on some grieving stranger's door or place a phone call to a victim's family. But Scott doesn't equivocate:

> Journalists plumb grief because of this truth: At some point, nearly everybody wants their loved one's memory honored. Reporters are the people in a community best equipped to tell those stories.[120]

By the story's halfway point, the narrative turns into a legal drama—a showdown between police and Mylo's family. "It was like watching a car sliding on ice down a steep hill," Scott writes, displaying a fluid use of metaphorical devices and descriptive details. He foreshadows how: "Competing versions of truth would collide. . . . Only time would tell how well anybody listened."[121]

Scott identifies two opposing theories, by the time the (federal civil rights) trial approaches in the fall of 2006, as to why Mylo died. The police experts would link his death to "excited delirium." A long and exhausting struggle with several officers, "driven by Mylo's drug-induced state, created lethal changes in his blood chemistry that stopped his heart." The plaintiffs (Mylo's family) would claim, via their experts, that the young man likely died "from a combination of being struck on the head with a police baton and having his chest compressed under the weight of struggling officers."[122]

As the trial nears, the Tulalip tribal members (some 4,000), through their board of directors, authorize financial support to assist Mylo Harvey's family in pursuing litigation. Scott as ethnographer describes the tribal culture's rituals. He attends a ceremony in a gymnasium and is given a medicine pouch (containing personal items, notably mementos of Mylo Harvey) to wear around his neck:

> Journalists usually don't accept gifts, but the *Herald*'s policy is also clear. Culture trumps code; the purpose of having ethics is to do the right thing. I was honored.[123]

The emotional ceremony causes Scott North to reflect on his career:

> I carry these memories along with the sights and sounds and smells from thousands of stories I've covered. As a reporter I've written about people struggling with fire and flood; homecomings, departures, trials and triumphs. Each memory is distinct, but they play off each other, in the way moving water, rocks and trees come together to form a river. Some memories become clear only when viewed from a distance.[124]

Scott also reflects on the grief he has experienced in his life, such as the death of his mother from cancer. She had raised him to work hard and to stand up for what he believed in. By being emotionally engaged in the story of Mylo Harvey, Scott North was vulnerable to his own feelings of loss: "Loving somebody means living with risk."[125]

Instead of a melodramatic (Hollywood) ending, Scott lays out the pragmatic conclusion to the Harvey's family quest for justice. He notes that the family and their attorneys took a suggestion from the presiding judge and attempted to settle the case. A federal mediator structured an agreement acceptable to both the family and the police. The city of Everett would pay the Harvey family $500,000 in an out-of-court settlement. Officials would publicly express remorse over Mylo's death. The police would also seek (crisis intervention) training as other departments had done nationwide to try and prevent another tragic death.

At a graveside ceremony in November 2006, the Harvey family, led by Mylo's mother, Diane, grandmother Donna, and aunt, Nilah, once again bid their goodbyes, believing that some measure of justice had been achieved. Most importantly, the family had supported one another "through the tough times, never turning back from what needed to be done."

> The family released eight balloons into the sky, seven white and one red in the shape of a heart. The balloons rose slowly, a cold wind pushing them west over the slate-colored waters of Tulalip Bay. I stood near the circle, an observer, connected but apart, at a distance where a journalist finds truth.[126]

That "truth," says Scott, includes acknowledging that immersion in trauma can transform a journalist and not always in positive ways. He says the hesitancy of those in the news media to openly discuss issues like the psychological effects of reporting is tied to the longstanding belief among journalists that the focus should be on others and not on the storytellers:

> That emotional separation is the place we've been taught to seek cover and also to maintain objective distances. What happens when evidence tells us otherwise; that the separation is a myth? Answer: You've got to rethink just about everything.[127]

In hours of conversation, Scott North speaks passionately about the "highest and best expression of journalism" amid cutbacks and closings of major news outlets. He encourages young reporters to see journalism as more of a craft than a profession, his rationale being that skill at a craft takes time and attention to develop. He notes one's progress is as much a product of mistakes as success.

"Much of what we know about good trauma reporting comes from people having made mistakes," he says, alluding to his journey and apprenticeship as a community journalist. "Learn from those and the ones you inevitably will make on your own."

CHAPTER FOUR

In Tragedy's Wake

In this chapter, I examine the impact of media coverage of six recent (1999 to 2010) devastating events—two international and four that occurred on North American soil. Because of their magnitude and the extensive news treatment each received, my emphasis is not on retelling these dramatic stories but in analyzing the effects of reporting on journalists, their sources, and their audiences. These case studies include commentary on the news media's performance, both in the execution of the craft under demanding circumstances and in ethical decision-making, offering lessons for current and future generations of trauma journalists.

Columbine: April 20, 1999

The psychological impact on journalists covering the massacre at Columbine High School and the extended aftermath were discussed in a 2000 dart-center.org article "Columbine: Reporter's Perspectives, Part 1." Author Audrey Lott Watkins quotes Ann Schrader, a medical/science reporter for the *Denver Post*:

> It scorched your soul. It made you really look down deep within yourself. . . . These were not just numbers; these were people. You had to try to be as sensitive as you could but yet still be competitive and bring people the news. . . . It was tough.[1]

In a follow-up article, Watkins focused on a journalist from a small weekly newspaper—*Columbine Courier* reporter Caren Boddie, who had arrived at the high school before other media and most emergency personnel on April 20, 1999. Boddie says it was "overwhelming" covering the Columbine story for months: "It was supposed to be this part-time job that was supplementing my other income, and it had become my whole life. I went up to full time and beyond." She admits confusing her priorities, putting too much emphasis on work, and trying to deal with ongoing stress. Ultimately, the toll became too great for Boddie, who was affected by the intense dislike and distrust for the media that resulted from the Columbine stories. She left her job at the newspaper.

> When you come from New York, and you cover the story and go home, it's not a biggie to you if you upset people. They weren't really upset about what I had written, just the media. The people here grew to hate anybody who had anything to do with the media. This is my community, and that just became way too much for me.[2]

A March 2001 article ("Stress on the Press: The Media and Violence") published in *Columns*, the UW's alumni magazine, cites George Kochaniec Jr., photographer, *Rocky Mountain News*, recalling how difficult it was taking photos near the makeshift triage area in the school parking lot on that dreadful April day. He talked about not wanting to "make it any worse for those kids," but he also spoke of having to do his job. More than a year after the tragedy, Kochaniec, the father of then-high-school-age boys, admitted to still being troubled by his Columbine experiences. "Little things trigger memories," he said. "Sometimes I think I just can't move on."[3]

Months after the deadly shootings in Littleton, Colorado, high school administrators, faculty, students, victims, and other community leaders planned a ritual to promote a shared sense of healing. They conceived a special event called "Take Back the School." According to *Columbine* author Dave Cullen, the ceremony to be successful needed an antagonist, and the news media were an easy target.

> The *Denver Post* and *Rocky Mountain News* were still running Columbine stories every day—several a day. As the fall (1999) semester beckoned, coverage shot back up: ten stories a day between the two papers. And the national outlets were back. "How do you feel?" everyone constantly wanted to know.[4]

> (Author's Note: In more enlightened journalism circles, such a question is considered an anathema to ethical reporting and among the worst, most insensitive questions to ask victims or family and friends.)

What had precipitated such a vehement reaction from this solid middle-class Denver suburb? First, mistakes, misinformation, and error-filled reporting in the immediate aftermath of the tragedy. Second, the relentless pursuit of media coverage and the often arrogant, patronizing, insensitive attitude of reporters, particularly from the national news organizations, who "parachuted" in, camped out at the high school and other community locations, and invaded people's privacy. Third, the continuous news cycle, which was allegedly retraumatizing children and their families, was arguably driven not by genuine news value but by the quest for local market dominance (by the two competing Denver newspapers—the *Denver Post* and the *Rocky Mountain News*) and broadcast ratings.

John Temple, then editor, president, and publisher of the *Rocky Mountain News*, says in a 2003 video (*Covering Columbine*), written and directed by Meg Moritz, University of Colorado School of Journalism and Mass Communication, and partially funded by the Dart Center for Journalism & Trauma and The Freedom Forum: "We were an obvious target—cause what did we do? We reminded them constantly of Columbine."

Denver-area reporters spoke on the video about the anger directed at the mob mentality of the "media circus" covering the tragedy. But the harshest criticism from Littleton residents, including direct threats to journalists, appeared reserved for the actions of scores of national news media, as was the case with other American communities struck by mass murders, including Lancaster, Pennsylvania, in the wake of the October 2006 Amish school shootings and the 2007 massacre at VTU in Blacksburg.

Some final reflections on the coverage of Columbine: Ten days before the first anniversary of the tragedy, photographers at the *Rocky Mountain News* won the Pulitzer Prize for spot news photography. The *Denver Post* also won a Pulitzer for its news coverage. A decade later, on February 27, 2009, the *Rocky Mountain News* published its last edition, closing after nearly 150 years in business.

In the acknowledgments of his book, Dave Cullen thanked Dr. Frank Ochberg (founder), Bruce Shapiro (current executive director), Barb Monseu (former executive committee vice president), and everyone at the Dart Center (for Journalism & Trauma) who helped teach him about "compassion for victims and for myself." As a Dart Center Ochberg Fellow in 2002, Cullen, a longtime freelance journalist, creative writing instructor, and former lieutenant in the US Army, had received weeklong intensive training in critical incident coverage.

9/11

If the Columbine tragedy revealed failings of the news media in covering a community crisis, then the reporting of the terrorist attacks of 9/11 in New York City and Washington, DC, undoubtedly showed many courageous acts and valiant efforts as journalists faced death, destruction, and trauma on an unprecedented scale. Repeated anecdotes document how reporters and photographers put themselves at risk as they moved toward Ground Zero and the Pentagon, bearing witness to the horror and chaos that surrounded them. In *Covering Violence: A Guide to Ethical Reporting about Victims and Trauma*, authors Simpson and Coté note how journalists as first responders often reach disaster scenes ahead of or along with emergency workers, balancing "the fear of unknown dangers against the search for the image or pieces of the story."

David Handschuh, photographer for the *Daily News*, was one of many who ignored his personal safety as he took pictures of his native New York City under attack. His story is among the 8 in-depth "Faces of Trauma Journalism" profiles in this book. Bill Biggart perished on 9/11 while photographing cataclysmic events in lower Manhattan. Dirck Halstead, digitaljournalist.org, provided this account of the man who took some 150 images as he walked toward the World Trade Center:

> People filled his pictures as they stopped, stunned, and reacted in disbelief and amazement. At 10:00:08, according to the time stamp on Biggart's digital photo, a cloud of debris from the tower collapse engulfed him. He walked farther, snapping the damaged Marriott Hotel. Two minutes later, Biggart died as the second tower collapsed.

Another impressive 9/11 account tells of Arthur Santana, a crime reporter at the *Washington Post*, who was one of the first news workers to reach the area of the Pentagon that had been struck by the crashed airliner:

> He stayed at the site for the rest of the day and into the evening, helping rescue workers and talking to those who had lost friends and colleagues. . . . Santana befriended Kenneth Foster, whose wife, Sandra, had worked in the damaged section of the building. Foster worked tirelessly in the rescue efforts, driven by an "awful mission" to find his wife alive. A day later, after Foster realized that his wife had died in the explosion, Santana invited Foster to talk about her for a *Post* article. "Ken saw it as a chance to honor the memory of his wife," Santana told the Dart Center. "He saw that I had laid down my notebook to help with the rescue efforts. He saw me as a human being and not a journalist."

In his award-winning documentary, *Breaking News, Breaking Down*, broadcast journalist Mike Walter, who was also in Washington, DC, on September 11, 2001, and witnessed the American Airlines jet slamming into the Pentagon, described how the events of that day affected him in ways he couldn't imagine. He said he was surprised at his emotions. "After that day, I was haunted by nightmares, gripped by depression, and lived my life in a constant fog," he writes in "Tears are Part of Telling the Story" in the winter 2009 issue of *Nieman Reports.*[10]

Walter, the writer, director, and producer of the 2008 film, states in his article that after 9/11, he felt "like a misfit as I asked myself why. Why me? Why was I there that day? Why was I reacting this way?" He says it would take years for him to "find a way to create something good out of the experience of witnessing such a tragedy." His film traces his journey as he meets other journalists "who were similarly affected by their work from coverage of 9/11 to Hurricane Katrina."[11]

The 2002 book *At Ground Zero: 25 Stories from Young Reporters Who Were There* features eyewitness journalistic accounts of 9/11. In her first year reporting for the *Washington Post*, Christine Haughney had interviewed relatives of those killed in the 1988 Pan Am Flight that exploded over Lockerbie, Scotland. During her career, she also had to question loved ones of murder victims, survivors of sexual assaults, and other traumatized sources. She says she often felt uncomfortable being so close to victims' emotions.[12] But the sights she lived through and the people she interviewed after the World Trade Center attacks were much more intense than her earlier experiences:

> It was nothing like running from crumbling towers and inhaling acrid smoke. It was nothing like interviewing heartbroken firefighters. These experiences don't go away when I file my articles. There is too much tragedy to process.[13]

For four months after 9/11, Haughney wrote or contributed to more than thirty stories relating to the World Trade Center attacks or the anthrax scare. Most of these stories required her to return to Ground Zero or to revisit that fateful day. She says she found herself thinking constantly about the logistics of death. Haughney had a steady stream of nightmares and restless nights that left her cranky and overtired. She didn't know how to share what she was going through with family and friends. It seemed as if everything she said about her work was depressing. She wept often. She said her boyfriend "couldn't understand the depths of my sadness about the tragedy I had witnessed." Haughney often found solace connecting with her sources—Tribeca residents and rescue workers.[14]

She concluded her chapter in reflection:

> The biggest lesson I have learned from this experience is not to judge how people process tragedy. . . . I can't expect my boyfriend, family and close friends to fully understand what it was like to live and work through the World Trade Center attacks. There's something comforting in that they don't share these recesses in my heart.[15]

In the aftermath of 9/11, Heather Nauert, general assignment reporter, Fox-TV News, had to interview victims' families. She thought it would be insensitive to intrude on people's grieving by asking for interviews. She didn't want to exploit them nor challenge their "false" hopes for their loved ones' survival. During her interviews, Nauert noticed that she and other reporters were weeping before, during, and after their questions. She wondered if journalists had ever covered a story like this, a story that touched so many of them. She kept pushing on through, telling herself that she would deal with her feelings later. "I tried to tell each person's story with compassion and professionalism without being too sappy, sensational, or cold. I was never sure whether I was striking the proper balance," she says.[16]

Nauert's employer, Fox News, like other media outlets, offered its employees access to grief counselors, but Nauert declined, claiming it seemed silly and self-indulgent to her. "Although I don't regret not seeking counseling, I wish I had realized then that even though reporters are supposed to distance themselves from a story, that doesn't necessarily work when you're covering something horrific in your backyard. You can't help but internalize the images of death and destruction."[17]

Like other New York journalism graduate students in the aftermath of 9/11, Chris Williams was assigned stories on the tragedy. But the 24-year-old Columbia University student had serious doubts: "I was smack in the middle of the biggest story I'd probably ever cover, and suddenly I wanted no part." Some of his friends argued that they needed to keep an emotional distance to be able to report on what was happening around them. Williams felt torn. He wondered: "How in God's name do you distance yourself from your subjects at a time like this?"[18]

Williams spent hours near Ground Zero, walking the streets, gathering quotes, trying to find an angle for his sidebar stories. He scribbled down everything he could, filling his notebook. But he wasn't sure where he was headed or what he would write about. On the evening of September 11, he called his mother and girlfriend. He cried because of the magnitude of what he had witnessed, and he cried because he wasn't sure that he wanted to pursue a journalism career: "The day had changed everything. I didn't want to be that detached, emotionally distant journalist . . . . I wanted to be more involved. I wanted to help."[19]

On September 12, Williams returned to the streets to conduct interviews. He admitted "chasing this story all over town was a great experience." He found the pressure of writing on deadline exhilarating. But once he had completed his assignment, his second thoughts returned: "I went home that night feeling like I needed to go to confession."[20]

At the end of the week, Williams called his professor who had assigned the 9/11 coverage. He says he "breathed a quiet, selfish sigh of relief" when the professor's wife answered the phone. Williams admitted how guilty he felt using the tragedy of 9/11 to get clips and enhance his portfolio. Professor Gissler's wife (Mrs. G.) reassured Williams, telling him how in many cases it helps victims to talk about their experiences. "You're helping them heal. You'll find many of them are thankful to have someone let them talk," she said.[21]

Closing his essay, Williams realizes the important role he and other journalists were fulfilling by providing information in the wake of the tragedy.[22] By writing personal accounts of victims and their surviving family and friends, reporters could help people "grasp the magnitude of what happened."

In his article, Michael Howerton, reporter, *Stamford Advocate*, says on 9/11, he "channeled my anxiety and fear into my reporting." He describes an adrenaline surge propelling him from one interview to the next as he moved uptown with the mass of people being relocated from lower Manhattan. Howerton writes that he was ashamed at the "giddiness" he felt on that tragic day:

> Maybe this is part of the pathology of being a reporter, this wanting to be where most people wouldn't, wanting to see what most would turn from. . . . A reporter has the privilege to feel included, but not consumed by events. It makes sense to me now that part of my exhilaration that morning was a defense against realizing the horror. As a reporter I could at least have the illusion of control and usefulness.[23]

For weeks, Howerton wrote stories about women in the suburban Connecticut community who had lost fathers, husbands, and brothers in the 9/11 attacks. He says he felt "ghoulish" and "exploitive" interviewing grieving families: "The reporter is asking them to expose themselves at their most vulnerable, to talk about their grief before they have processed their loss. . . . I benefit from the tragedy by being the one who gets to tell the story. I get to sit next to horror, examine it up close, but not be crushed by it." In one interview, he broke down and was comforted by a widow whose husband had died when he was trapped on the 105th floor of the second tower. "I was embarrassed of my tears; crying was not professional. Yet in her company I finally felt the stress and sadness of the past week."[24]

Howerton says he came to terms with the realization that his fear on 9/11 had been unrecognizable. He had not only been a reporter but also a scared bystander. In the weeks following the tragedy, as he wrote and heard more stories, he began to understand his emotions: "My story of the attacks became clear only after I heard the stories of others. It was as if I had to hear it to feel it."[25]

As a reporter for the *Staten Island Advance* (New York) for five years prior to 9/11, Heidi Singer had covered fires, building collapses, and natural disasters, and death by suicide, homicide, disease, and accident. But she soon realized that the stakes were higher as a journalist covering the World Trade Center attacks: "The tragedy was worse, and I was a part of the story, the buffer of objective listener torn away."[26]

She says she felt powerless to describe some of the horrific images she had seen. However, she also felt proud that people trusted her to be the "objective recipient of dangerous thoughts." But there was dissonance mixed with the pride: "Did they really think I had no emotions?" she mused.[27]

Days after 9/11, Singer remained conflicted. She wrote that she felt her reporting had fallen short. But she was also uncomfortably aware that in some instances she had gone too far ("in short bursts of remembered ambition"), such as hoping to find a body part sticking out of the rubble because it "would make great copy." She wondered if she was being a good reporter or a crass voyeur?[28]

After a heart-wrenching interview with a victim's family, Singer felt "a rush," having captured something important in the family's words and recollections. Feeling stressed and exhausted, she probed deeply into the family's feelings of loss. She finished the story, though later wondered: "But I still don't know whether I exploited the situation, wrote down things too personal for the world to see."[29]

Singer confronted her pain and sadness. She realized the trauma had surfaced in her writing—the quotes she chose, the passages she lingered over, the overdone descriptions that "glared off the page." She said she was exhausted and overwrought in that first week and wrote things that now make her wince. She knew that she might have added to some people's suffering by the stories she wrote. But she took solace in the fact that though she may have gone "too far," at least she didn't "cheat anybody" in her reporting. She says she had tried to do her best to get the story right during that most difficult time.[30]

South Asian Tsunami: December 26, 2004

If the events of 9/11 were unprecedented, then the 2004 tsunami that killed an estimated 200,000 people was unfathomable. Journalists covering this natural disaster, which struck 11 countries, struggled to find ways to describe what they saw, heard, smelled, and felt in the aftermath. Words like overwhelming, heartbreaking, devastating appeared in many stories. Reporters and photographers also said they felt helpless and guilty in the face of such incredible loss.

BBC correspondent Ben Brown personalized his experiences in Meulaboh, Aceh (an Indonesian province), where the tsunami had struck shortly after 8 a.m. on December 26, 2004, with waves estimated at 80 feet. Brown, whose story was published in the *Observer* (United Kingdom) on January 16, 2005 (and later reprinted on a dartcenter.org website), focused on one of the survivors, a woman named Rohati, who lost her husband and four children in the tsunami. Her family was among the 40,000 (about half the population of Aceh) who perished within minutes as giant walls of water swept over the once bucolic beachfront community.[31]

Brown, who had interviewed countless victims in his career, strolled on the beach with Rohati. But this typical "walking shot" turned extraordinary as the woman became "hysterical with grief, her body jerking and shaking." When Rohati began sobbing uncontrollably on Brown's shoulder, he was "stiff and uncertain how to respond."[32]

The journalist tried to console her, but he was unprepared for the depth of Rohati's emotions. His interpreter, Sonny, also Indonesian, was sobbing as he spoke her words: "I have lost my children! How can I live now? What am I to do and where am I to go?" As Rohati wailed and flailed with "a frenetic energy," Brown tried to gently hug her. "But it all seemed so absurdly, pathetically inadequate," he wrote, adding that as she broke away from him, he could only stutter: "I'm so sorry for your loss."

> But I fear the pain etched on Rohati's face will always haunt me, as will the vision of grotesquely bloated bodies lined up at a makeshift morgue in Thailand, the stench of death there so bad it made me want to retch. For many of us in the media, this has been easily the most harrowing story we have ever covered. . . . With relentless deadlines there is not much time to pause or reflect on the daily horror that we witness as soon as we venture into any street in any town or village here. Perhaps it's better if we don't dwell on it too long.[33]

About a month after Brown's article was published, a group of journalists, mental health professionals, and aid workers met at the Frontline Club in London in a discussion ("Covering the Tsunami") moderated by then-director of Dart Centre Europe Mark Brayne, who had been a correspondent with Reuters and the BBC for decades before becoming a therapist. In response to Brown's on-air report, BBC colleague David Loyn, who also covered the tsunami's aftermath, challenged the role of emotion-based reporting: "I would make a plea for disengaged journalism," he said. "We need to keep ourselves intact. We're faced with daily horror and a thousand dilemmas."[34]

But CNN correspondent Nick Wrenn disagreed with Loyn:

> I'd argue that I like to see that engagement. The Ben Brown incident really brought it home to me—just the raw emotion of it. . . . I think sometimes you have to engage. To me that was one of the most powerful packages that I saw out of all the broadcasters.[35]

The debate on issues such as emotional engagement in reporting, hostile-environment training, and trauma counseling for journalists intensified in the weeks and months after the tsunami coverage in South Asia. It was as if this tragedy had brought heightened attention to controversial topics rarely discussed openly in newsrooms in previous years.

Brian MacArthur wrote an article ("Journalists Find Ways to Cope with Tsunami") on January 7, 2005, in *The Times* (London) in which he admitted: "I belong to a generation that inwardly sneers at any thought that a reporter would need counseling, even after witnessing the many horrors wreaked by the tsunami, but nowadays there are those who think that they do."[36] MacArthur discussed the Dart Centre for Journalism & Trauma and its concern that journalists may be wounded emotionally due to prolonged exposure to tragic scenes. He appeared to scoff at Dart's Mark Brayne, who said those journalists returning from their tsunami coverage would deserve "some tender loving care (TLC) when they return" (MacArthur's words).

> Reporters may sometimes seem ghoulish, but they remain human. (Catherine) Philip admits to feelings of guilt at the end of the day when she relaxes with colleagues over a glass of wine away from all the rubble outside. If reporters aren't capable of being moved—for instance, by a father kissing a picture of his dead daughter and starting to cry—and can't shed a tear, they shouldn't be journalists, says (Daniel) McGrory. But he won't be asking for any TLC.[37]

On April 15, 2005, the Dart Center at the UW sponsored the conference "The Tsunami Aftermath: Consequences for Journalism and the Region." Matt Ironside subsequently highlighted the intense recollections and reactions of several journalists, including Barry Peterson, Tokyo bureau chief for CBS News, who discussed the "pressures of working amid the 'psychic onslaught' of devastation and loss, and the sights and smells of death and decay."[38]

Those at the forefront of the trauma journalism reform movement would say that significant craft issues had emerged during and after the tsunami coverage. Chris Cramer, then-CNN International's managing director, was quoted in a March 1, 2005, online article "The Emotional Toll of Disaster Reporting" by Australian journalist (and Southeast Asia correspondent) Kimina Lyall. Cramer had written an article published in the *Australian*'s Media section on January 27, 2005, stating:

> What has been different about much of the reporting, particularly on TV, has been that the emotional attachment between reporter and victim has been obvious. Gone is the professional, some might say, artificial detachment . . . . Now, for the first time, media professionals are starting

to tell us how they feel about some stories. And it will probably make them better journalists.[39]

Lyall, who had been visiting a coastal village in Thailand, where she and her partner owned a vacation home when the tsunami hit, became a part of the story as both a devastated resident of the affected area and an experienced journalist expected to report on the disaster.

> Much as we like to sanctify this to laypeople, the reality is that often the greatest stress in stories like this is simply the pressure to deliver, preferably exclusives or a dramatic news angle. . . . These stories are career makers or breakers for journalists—and we know it. This is why we, as a group, cling to an outdated culture that values toughness over sympathy, cynicism over understanding, and a fight-to-the-end attitude to a news assignment. We all fear that any sign of weakness (and let's face it, that's what tears are) is an indication that we shouldn't have been sent on the assignment, that we aren't coping with it and that ultimately, that we ought not be given such a task again. In other words, a career-breaker. . . . For my money, the best journalism from the tsunami came from reporters that allowed themselves to "feel" inside and outside of their copy.[40]

She said she was given "an enormous amount of support by her news desk" and colleagues in the field. Although many of her fellow media workers told her about "turbulent dreams, irrational anger, and difficulties in making decisions in the wake of their reporting on the tsunami," she "was one who took up the option of postsituation counseling. But I fear other journalists still feel hesitant to do so, fearing it reflects a sign of weakness, a lack of that steely resolve so prized in newsrooms."[41]

CNN's Anderson Cooper, in his memoir, *Dispatches from the Edge*, discussed his reporting on the tsunami's devastating impact in January 2005, when he at first seemed to be more concerned with being scooped than being empathetic, with packaging his reports, rather than being sincere to those he encountered:

> There was a time many years ago, when I first became a reporter when I thought I could fake it. Go through the motions, not give away pieces of myself in return. . . . When I had what I needed, I'd pull out. I thought I could get away unscathed, unchanged. The truth was I hadn't gotten out at all. It's impossible to block out what you see, what you hear. Even if you stop listening, the pain gets inside, seeps through the cracks you can't close up. You can't fake your way through it. I know that now.

You have to absorb it all. You owe them that. You owe it to yourself as well.[42]

Commenting on her eighteen years of covering stressful and shocking stories as a newspaper reporter, Dawn Fallik, in a June 28, 2010, e-mail wrote: "It sounds a little crazy, but it's an honor and a privilege to cover the horrific events. It's someone's kid. It's some nightmare halfway around the world. It's my job to make it mean something to everyone I can." Five years earlier, Fallik had gone to India on a several-week assignment from the *Philadelphia Inquirer* to cover the impact of the tsunami. Her focus was on the role of doctors (including volunteers from the United States) who were treating the injured across South Asia. She said there wasn't time for any specialized training, and her preparations consisted of getting shots, securing a visa and satellite phone, and making countless other arrangements.

By the time Fallik arrived in the areas hit by the tsunami, most of the dead had been buried, "but the living were kind of dead too—they didn't know what to do with themselves." As a reporter, she felt helpless and often overwhelmed by the scope of the disaster and by the trying living and working conditions. She was driven by the desire to "do right by these people" and to make her readers back in Philadelphia care about the dreadful situation.

She said she learned from the doctors she traveled with that it was OK to shut down at the end of the day. "You can't suck in that kind of horror 24/7." To cope during her time in South Asia, she sent daily e-mails to friends and family back home, sharing anecdotes and doses of dark humor. But mostly, as she had done throughout her career, she worked her way through the emotional days and nights.

Upon her return to Philadelphia, she went directly to the *Inquirer* newsroom to file her final story in a series of articles. She says she received mostly overtime instead of time off, as union rules did not require the paper to offer both financial and time-off options. Within a couple days of returning from weeks of trauma journalism in South Asia, she was covering the latest *Harry Potter* book release.

Since 2007, when Fallik left the *Inquirer* after scores of news staff were laid off, she has shifted her career to academia. The New York native, who was raised in Columbia, Maryland, and holds degrees from the University of Wisconsin and University of Missouri, is an assistant professor in the English Department at the University of Delaware. She continues to write medical stories for the *WSJ* and other publications. She also encourages young journalists to have a "safety valve"—writing a blog, listening to music, something to allow them to escape for a while. Fallik reminds her students to: "Be fair, do your job, but be human. A smile goes an amazingly long way." When asked what it will take for more journalists to come forward and openly discuss trauma-related issues, the former reporter-turned instructor replied:

> It will change on an editor-by-editor basis. One day, one editor will pause for a second before sending a reporter to cover some horrible fire, where three kids have died, and say: "Come talk to me for a second when you're back." But I'm not holding my breath.

Hurricane Katrina: August 29, 2005

American journalists who covered the tsunami couldn't have imagined that nature's wrath would devastate portions of their own country less than a year later. But some would draw comparisons to the horrible conditions and loss of life in places like New Orleans and Gulfport as they had witnessed months earlier across South Asia. Others in the media would speak of the physical and psychological effects that resulted from their reporting on the natural disasters, the human tragedies, and the series of crises and catastrophes that befell the Gulf coast region of the United States.

Michael Perlstein, a reporter with the New Orleans *T-P* for twenty years, spoke with author Jim Willis about his experiences covering the impact of Hurricane Katrina during the late summer and fall of 2005.

> More than half of us at the *Times-Picayune* lost homes to flooding. While working feverishly in the first week to write and publish stories, we somehow found time to canoe into our flooded homes, rescue pets, ferry neighbors to safety, and check on the homes of friends and colleagues. All the while, for those of us in New Orleans, getting in touch with family was impossible for several days and difficult even then.[43]

Perlstein, now on the faculty of Loyola University of New Orleans, discussed how journalists witnessed crimes, such as widespread looting, found dead and bloated bodies, and learned of the loss of friends and colleagues. While coping with a range of intense feelings, including "sadness, anger, frustration, disorientation, grief, and anxiety," he and his *T-P* colleagues displayed their tenacity and some novel approaches to their craft:

> Objective reporting quickly gave way to subjectivity (and even advocacy) in the storm's aftermath, and the immense scale of the calamity and our personal immersion also gave rise to another level of journalism that I have coined "hyper-objectivity." Those of us in the floodwaters also were fueled heavily by reporting instincts, journalistic training, sense of duty to get the story out, loyalty to our newspaper, and the realization

that this was "the big one," the story of a lifetime in which our words carried immediate weight and urgency and, eventually, would become the first draft of this history of tragedy. . . . Clarity slowed us down—made sure we got it right, understood the complexity of New Orleans, knew the landscape, informed enough not to fall for easy stereotypes.[44]

Some would say that his passionate coverage of Hurricane Katrina made CNN anchor Anderson Cooper one of the most recognizable of today's journalists as he blended disaster reporting with empathy, confrontation, and advocacy. As he recounted in his memoir, *Dispatches from the Edge*, he conveyed to audiences his shock at conditions in the region—"the worst I've ever seen in America," comparing Gulfport, Mississippi, to Sri Lanka after the tsunami.[45] His anger was directed at equivocating politicians who failed to be accountable.

Cooper in frustration wrote: "Here, you grow up believing there's a safety net, that things can never completely fall apart. Katrina showed us all that's not true." He described New Orleans as a "fresh wound, sliced open by the shrapnel of a storm."[46] As his reporting continued, Cooper drew strength and reassurance from the belief that maybe he could be of some help—he could make a difference. ("I don't want to let these people down, this city, down.")[47]

Driving through the deserted streets, the SUV's headlights shine on splintered wood and collapsed homes. I don't want to leave these colorless streets, the mud and debris, cars hanging from trees. I don't want to return to the cleanness, the convenience, the traffic rules. I want the roadblocks, the hassles, the heartache, the look in peoples' eyes—thankful you're here. There is no good that comes from the storm, no silver lining, no Hollywood ending. Death descends. Lives are lost. No good comes of it, but you meet good people along the way. They open up their homes, they cook you food, give you a cot to crash on. I was honored to be here, privileged to have been a witness to so much feeling, so much kindness, so much heroism.[48]

If Anderson Cooper and Michael Perlstein conveyed intense emotions as broadcast and print reporters dealing with the aftermath of Hurricane Katrina, then *T-P* columnist and book author Chris Rose (*1 Dead in Attic*) revealed the extreme depth of a person's traumatic reactions as he chronicled life in a devastated, distorted community he had grown to love after residing there for more than two decades. When others abandoned New Orleans, Rose, a popular local journalist, chose to remain, becoming "a soldier on the front lines of a battle to save a city, a culture, a newspaper; my job, my home."[49]

For eighteen months, he wrote intimate stories of victims and survivors. But the longer he covered the shocking conditions in New Orleans, the more damage he suffered:

> I also submit that if you don't have this affliction, if this whole thing hasn't sent you into a vicious spin of acute cognitive dissonance, then you must be crazy and—as I said—we're all whacked. How could you not be? Consider the sights, sounds, and smells you encounter on a daily basis as you drive around a town that has a permanent bathtub ring around it.[50]

What makes Rose's narratives different from most media accounts is that he shares with readers his feelings, fears, and intimate experiences as he documents the destruction surrounding him and his fellow residents:

> Basically, I spend my days like everyone else, lurching from one "episode" to the next, just trying to live, just trying to survive, just trying not to crack up and publicly embarrass myself, my family, and my newspaper. It's hard, man. It's hard, just to live. I don't mean to be overly confessional here, but sometimes I feel I am no longer fit for public consumption, no longer fit for publication, and definitely no longer fit to operate heavy machinery.[51]

He writes of the impact of the disaster on ordinary people, and he pleads with the community at large: "We need to be civil. We need to be clean. We need to change. We need to respect ourselves and our city."[52]

As a journalist, Rose goes beyond reporting to interpret the world around him, including analyzing national media coverage, which "has largely been played out to pit the rich white folks of Lakeview against the poor black folks of the Lower Ninth, never mind that the flood itself ignored such devices and claimed lives, property, and peace of mind indiscriminately and equally across race, class, and gender lines and across hundreds of square miles." Rose wants to help others understand the scope of human suffering that occurred before the tragedy and occurs still in New Orleans. But he also shares stories of "the triumph of the human spirit."[53]

In his most personal sections of his book, Rose writes openly about his psychological battles: "After living in the specter of curfews and military troops and arson and desperate squalor, maybe for the first time in my life I get a hint of what posttraumatic stress really is."[54] Toward the end of his book, in the section titled "Falling Down," he notes that after documenting his struggles in the post-Katrina world: "In many ways, I feel as if I have become the New Orleans poster boy for posttraumatic stress, chronicling my descent into madness for everyone to read."[55]

When his condition worsened, Rose describes his editors at the newspaper as kind. ("They cut me slack.") But all the empathy in the world couldn't curtail Rose's decline into a clinical depression, which he couldn't understand.[56]

> Early this summer, with the darkness clinging to me like my own personal humidity, my stories in the newspaper moved from gray to brown to black. Readers wanted stories of hope, inspiration, and triumph, something to cling to; I gave them anger and sadness and gloom. . . . Hopeless, helpless, and unable to function. A mind shutting down and taking the body with it. A pain not physical but not of my comprehension and always there, a buzzing fluorescent light that you can't turn off. No way out, I thought. Except there was.[57]

Rose, who admits that he had previously regarded the concepts of "depression and anxiety as pretty much a load of hooey," finally relents. He realizes that the impact of his reporting on so many heartbreaking stories of people's pain ("a full-time chronicler of sorrowful tales") has driven him into a full-blown mental health crisis.[58]

After enduring months of problems for himself and his family, Rose sought medical care. He was prescribed antidepressants, which he says, along with therapy, saved him: "It boggles the mind to think of how many among us are holding on by frayed threads, just barely, and trying to hide it as I was for so many months."[59]

Critics may claim that Chris Rose's personal story is melodramatic or self-indulgent. He might be viewed as the exception to the stereotype of the strong, detached, resilient journalist. Regardless of such opinions, Rose's account offers readers and fellow news workers valuable insights into the potential for experiencing serious psychological effects.

Jed Horne, who was metro editor of the *T-P* during Hurricane Katrina, is quoted in an article "Trauma in New Orleans: In the Wake of Katrina" as saying: "Other reporters went bonkers in print—notably Chris Rose, who wrote in a fascinating and courageous way about his breakdown."[60] Horne describes his concern as a newsroom manager during the dark days in 2005 of trying to keep staff from overworking (as a means of coping with stress), burning out after their manic energy had dissipated, and "disintegrating." He characterized the ordeal his newspaper went through as "the intimacy of our experience: Intimacy in the sense of the obscenity of what had happened and also in the sense of being stripped away and laid bare in the eyes of the world and brother and sister media operatives."[61]

In the introduction to his 2008 film, *Breaking News, Breaking Down*, Mike Walter says the documentary is about "a growing wave of journalists who understand that trauma journalism can be dangerous and emotionally devastating." The film is dedicated to the journalists "who lived through Katrina and told the story."[62]

Walter talks of his depression, triggered by his experiences in Washington, DC, on September 11, 2001. But the central character in his film is *T-P* photographer John McCusker, a journalist severely affected by the stress of his work and by his extended exposure to tragedy. McCusker had a violent episode on the first anniversary of Katrina in 2006, resulting in a confrontation with New Orleans police, his arrest, and in-patient psychiatric treatment.[63]

Breaking News, Breaking Down depicts journalists from across the country and internationally who were drawn to New Orleans in 2006 to offer support for McCusker, for the city, and for each other. As Walter narrates:

> That's how "Target New Orleans" was born. The idea was simple. We'd rent this tiny home in New Orleans [Lower Ninth Ward], and trauma journalists from around the world would come here to stay and work. We'd gut homes, tear down walls, and, hopefully, tear down emotional walls journalists had erected. It would give them the chance to open up to someone who understood.[64]

The driving force for the effort was provided by the Dart Society, an organization of dozens of journalists who had received extended education and training in the effects of crisis coverage. Natalie Pompilio, who reported on Hurricane Katrina for the *Philadelphia Inquirer*, had covered New Orleans' stories earlier in her career. She had volunteered for the Dart Society project, drawn to the city she loved and appreciative of the opportunity to be with colleagues who "know what it's like to be traumatized or go through something traumatic . . . and feel like you're not alone." Penny Cockerell was another former Ochberg Fellow participating in the "Target New Orleans" project. She had covered the Oklahoma City bombing in 1995 and understood the need for a community-based effort to promote healing. Australian journalist Gary Tippet, who had been in the same class of Ochberg Fellows as Cockerell in 2000, states in Walter's film: "People all around the world have a fairly low opinion of journalists. They forget that we're human first and journalists second, and that we can be affected by the things we do."[65]

Photographer John McCusker, in concert with Tippet, says eloquently:

> Nobody understands what we do better than other journalists. We understand that when you see a picture, there's a beating heart and a human being behind the photograph that was shot. When you read words from a disaster area or a war, there was a human being writing

that down. And I don't know that I fully appreciated it until I became that human being and the experience debilitated me.[66]

At the end of Mike Walter's documentary, it is 2007, a year has passed, and "Target New Orleans" has ended, leaving many of the journalists with a sense of hope. John McCusker's criminal charges, from his erratic actions in August 2006, were reduced to misdemeanors—providing a happy ending to what had been a nightmare. Walter refers to McCusker and himself as two journalists who had "broken free of the depression that had gripped us." Walter describes the making of the film as being therapeutic, as he reviews the journey and his meaningful encounters with fellow trauma journalists along the way.

> I once had a trauma specialist tell me: "In order to put something behind you, you must first put it in front of you, examine it and come to terms with it." This film has helped me do that.[67]

Virginia Tech: April 16, 2007

One of the most remarkable narratives to emerge from the tragedy at VTU in 2007 was the work of student journalists at the *Collegiate Times* (*CT*) newspaper. Their concern for their community of readers—on campus, in Blacksburg, and those affected in the Virginia Tech "Hokies family" nationwide—became the leitmotif of their journalistic accomplishments. These twenty-something editors, reporters, photographers, graphic designers, and production staff were praised for their efforts, while those representing the "outside" media were often criticized:

> Families of victims were furious at news organizations and NBC in particular for airing [the murderer of thirty-two students and faculty] Cho's photos and rantings. Tech students said it felt as though he had reached out from the grave to continue manipulating the campus.[68]

By contrast, *CT* editor Amie Steele in an article "Story of Their Lives," published in 2007 by SPJ in the *Journalist*, a supplement to *Quill* magazine, wrote:

> We weren't printing a paper for the rest of the world; we were printing a paper for the Tech community. . . . We chose to only print a headshot of the alleged perpetrator. We thought it was important to not buy into the sensationalism and the attention he so desperately craved in sending

the manifesto to NBC. I strongly believe our readers thought our paper was a safe place for them to get their news about the entire tragedy without having him pointing a gun at their face. That portrayal of anger and hate was the last thing the Virginia Tech community needed to see.[69]

The *CT* staff, including Steele, two managing editors, Joe Kendall and Bobby Bowman, sports editor Ryan McConnell, and the paper's faculty adviser Kelly Furnas, and many others, performed admirably in the hours during and after the deadly campus shooting. Forty-five minutes after hearing reports of gunfire at Norris Hall, the *CT* staff had posted the breaking news on its website. The morning after the crisis (April 17), the sixteen-page edition of *CT* was on news racks.[70]

Print and web editions of the *CT*, which received millions of hits, were produced for days in the aftermath of the tragedy, despite the constant calls from national and international media and the fact that student reporters were leaving because classes had been canceled and parents wanted their children home.

"We did a good job of covering it not only for the victims but especially for their families," said Bobby Bowman. "It was close to all of us."[71]

What was unprecedented about this deadline reporting was not only the extreme emotional stress the college journalists faced or the fact that several on the newspaper staff were inexperienced. Most impressive was how these individuals performed while having to deal with the demands of scores of news organizations and individuals. In an April 20, 2009, online article "Virginia Tech: Tips from a Newsroom Adviser," Kelly Furnas described the "barrage of requests from outside media":

We had national news outlets seeking stringers. . . . We had dozens of other publications seeking permission to reprint [student] photos or stories. We had other news organizations seeking space and computers. Every phone in the newsroom was ringing (not once with a news tip, and always with someone wanting something), so the staff ended up forwarding all the phones to the editor's office. Yet every time she would hang up the phone, it would literally begin ringing again. At 11 p.m. on the day of the shootings, she decided to leave the phone off the hook. . . . We were overwhelmed with more than 100 calls from different media and agencies [for photography].[72]

The *CT* editors credited Furnas, a former print journalist, who had been at Virginia Tech since 2005, for guiding them through the crisis coverage, for urging them to take care of themselves—either by seeking counseling or informal debriefings, if necessary, and for giving them practical (emergency) skills training. A *Poynteronline* article "Massacre on a Managing Editor's

First Day" documented the experiences of the *CT*'s Bobby Bowman, who had addressed the National Writers Workshop in Wichita, Kansas, on May 20, 2007: "Kelly Furnas, our adviser, he's the only reason we did as well as we did. He gave us a 30-minute workshop on how to contact families [of victims] in a nice way to ask for stories about these people."[73]

According to Joe Grimm's article, Furnas had assembled "32 packets that contained background on the individual victims—one for each person slain—to be distributed to staff far smaller than that number. . . . The *CT* staff worked through the night to write vignettes that would dignify the 32 killed."[74] In celebrating the lives of the victims rather than their deaths, this college newspaper was following in the tradition of the *Oklahoman* (1995) and the *New York Times* (2001).

The Virginia Tech tragedy, as seen through the eyes of collegiate media workers, is a meaningful case study of trauma journalism. Compare the words of *CT* editor Amie Steele in her article in the 2007 SPJ publication the *Journalist* with her reflections two years later (April 20, 2009) in an online article for the Dart Center ("Virginia Tech: Tips from Student Journalists").

> **2007:**
> The job of a journalist is to report the news. Without opinion, without emotion, without bias—just report the news. Sometimes the news is heartwarming; other times it is gut-wrenching. . . . How do you deal with your own personal emotion and attachment to the story when you're supposed to remain neutral?[75]
> **2009:**
> The whole week had been spent running around, worrying about stories, Web updates, headlines, interviews and the like. I think a lot of the staff members never took a step back and thought about the emotional toll the shootings would have on us. We were so concerned with coverage that we never took time for ourselves to deal with our own grief. While counseling was readily available to all of us, many of us were so busy that we didn't take the time to talk about our emotions.[76]

Steele then describes how affected she became when interviewing a student who was talking about his former French instructor, Jocelyn Couture-Nowak, who had been killed on April 16, 2007. Steele said she sat in her car crying after the interview.

> I realized there was a story behind the victims. And while we had our notebooks and recorders out during those weeks writing about people's emotions, we weren't dealing with our own. Journalists are too often covering heartbreaking, emotional stories. At the end of the day, I think

it is important for journalists to come to terms with the grave things they may see while covering a story—not only for their sanity, but for their reporting. While it is important for you to tell that person's story, your health is important too.[77]

Meg Spratt, associate director of academic programs, Dart Center for Journalism & Trauma, put the demands of this type of reporting in context:

Mass shootings and other attacks at schools and universities present a grim yet classic challenge for even the most seasoned media workers. How do journalists insure accurate, informative, ethical and sensitive coverage in the midst of danger and chaos, on the most emotional terrain for students, parents and journalists alike? And if mass-casualty attacks at schools are horrifying for all journalists, the challenges are even more profound for student reporters and editors. The nightmarish 2007 shooting spree at Virginia Tech University and a similar tragedy at Northern Illinois University less than a year later [February 14, 2008] immediately involved student journalists and their faculty advisors in frontline crisis coverage, and in news choices of deep consequence. . . . In both cases, student media workers [*Collegiate Times* and *Northern Star*] faced a crash course in maintaining professional journalistic standards under dangerous conditions and intense emotional stress. Student news staff not only covered the tragedies, they were part of the news themselves. Student media workers lost friends, colleagues and teachers.[78]

(Author's Note: Educational and training materials from collegiate media involved in the Virginia Tech and Northern Illinois University tragedies are featured in Chapter 7: News Reform 101.)

Haiti: January 12, 2010

When the international news media covered the earthquake that befell the poverty-stricken island of Haiti on the cusp of a new year and decade, issues central to trauma journalism received heightened discussion and scrutiny. It was as if in the reporting of this massive tragedy, the journalistic community was striving to demonstrate how it had evolved in recent years—not only in terms of technology (e.g., the use of social media)—but also in its temperament. Could reporters balance fact and reason with empathy and emotion? Would news organizations offer postevent intervention programs for its staff in the field and back in the newsrooms? Arguably, the Haitian earthquake marked a coming of age for journalists regarding disaster coverage and a tipping point in the movement toward establishing a "culture of caring" among news media worldwide. Such alleged progress, however, was accompanied by healthy and vigorous debate.

In a January 19, 2010, online article ("Emotion in Reporting: Use and Abuse"), Stephen J. A. Ward, a professor of journalism ethics at the University of Wisconsin, critiqued broadcast media coverage of the earthquake, such as when Dr. Sanjay Gupta, CNN's chief medical correspondent, was shown running through the streets of Port-au-Prince to minister to an injured infant. He asked whether such emotion-based reporting was a "true expression of compassion? Or is it self-promotion? Is it compassion or self-congratulation?" Ward's response was that people should be skeptical of journalists using emotional reporting (i.e., self-aggrandizement) to attract audiences and boost ratings. But he also provided a template for news coverage where reason and emotion converge:

> Good coverage of disasters is a skillful combination of the emotional and the objective sides of journalism. The issue is not whether journalists should display emotions. The idea that journalists must be detached and neutral in the middle of chaos is outdated and wrong. In a disaster zone, journalists are not neutral observers. They are part of the world's response, an essential communication channel for the rescue effort, and for the raising of funds for humanitarian agencies.[79]

He believes that journalists' feelings in covering a story may lead to more diligent reporting, while encouraging more audience engagement. But he cautions that a reporter's strong emotions should be balanced by verification of facts and critical analysis.

> The best disaster journalism is engaged and objectively tested journalism. Journalism based only on emotion can be incorrect or manipulated. Journalism based only on a studied neutrality is not only an inhuman attitude toward a disaster. It fails to tell the full story.[80]

And, the full (factual) story, in the hands of an accomplished journalist, may be as evocative as any work of art. In a photo essay ("Out of the Ruins"), published in *TIME* magazine on February 8, 2010, photographer James Nachtwey, 62, whose career has been marked by decades of notable coverage of tragedy and trauma, compares the destruction in Haiti to being "lost inside a walking nightmare."

> The markers on this mapless journey are the swarms of looters, children with chopped-off limbs, cities fabricated of sticks and bedsheets,

pulverized cathedrals, dogs circling the dead in the streets. Most Haitians have always lived in a society constructed along a narrow ledge on a precipice above the abyss. . . . Their nation was born in the conquest of slavery; it has been shaped by poverty, struggle and faith.[81]

Nachtwey reflects that the bulk of his photojournalism during the past thirty years has focused on "wars, conflicts and social injustice. It's been fueled by anger, driven by the belief that if people are informed, they will be inspired by compassion and will share a sense of outrage at violence, aggression and the unacceptable deprivation of fundamental human rights."[82] Such disclosure of a journalist's emotional and activist impulses would have been rare (or likely missing) in a major news publication in the not-too-distant past.

Fox-TV News anchor Bill Hemmer, in the spring 2010 issue of his Miami University (Ohio) alumni magazine, noted the horrific numbers of dead in Haiti (estimates as high as 200,000) and scope of the tragedy.

But it isn't so much the dead that haunt you. It's the living and the fact that a week after such a tragedy there were still people walking the streets looking for a doctor to set their bone or for someone to stitch an enormous gash and to do it without anesthesia or proper medical tools. This is Civil War medicine. I think, in general, I have thick skin, and I'm able to shut out a certain portion in order for me to do my job. However, on this story, it was as haunting an experience as I have likely ever had. At nighttime when you close your eyes and all those images come running back through your brain, you throw your eyes open again as if not to go there . . . don't go to that dark place.[83]

Veteran war correspondent Jon Lee Anderson wrote about his experiences in Haiti, less than a week after the earthquake. In an article "Neighbors' Keeper," published in the *New Yorker* on February 8, 2010, Anderson uses vivid detail in describing a scene at the main cemetery in Port-au-Prince:

As we approached, I saw three bodies lying face down on the dirt in a gap in the wall. Two of them appeared to be women, one very young. The other bodies I had seen in Port-au-Prince were distended and blistered from the heat. These were fresh, with no visible injuries. They reminded me of photographs I had seen of victims of death squads in El Salvador. An overwhelming stench permeated the air, even inside the truck.[84]

In his review of Haiti earthquake reporting, Stephen J. A. Ward discussed the challenges facing news media early in the crisis:

Parachuted into a disaster, journalists struggle to absorb what they experience, recoiling from the stench of death and the suffering of dazed and wounded souls. In a 24-hour news world, reporters are always "on." They don't have time to collect themselves and then report. Instantaneous and continuous reportage means journalists' raw emotions inevitably surface in the middle of on-air conversations and interviews. . . . Among major U.S. networks, there have been valid expressions of emotional tension. For example, NBC anchor Brian Williams explained on air that his news crew in Haiti struggled with the fact that they were about the only ones with food, water and electrical power. Yet they needed these resources to tell the world about the disaster.[85]

How do trauma journalists handle such dilemmas, if not outright exhaustion and posttraumatic stress? Bruce Shapiro, executive director, Dart Center for Journalism & Trauma, addressed news organizations in a January 21, 2010, online article ("Haiti Quake: Watchful Waiting"). While noting the need to sustain "exhausted news teams who arrived in Port-au-Prince with emergency crews" and who were preparing to rotate out as the Haitian disaster moved from breaking news coverage to an extended recovery story, Shapiro reminded managers to pay attention to those photo editors, technicians, and producers who had spent hours, day after day viewing disturbing pictures and video footage.

Simply put, a steady diet of graphic and horrifying images or audio can be overwhelming. Psychologists have long recognized vicarious traumatization—the symptoms of traumatic stress or other psychological distress in individuals who absorb toxic levels of horror through the eyes—or camera lenses—of others, such as psychotherapists, human-rights investigators or journalists. While the source of distress may be second-hand, the impact is real and sometimes enduring. On a 24/7 story like Haiti, it's important that in-studio personnel pace their work, take frequent breaks, share concerns that arise and be on the lookout for colleagues who may be unexpectedly derailed by distressing images.[86]

Dr. Anthony Feinstein, who has pioneered research on posttraumatic stress among war correspondents, consulted with CNN in February 2010 after weeks of Haiti crisis coverage, at the suggestion of the cable TV network's human resources department. He conducted 2-hour presentations and Q&A sessions with an estimated thirty to forty news media workers in both New York and Atlanta. He also referred a fellow therapist as a post-Haiti consultant to the *New York Times*.

Bruce Shapiro applauded such responsive efforts, while recognizing other media entities, such as the BBC, the Australian Broadcasting Corporation, and NPR, who "routinely arrange expert trauma-awareness briefings for their managers." At the close of his January 2010 online article, he wrote:

> Don't assume that everyone on your Haiti team immediately needs to see a mental health professional. Instead, focus on public and private acknowledgement of the assignment's importance; make it clear to the whole newsroom that emotional responses to a story like Haiti, whether by those reporting or those working on the desk, are normal human reactions, not a sign of weakness. Encourage news teams to talk among one another as colleagues, and with you in private; and make it clear that management supports anyone who seeks confidential professional counseling.[87]

Faces of Trauma Journalism:
Amy Dockser Marcus

Photo by Ronen Marcus

If your image of a trauma journalist who has covered war, disaster, and death is a dysfunctional loner, consider the real world of Amy Dockser Marcus. The 44-year-old Harvard grad and Pulitzer Prize-winning reporter for the *WSJ* has a contented family life to accompany her successful career. She considers her work a calling that can change and possibly even save lives. Her advice to young journalists who may wish to follow her example: Don't turn off your humanity.

I first met Amy in 2005 when she came to Ball State University to accept the Eugene S. Pulliam National Journalism Writing Award for her story of the O'Donnells, an Indiana couple coping with "a life lived after cancer." Her article revealed a rare level of access and telling details that resonated with readers.[88] It was part of a nine-article series on terminal illness that Amy wrote in 2004, earning her a Pulitzer Prize for beat reporting.

I remained in touch with her over the years, and traveled to Greater Boston in March 2010 to learn more about the intersection of her personal and professional lives.

On this particular sunny, brisk Sunday morning, I am at a Star Market in the tony suburb of Chestnut Hill, awaiting Amy and her husband, Ronen, and their children, Eden and Yuval. This is Mitzvah day for Eden, 13, Yuval, 11, and their fellow K-8 grade students at Solomon Schecter Day School in Newton, Massachusetts. The students are volunteering in a number of community projects today, including assisting at homeless shelters and nursing homes, participating in environmental issues, and raising funds for worthy causes such as childhood cancer research through an organization called "Alex's Lemonade Stand." That has brought the Marcuses to Star Market today. They are enthusiastic volunteers for an issue close to Amy's heart.

For 3 hours, Amy will sell cups of lemonade to shoppers, while overseeing the activities of her children—ensuring that 11-year-old Yuval smiles as he holds the promotional sign outside the door and praising Eden for her tee-shirt artwork. Amy talks comfortably with fellow parent volunteers and suburban donors, smiling easily and hustling on her appointed rounds this morning. Later, she will help Eden prepare for her upcoming two-week class visit to Israel, while working on one of four health-related feature stories due by Friday. Over this spring weekend, she chronicles her experiences with trauma journalism and comments on contemporary efforts to reform newsroom culture.

Amy is brisk and concise in her speech (no Boston "arrhhs" for this Lexington native), her gait, and her writing. Initially, she viewed the *WSJ* health beat as a respite from her seven years as a foreign correspondent in the Middle East, covering the Israeli-Palestinian dispute and "the endless conflict over land, religion, legitimacy, and identity." Amy says reporting on life-threatening diseases, where the specter of death hovers, is as stressful and brutal as the longest war. In 2004, she embarked on a yearlong project, immersed in the lives of six cancer patients and their families. Her efforts resulted in the award-winning nine-part series.

"I think reporting about fatal illnesses is often overlooked in the typical definitions of trauma," she says, noting how as a journalist "you embark on profound relationships with people that can last years."

Two of the most personal stories in the series were published less than three weeks apart in June 2004. The first of these was about 8-year-old Jack Streeter, a Natick, Massachusetts, boy who had been diagnosed with leukemia five years earlier. Amy wrote, "Children with cancer pose special challenges of survival, since their experience also transforms the lives of their parents, and often their wider community."[59] A sobering twist on Jack's story was the fact that his father, Larry, was a twenty-year cancer survivor.

Recalling the Streeter family some six years later, Amy says it was very difficult to write about someone who was about the same age as her own children at the time. She was struck by how the Streeter parents constantly worried that a new illness was not a routine childhood sickness but the return of the cancer and the real possibility he might die. "I remember coming home after intensive reporting sessions, hours spent with Jack at school and with Jack's family, and rushing to hug my children."

The second story published in June 2004 concerned 45-year-old Lori Monroe of Bowling Green, Kentucky, who had been diagnosed with terminal lung cancer three years earlier. Amy chronicled how Monroe had chosen the risky option of surgery and other aggressive treatment in the hopes of staying alive long enough to see both of her daughters graduate from college. As a devoted mother of two children, Amy identified with Monroe's determined spirit. Her descriptive writing enhanced the story of this courageous woman:

> Ms. Monroe says she always made a point of looking her best before seeing her doctors. "I want them to look at me and know that I am viable," she said, "that my life is worth saving." On this day, it was hard to tell how seriously ill she was. Toenails painted bright pink peeked out from sandals. She wore dangling earrings with blue stones that matched her V-neck blouse. Her short brown hair brushed just past her ears. She was quick to smile.[90]

Amy spoke often about her feelings with her husband, children, and parents while working on the cancer series. If her children noticed she was sad while writing a story, she would explain to them that sometimes she wrote about sad things, and this was part of life. Amy also credited editors at the *WSJ* for being willing to talk about the stories, asking how she was feeling, and encouraging her to take breaks and time to decompress. (It should be noted that in discussing newsroom culture with other women reporters in print and broadcast positions, several claim that this level of care and concern is often missing during and after stressful news cycles.)

"There was a huge sense of camaraderie in doing these stories," Amy recalls. "Even though I was working alone in terms of the reporting and writing, the editing process was very collaborative."

Within days of her final story in the series being published in December 2004, Amy had to confront news that overshadowed any assignment. Her beloved mother, Golda, was diagnosed at 62 with gallbladder/bile duct cancer, an "orphan" disease that strikes fewer than 10,000 people annually in this country.

In an article published in January 2010 in *Health Affairs* magazine, Amy discussed her mother's rare cancer.[91] Because of the relatively low numbers of people contracting certain forms of cancers, pharmaceutical companies don't concentrate on new drugs to address such unique diseases, and researchers find it very difficult to secure funding from the government or corporations. Using her excellent contacts in the medical community as a result of her *WSJ* reporting (experts such as Dr. Judah Folkman), Amy spent years exploring how patient advocates could enhance therapies developed for orphan cancers (like her mother's) and influence health care policy changes to spur development of new drugs. She hoped that her mother's treatments would inhibit the spread of the cancer. But, ultimately, despite Golda's determined spirit, the disease took its toll, and she died in May 2007 at age 65. Amy recalls:

> She did all she could. For me the experience had been like standing on the shore, watching someone you love drown before your eyes as you frantically threw rescue buoys that always fell short.

"My mother's death was a life-changing event," says Amy. "We were extremely close. She was incredibly supportive and loving, and her death left a huge hole in our family."

Although she admits to managing the emotional effects of her work well over the years thanks to a strong network of family and colleagues, Amy was unprepared for the impact of Golda's passing.

Amy had "sleep issues" and anxiety during the two and half years after her mother's diagnosis until her death and afterward. There was frustration and anger along with deep grief to process. But Amy tried to channel those feelings into life lessons for her children. "Part of being an adult is finding a way to stay resilient," she says, noting how the death of a loved one "teaches you to cherish every moment with people whom you love."

She also coped by maintaining weekly religious and family dinner routines with her father, Bob, and younger sister, Lynne, and her family. She sought comfort in her books, in cooking, and in regular exercise. And she drew on her close-knit community ties.

Dealing with her mother's bout with cancer reinforced what Amy had learned during her yearlong reporting on terminal illness. She resolved to try to help others through her work as a journalist. Amy had written several stories on rare diseases and the patient-driven research initiatives and venture philanthropy required to raise money and create vital collaborations within the medical community. One of the patient advocates she profiled was Amy Farber, then a 36-year-old social anthropologist on the faculty of Harvard Medical School, who had been diagnosed a year earlier with an orphan disease known as Lymphangioleiomyomatosis (or "LAM"), a progressive and fatal lung condition. Farber says at first she wasn't quite sure how to make sense of Amy's commitment to these issues as a journalist. She was soon struck by the depth and rigor of her professional curiosity, commitment, and follow through. During months of interviewing, the two Amys connected on a personal level, discovering mutual values, motivation, and determination to effect change.

"Many of our conversations were exciting because of the shared focus on problem solving," says Farber, who founded the LAM Treatment Alliance organization, headquartered in Cambridge, Massachusetts.

Amy Dockser Marcus speaks of the intensity she has felt as a journalist—not from confronting danger (as she often did as a "nervous" Middle East correspondent) but from the intellectual thrill of "recognizing something important that you thought other people weren't seeing yet." She says she felt that sense of meaning and mission in reporting on patients and fatal illnesses because the subject was not covered as dramatically as war or crime. Amy has witnessed the trauma felt by people who face imminent death not from violence but from disease.

She has also realized a unique perspective by spending so much time with cancer patients. "They're not dying. They're living," Amy says, her voice rising with emotion. "When you see life lived, valued, and fought for, it's not depressing; it's inspiring."

In 2006, while she wrote about advocates like Amy Farber and dealt with her mother's cancer, Amy had applied to the Robert Wood Johnson Foundation for an Investigator Award in Health Policy Research. The awards are designed to sustain research and investigation into health policy issues that are overlooked. Amy received the grant, and from September 2007 until September 2008, she took a leave-of-absence from the *WSJ* and researched and wrote about patient advocates, scientists, researchers, and clinicians who were targeting a wide range of rare diseases. Her work included documenting efforts by patient advocacy communities to spur drug development.

Amy has written two books (*The View from Nebo: How Archaeology is Rewriting the Bible and Reshaping the Middle East* and *Jerusalem 1913: The Origins of the Arab-Israeli Conflict*) based on her years as a foreign correspondent.[92] She sees her latest efforts writing about advocacy for curing rare diseases as trauma journalism: "I continue to tell the stories of communities in conflict, and the choices people must make when they find themselves locked in life-and-death situations for which there are no clear solutions."

The energetic reporter, who began her media career as a 12-year-old columnist for her hometown weekly newspaper, believes that journalism is a tool that empowers people, especially those outside the system. She says her crisis coverage has made her more compassionate:

The essence of telling these stories is to be humble. My obligation is to bring issues to light and to help people look at things in a new way. I'm grateful for the work that I can do.

CHAPTER FIVE

Traumatic Stress Studies

Accounts of journalists covering conflict, tragedy, or trauma date back centuries, but social scientific research examining these issues is a recent phenomenon. One of the earliest such studies (1994 *American Journal of Psychiatry*) concerned the stressful psychological reactions of fifteen journalists who had witnessed an execution of a man found guilty of the murder of two 16-year-old boys. The results indicated that "merely witnessing violence may be sufficient to promote the development of dissociative, anxiety, and other symptoms, even in the absence of physical risk."[1]

As noted in Chapter 2, in 1999, UW Professor Roger Simpson published a significant study about trauma journalism, based on the responses of 131 reporters, photographers, and editors. Although journalists indicated they often had experienced gruesome scenes, only 30 percent said the employer had helped them or others handle the stress of such coverage.[2]

During the next decade, new research focused on war correspondents and journalists—print and broadcast reporters, photographers and videographers in the United States, Canada, Europe, and Australia—who had covered violent and catastrophic events at home and abroad. One 2001 study of sixty-one journalists from Europe and the United States concluded that 92 percent of participants had covered at least one story in their career that had caused intense feelings of fear, helplessness, or horror.[3]

Another 2001 study by researcher and current Australasia Dart Centre director, Cait McMahon, of fifty-seven journalists in Australia revealed that 35 percent of those surveyed were suffering from long-term trauma symptoms. She studied two groups of journalists—thirty-two who had reported on traumatic stories in the past three years and a contrast group of twenty-five who had not reported on trauma during the same timeframe. Types of trauma-related incidents covered included war, bank robberies, riots, natural disasters, domestic violence, child abuse, fires, vehicle accidents, rape, and murder. Her findings showed that "a large majority of the journalists surveyed experienced the intrusiveness, avoidance and depression symptoms between one and three years following reporting on the traumatic story."[4]

McMahon also noted that the predominant symptom experienced by many trauma journalists were high levels of anxiety—although there were differences in the reactions of older, more experienced reporters (more intrusive thoughts and avoidant behaviors) versus younger journalists (more anxiety and insomnia). There were other variations based on gender (women reported more anxiety and insomnia than men) and marriage status (single journalists reported more depression and social dysfunction at time of reporting on trauma). In interpreting the results, McMahon observed that influences may include the traumatic incident itself, general health and lifestyle factors of the journalists, personality differences, lack of training in trauma and stress management, or a combination of all of these factors. A final, significant finding in this 2001 research was that a majority of journalists expressed a desire to debrief or talk about their experiences following coverage of "trauma, tragedy and disaster."

In 2002, Canadian psychiatrist Anthony Feinstein and colleagues studied 140 war correspondents. Their landmark research compared questionnaire responses of the 140 subjects with 107 Canadian journalists who had never covered war. Results showed a lifetime prevalence of PTSD (among war correspondents) of 28.6 percent, and rates of 21.4 percent for major depression, and 14.3 percent for substance abuse. Though these rates compared with those of combat veterans, the researchers noted that journalists were unlikely to receive counseling or intervention of any kind.[5]

The potential for media workers to experience PTSD due to exposure to work-related traumatic events was the focus of an extensive 2003 study of 906 American newspaper journalists. Interestingly, despite high rates of traumatic exposure, relatively few journalists described a level of symptoms sufficient to be classified as disordered. This study concluded that for those journalists experiencing enduring stressful symptoms (e.g., PTSD), cognitive (behavioral) therapy interventions might be useful in dealing with work-related symptoms.[6]

Also, in 2003, Elana Newman, a Tulsa University psychology professor and Dart Center research director, coauthored a research study with colleagues Roger Simpson and David Handschuh, who had been injured while photographing the 9/11 World Trade Center attacks. The study surveyed 875 photojournalists, 98 percent of whom had covered traumatic events (e.g., automobile accidents, fire, and murder) in their careers. The research addressed the results of assignments involving exposure to death and injury, and the psychological consequences of these stories. Only 11 percent of the respondents said they had been advised of potential for emotional effects of such coverage, and just 25 percent stated their employers had offered counseling. The findings also revealed that approximately 6 percent of respondents "met the criteria for a diagnosis of post-traumatic stress disorder (PTSD)." The number of assignments involving critical incidents, the journalist's personal trauma history, and decreased social support increased the risks of PTSD.[7]

Occasionally a study will be distinctive on the basis of startling generalizations such as the abilities of journalists to endure exceptional stress in their work. Such was the case in 2002 when researchers used psychological analysis based on Freudian concepts, specifically the ego functions of four broadcast journalists (two American and two Finnish) who had extensive experience covering catastrophic events.[8] The methodology featured lengthy (e.g., 8 hours) interviews with the journalists and an American psychiatrist who had studied news media burnout and vicarious traumatization. Researchers praised the four journalists for their coping skills and "concern with the human condition and desire to contribute to its improvement whenever possible inevitably involve an underlying altruistic motive based on empathy for human suffering, ignorance and confusion."

The study noted: "Truly professional journalists have a superior aptitude for abstract thinking related to synthetic-integrative functioning and requiring a high degree of discipline and focus." Whereas other research on the adaptive strategies of trauma journalists addressed the difficulties often faced by news media workers, this 2002 study cited how successfully those reporters who were interviewed demonstrated strength "of their object relations" and "opportunities to ventilate or share their experiences," which have been "central to their maintaining inner balance when often in the midst of chaos." In a singular excerpt of hyperbole, the researchers later proclaimed: "These superior coping mechanisms allow them to file reports that are informative, often intellectually and artistically inspired, and sensitive to the emotional needs of their interviewees and their audience." The study concluded with a sensible discussion of the various in-house counseling, debriefing, psychological intervention, and training programs offered by major news media, such as the BBC, the *New York Times*, Fox News and CBS News, plus a recommendation that journalism students "develop or strengthen specific ego functions that will be essential to the performance of their tasks" when covering traumatic events in their careers.

In 2005, an engaging article on "War Correspondents as Responders: Considerations for Training and Clinical Services" was published in *Psychiatry*. The authors demonstrated a thorough knowledge of the challenges facing those journalists who cover war, terrorism, and conflict. They noted long-held norms that often result in reporters suffering in silence for fear of revealing any weakness or reaction to an assignment that might compromise their career progress, as well as newsroom behaviors that intimidate those with work-related concerns. The article's authors recommended psychological preparedness and training, not only for full-time reporters but also for independent (freelance) journalists: "While stimulated by their work, war correspondents on assignment may suffer from compassionate reactions, vicarious traumatization, and burnout."[9] The study also called for the destigmatizing of mental health services for "trauma" journalists and their families, as well as prioritizing "helpful interventions" with journalist peer groups (i.e., surrogate family members).

A 2008 Canadian study of twenty-nine print and broadcast journalists explored stress injuries caused by dangerous assignments.[10] Participants had covered domestic and international crime, violence, natural disasters, and accidents. A primary desire of many respondents was to time to reflect, decompress, and understand what they had witnessed, and thereby perhaps preventing cumulative stress. Interestingly, the journalists who participated expressed skepticism about the effectiveness of peer support groups in discussing people's distress. They cited the high level of distrust that existed in their workplace toward such disclosure. One popular suggestion was to take time to do a "lessons-learned exercise" after stressful assignments, educating both journalists and editors alike.

In recent years, an active researcher in the trauma journalism field has been Gretchen Dworznik, a former TV reporter and anchor for eight years in northern Ohio, and an Ashland University assistant professor since fall 2006. That year, Dworznik published a study on journalism and trauma that utilized the methodology from psychological literature on PTSD and traumatic stress to explore the coping mechanisms of twenty-six TV reporters and photographers from a large Midwestern market. Her focus was on the emotional effects of repeated exposure to fatal auto accidents, murders, kidnappings, and other violent crime on local journalists. But rather than use a survey, Dworznik used the journalists' own personal narratives about their experiences to demonstrate how they adapted to their stressful work and found constructive meaning in their efforts.[11]

A year later, she published qualitative research on attitudes of under-graduate journalism students regarding awareness of the effects of trauma coverage and the need for more specialized training in the classroom.[12]

Dworznik's current study includes results of an in-depth survey from her 2008 doctoral dissertation regarding PTSD and compassion fatigue (i.e., secondary traumatic stress and burnout) with television news work-ers, featuring the opinions of two hundred eighty reporters, photogra-phers, and live truck engineers working at local television stations across the United States. In her sample, twenty journalists (7.1 percent) met the criteria to be diagnosed with PTSD. Nearly all of these twenty respondents indicated that the symptoms were severe enough to impair their daily lives. Nearly 30 percent of the sample (about eighty journalists) reported being bothered in various degrees by symptoms of compassion fatigue, a situa-tion common among counselors and therapists and professionals who deal with traumatized individuals. In this study of TV news workers, women had higher compassion fatigue scores than men. Dworznik and Wearden concluded by advocating for greater awareness of the psychology of news coverage:

> Understanding traumatic stress reactions in journalists can provide information to help improve not only the training of new journalists, but the practices of the news industry as well. Training future journalists to recognize the elements of their jobs that can contribute to traumatic stress reactions will help them to cope with what they see and better protect themselves physically and psychologically. This is training that student-journalists are already asking for. In the professional news industry, knowing the possible reactions reporters and photographers could have to certain stories might lead to changes in news gathering practices that would give journalists a better chance at coping and processing what they see. This could cut down on absenteeism and turnover related to unprocessed trauma and lead to better journalists producing better stories overall.[13]

In 2009, former Dart Centre Europe director Mark Brayne and his colleagues published an article in the *Journal of Mental Health* (United Kingdom). Although the focus of the research was similar to earlier studies regarding media professionals' awareness of the risk of develop-ing mental health problems including PTSD as a result of their work, this study surveyed mostly management-level employees of a major news organization before they completed a one-day trauma-awareness work-shop. The researchers were interested in the options (i.e., help-seeking) explored by those media workers dealing with trauma-related problems, notably the perceived role of immediate supervisors. Of the 124 participants, 64 percent were males, half between 35 and 45 years of age, and 66 percent had been employed at the organization for a minimum of 10 years. The respondents, who held relatively nonstigmatizing attitudes toward PTSD and related issues, claimed that affected journalists in their news organization were more likely to turn to family members than managers or colleagues for support after traumatic incidents. The researchers posited that the reluctance of journalists to seek help from organizational sources, such as EAPs, was evidence of a "culture of silence" among news media workers. These employees need to be reassured that seeking in-service support is acceptable and will not damage their careers.[14]

Noting the comparison of the military to journalism concerning the stigmatizing of psychological problems, the authors of the study referred to a Trauma Risk Management (TRiM) program developed by the British military. TRiM is defined as an intensive psycho-educational posttraumatic management strategy based on peer-group risk assessment. It employs a cognitive behavioral therapeutic approach to modify attitudes about PTSD while providing support and education. Recent research has shown this program to be effective in identifying at-risk personnel and referring them for early intervention. In the article's conclusion, the authors called on news organizations to be more progressive in managing the psychological care of their employees.

The impact of management attitudes concerning news workers was the focus of a 2009 detailed telephone survey conducted with 400 US journalists examining the role of coverage of violent or traumatic events with regard to job satisfaction, workplace morale, or career commitment; the perceptions of journalists about management attitudes toward news workers who are experiencing emotional difficulties as a result of traumatic news coverage; and the effect of dangerous work experiences in journalists' job satisfaction or perceived workplace morale.[15]

The study included an overview of trauma journalism findings from earlier research, such as the exposure of news workers to primary and secondary trauma, the vulnerabilities and coping mechanisms of journalists, and the concerns of journalists about newsroom reputations and job security that inhibit disclosure of emotional effects resulting from trauma coverage. Other data in the 2009 study concerned the "inconsistent" and "enigmatic" research findings on journalists' job satisfaction, noting that younger journalists and women reporters tended to be more dissatisfied in their work than older male journalists. While 69 percent of the 400 respondents felt "fairly well or very well prepared" to deal with trauma journalism coverage, 40 percent believed that showing signs of emotional distress would harm a journalist's career. Adding to the equivocal results of the attitudinal survey was the fact that:

> As a group, respondents tended to see the management of their news organization as generally sympathetic on issues related to violent or traumatic events. Most agreed that management was supportive of journalists who were struggling emotionally after covering a violent or traumatic event and that management cared about the physical safety of its news workers.

The researchers stated that a supportive approach to trauma journalism coverage was not only a moral obligation of an employer but also smart from a business standpoint—by helping to maintain positive attitudes among news workers.

The ethics of covering tragic and traumatic stories was analyzed in a provocative 2010 study that asked seventy-two members of the "reading public" to assess photojournalist behavior.[16] Researchers explored whether people believed photojournalists were ethical if they chose to act as dispassionate (professional) observers rather than "Good Samaritans" when confronted with life-and-death issues, such as the public suicide of an individual. The authors wrote that although codes of ethics guide photojournalists (as well as reporters) to treat vulnerable subjects with compassion and consideration, craft attitudes guide journalists to perform as detached observers. Using news photos from a publicized suicide of a woman in Seoul, South Korea, in May 1991, the research interpreted the effect of three situational characteristics: the presence of other helpers, the intention of the victim to engage in political speech, and the possibility of intervention by the photographer.

The findings demonstrated that respondents supported the notion of moral relativism, believing that evaluation of photojournalists' actions required careful consideration of situational factors particular to each case. The study's authors stated that these conditional characteristics might be used to help decide whether "professional ethics can supersede the moral compulsion to help a fellow in distress." Beyond the scope of specific research findings, the actions of journalists are judged most harshly by the public when there is the perception that these individuals are exploiting others' misfortunes, maladies, and tragedies to sell copies, boost ratings, or advance careers. Photojournalist James Nachtwey's poignant quote at the close of the 2010 study provided an apt coda on situational ethics: "It is something I have to reckon with every day because I know that if I ever allow genuine compassion to be overtaken by personal ambition, I will have sold my soul."[17]

(Author's Note: An October 31, 2010, online article announced the launch of the Dart (Center) Research Database to gather "interdisciplinary scholarship on journalism and trauma in a single location.")[18]

Faces of Trauma Journalism:
David Handschuh

Fifty-one-year-old photojournalist David Handschuh is of medium stature, but he has an impish quality about him. Maybe it's the full head of curly dark hair, the mischievous eyes behind the glasses, or the full beard that masks a boyish face. You know David is in the room when you hear his distinctive chuckling. A native New Yorker, he has a streetwise vernacular and a sense of the dramatic when emphasizing his words. He is likely to throw an arm around you in recognition. But he is also liable to slip quietly away, a hitch in his step. Like so many others who were injured in New York City on 9/11, David carries the physical and psychological scars of his death-defying encounter with terrorism on that awful blue-sky morning a decade ago.

That tragic day, David Handschuh, award-winning photographer for the *New York Daily News* was en route to teach his graduate course in photo-journalism at NYU, where he had been an adjunct instructor since 1995. He wouldn't return to the classroom for more than a year as a result of the injuries he suffered photographing the attack on the World Trade Center. In

At Ground Zero: 25 Stories from Young Reporters Who Were There, the introduction to David's chapter, "A Lens on Life and Death," reads:

> There he photographed the previously unimaginable, even for a veteran chronicler of horror: falling debris, flaming buildings, body parts, images that to this day he has never shown another human being. As the second plane slammed into the north tower, he snapped a shot he still does not remember taking. As the first tower collapsed, a thunderous wave of hot gravel and glass catapulted Handschuh an entire city block, trapping him under a car. ("I thought I was going to die, scared and alone, facedown in the gutter of a lower Manhattan street," he wrote in his memoir.) After rescue workers carried his unconscious body to safety, he became trapped again in a deli as the second tower came down. Handschuh, who broke his leg, was evacuated across the Hudson. His only regret: he had relinquished his camera in the chaos.[19]

The book chapter first appeared as an article on *Poynteronline* (January 8, 2002).[20] In the initial paragraph, David describes how the desire to document a tragedy is often stronger than the impulse to flee a life-threatening situation. "It's not a feeling of being invincible," he writes. "It's just a need to keep recording the truth."

In David's case, that "need" appeared when he first picked up a camera as a precocious 13-year-old from Manhattan and soon began selling photographs of breaking news to media outlets across New York City. His specialty was capturing images of violence. David quickly built a reputation for photographing "car crashes, fires, and murders" that he tracked by listening to police scanners.[21]

His talents led him first to the *New York Post* and then the *New York Daily News* by the late 1980s. He describes his work before 9/11 as "chasing something, catching something, and bringing it in." He says he liked the variety of spot news and the opportunity to take a "good look at the underbelly of New York City" at a time when then-Mayor Giuliani's administration was touting the significant decrease in violent crime in the city.

David has rarely left New York during his career. When I asked him if he had ever been a war correspondent, he replied wryly, "No, just shootings in the Bronx." However, David covered the tragedy of Pan Am Flight 103, which exploded over Lockerbie, Scotland, in December 1988. He also journeyed to Littleton, Colorado, in April 1999 after the killing spree at Columbine High School. The father of three children, who has been married for more than twenty years, recalls crying at Columbine and engaging in self-reflection, questioning his line of work along with some of the other photographers at the scene.

Later in 1999, David received an Ochberg Fellowship from the Dart Center for Journalism & Trauma, which was an integral part of his consciousness-raising on the effects of critical incident reporting. Then came the devastation of 9/11, David's struggles to heal from his injuries, and the onset of a decade of trauma journalism activism. In an article ("Helping Another Breed of Foot Soldier") written for the American Press Institute, Handschuh stated: "The first step to assistance is for journalists to admit that we are not machines, we are people and that it's OK to get some kind of stress debriefing whether it's talking with a friend, a member of the clergy, a psychologist, psychiatrist, a mental health worker or a peer."[22]

During his recovery, David developed programs to address long-term physical and mental health issues for journalists, arising from coverage at Ground Zero. He also was one of the lead researchers in the first extensive study, involving 875 respondents, of the effects of stress, trauma, and PTSD among photojournalists.[23] David returned to work in March 2002 and told his editors he would no longer cover breaking news ("I'm not photographing any dead bodies any more").

> Handschuh realizes that few journalists have the clout to tell their bosses that they won't cover news. Most cannot even admit publicly that they sometimes suffer from the trauma they encounter in their work. "Not only can we not admit it to ourselves, we can't admit it to our management," Handschuh says, "and the main reason for that is fear there will be career reprisal for admitting that covering the news might affect us."[24]

Nine years after the horrific event, David tells me, "I became the poster child for this event because I had a physical injury (e.g., broken leg), and it allowed me to try to nurture my emotional issues to the best of my ability." But David, who was officially diagnosed with PTSD and spent a couple years in therapy, becomes emotional when he speaks of the well-being of his colleagues: "plenty of other people that were hurt but just didn't have the physical injuries and the scars to show for it. But they were still wrestling with devils."

Today, David serves on the board of directors of News Coverage Unlimited, an international organization providing trauma support services for journalists. He is a former president of the 10,000-member National Press Photographers Association (NPPA) and a Poynter Institute Media Ethics Fellow. David has been nominated three times for a Pulitzer Prize and has won several local, state, and national photography awards.

One of his proudest achievements was being recognized by the National Public Health Information Council for establishing and promoting peer-counseling workshops, where journalists are trained to assist colleagues in debriefing sessions and other postevent interventions. David says that as a result of monumental disasters such as the 2004 tsunami, Hurricanes

Katrina and Rita, as well as the ongoing conflict in Iraq and Afghanistan, we are experiencing a "light bulb moment" for the industry and its practitioners. "Newsgathering can be hazardous to your emotional health," he says. "I'm a big believer that we journalists have the tools and the authority. We just need to have the desire to look after each other."

He challenges those in the news media who are skeptical of debriefings and counseling to look at the example of the military and the public service sector (e.g., police, firefighters, and emergency medical technicians), where intervention after a crisis is "an ever-present part of life." While acknowledging the growing awareness of the emotional effects of trauma journalism ("It's a good thing, and it can only go to help each other and create better stories for our audiences"), he recognizes the absence of training and support services for daily coverage of critical incidents at most newspapers nationwide. "It's not just the really big, scary stories that mess with your head," he says, when talking with young and aspiring journalists. "The work you do every single day on a local level can affect you."

David Handschuh's life was forever changed on one of the darkest days in American history. The events of 9/11 transformed him from a journalist driven by the adrenaline rush of violence into an advocate. He continues to raise awareness of issues affecting all newsrooms. "The most satisfying results come from conversations where you discover that the work we are doing is helping people."

CHAPTER SIX

Media Training and Intervention

Efforts to improve trauma journalism coverage focus on the empathetic/ ethical treatment of sources and the provision of training/intervention programs for news media workers. Responsibility for such change lies with journalists themselves (e.g., using proper interviewing techniques and adopting self-care practices) and with their newsroom managers.

Interviewing

Specific guidelines exist for handling interviews under stressful circumstances. In the article "How to Do an Interview—When Trauma is the Topic," Ruth Teichroeb and Karen Brown, wrote about the special situations when talking with people who have been affected by tragedy. Teichroeb, an investigative reporter for the *Seattle Post-Intelligencer* for twenty-two years, spent much of her journalistic career "covering social issues involving vulnerable people":

> It's just a totally different landscape when dealing with someone who's traumatized. They don't know the rules, and what's so essential in these interviews is to give the person choices about a whole host of things— from logistics like where the interview is going to be done and who's going to be there, all the way to what's going to appear in print. Time is crucial. I think it's insulting to a victim to go in and take their story and leave and put it in the newspaper without having that relationship— without them being able to say this is OK and this is not.[1]

Brown, a public radio reporter for WFCR (the NPR affiliate in Amherst, Massachusetts) for eleven years, discussed trust, access, and ethics in trauma interviews:

> The most important thing is to let people tell the whole story so they know that you're willing to listen to it. . . . I want to make sure that people I am going to interview understand that they could go through a pretty emotional experience. I try not to talk them out of it, but I just want to make sure that there's full disclosure about what they might go through.

Those experienced with interviewing victims understand that making the person feel as comfortable as possible is essential, particularly before asking difficult questions, such as about the details of a violent crime, a horrific disaster, or a tragic war scenario. According to an article by Lori Luechtefeld in the May/June 2003 *IRE (Investigative Reporters and Editors) Journal*, reporter James Neff of the *Seattle Times*, conducted several interviews with rape victims prior to exploring details on the crimes. "Before contacting the women, he met with a rape crisis counselor who was then able to vouch for his good intentions to the women before he interviewed them," Luechtefeld wrote.

In "Five Steps to Covering a Disaster Effectively," Joe Hight, former president of the Dart Center for Journalism & Trauma, told newsroom managers they must teach their reporters and editors about approaching and interviewing victims. His recommendations include:

- Emphasize that victims must be treated with dignity and respect.

- Approach victims politely with a clear introduction, identifying the reporter and his or her news organization. If the request for the interview is denied, the reporter should not badger the person but simply leave a business card or a telephone number.

- Try calling funeral homes or representatives first to connect with a family member.

- Remember to call victims to verify facts and quotes; return photos promptly.

- Never ask, "How do you feel?" or say, "I understand how you feel." Simply state, "My name is . . ." and "I'm sorry for what happened." Then ask questions that relate to the *life* (not death) of the victim.

In 2007, Hight also discussed the interviewing of "profoundly affected" soldiers and Marines in an online article published by the Dart Center and the Association of Health Care Journalists. He quoted experts who advised that reporters should allow returning troops time to decompress before asking tough questions. This situation typically requires extended "hanging out" time, a challenge for journalists working on a deadline. The article recommended that a sensitive interviewer of military personnel should focus on pragmatic and short-term queries rather than on more abstract, future-oriented questions (e.g., What do you plan to do with the rest of your life?). Hight cited journalist Curt Guyette's profile of an Iraqi war veteran (Chris Killion) who had earned three Purple Hearts and was combating PTSD: "However, Guyette said he was able to interview Killion because he got to know him, tried to relate to some of his veteran's experiences and researched PTSD. He was also able to use his experience as a journalist to relate the plight of the veteran to victims of violence, as a police reporter would."[5]

The ethics of interviewing victims of trauma become even more stringent when covering incidents involving children. A 2006 guide for journalism professionals (*Covering Children & Trauma*) by Ruth Teichroeb outlined several special requirements for journalists conducting interviews with children, such as:

- Seeking permission from a parent or guardian before interviewing or photographing a child (i.e., a person under 18 years of age). Exceptions to this condition should be discussed with an editor.

- Explaining to a parent and child what the story is about and how the interview will be used (i.e., informed consent).

- Having a parent or someone the child knows and trusts present during the interview.

- Emphasizing that the child can choose not to answer a question or ask the reporter not to use sensitive information.

- Avoiding interviewing at the scene of the tragedy or trauma. Be willing to wait until the parents and child are ready to talk, even if that is weeks or months after the crisis.

- Researching as much background information as possible before interviewing children about previous trauma by talking with parents, counselors, teachers, and medical personnel, and by obtaining documents, such as police reports and court records.

- Being aware that retelling a traumatic event can trigger intense emotions in your interview subject, even years later.

- Using sound judgment and discretion when deciding what information and images are central to the story and what material will embarrass or hurt a child and his or her family.[6]

Mark Brayne, who spent thirty years as a foreign correspondent and senior editor for Reuters and the BBC World Service before becoming a psychotherapist and trauma training specialist, discusses sound interviewing techniques in the 2007 publication *Trauma & Journalism: A Guide for Journalists, Editors & Managers,* which he compiled and edited while serving as director of the Dart Centre in Europe. The guide is well suited for any news organization interested in the welfare of its journalistic staff. Brayne tells journalists to acknowledge that they may be feeling nervous, fearful, and even angry about the story they're reporting. They should let their emotions inform their actions rather than clouding their understanding or judgment. He also advises the use of active listening skills—paying attention to mannerisms, cues, and the body language of sources—when conducting interviews. He suggests open-ended questions to explore attitudes and emotions (e.g., "What happened next?," "How did you deal with that?," "How are you now?"). Other recommendations include reflecting back and paraphrasing, as well as allowing for silences and pauses. Although Brayne urges journalists to be sensitive to sources, he cautions against "an inclination to 'over-empathise'." He believes reporters should not try to "rescue" the interviewee, or cross the line and become a confidante.

Brayne writes: "Trauma is at the heart of news—and of the human condition. How it's reported gives those who weren't there their first understanding of what a traumatic event means." Among the most outspoken international advocates for compulsory survival training for reporters and producers working in hostile environments, he adds: "Journalists are professional first responders to crisis and disaster. But they're among the last of those groups to recognize the psychological implications of that responsibility."

Journalist Training and Support

In the early 1990s, Brayne helped establish the BBC's first confidential counseling program, challenging the prevailing journalistic notions of discussing emotions in connection with newsgathering even under the most demanding conditions. Believing that "journalists are at risk for emotional injury," he says managers and editors need to identify the signs of psychological trauma among their staff, similar to the TRiM assessment of military officers in the field supervising combat stress issues. In the late 1990s, Brayne worked with the British Royal Marines in introducing such techniques to the BBC—"vaccinating the newsroom with trauma awareness." His advice to managers: Hold structured conversations with those covering traumatic stories; social interaction is often more important than formal counseling.

Brayne admits that, "Even the most seasoned and professional journalists can be affected and possibly distressed by exposure to tragedy." He recommends that people who have lingering emotional problems as a result of their work, should seek professional support, if necessary. But he also reassures those in the news media that, "Most people cope well with trauma—especially if they have good social, family and team support."

To deal with potentially traumatic events, Brayne offers the following pragmatic suggestions on self-care:

- Knowing your limits. If you've been asked to undertake a difficult or dangerous assignment that you'd rather not do, don't be afraid to say so.

- Acknowledging feelings and choosing to talk about emotions at the appropriate moment is not a sign of weakness. It is a way to help the person make sense of trauma and tragedy.

- Finding someone who is a sensitive listener—whether an editor, peer, or partner.

- Understanding that, sometimes, what you've been through may overwhelm your capacity to cope—and keep an eye out for delayed reactions. Talk to colleagues, and, if necessary, seek professional support.[8]

Trauma risk awareness for journalists is an emerging twenty-first-century issue. As discussed earlier in the text, Dr. Anthony Feinstein, a prominent Canadian psychiatrist and trauma journalism scholar, has developed an anonymous online diagnostic instrument on the INSI website. Under the headline, "How is Your Emotional Health? Test Yourself," the site states: "To assist news media professionals who suspect they might be experiencing some form of post-traumatic stress, INSI is making available an online self-help program . . . that allows journalists to assess their emotional health."[9]

Professor Patrice Alison Keats at Canada's Simon Fraser University in British Columbia has created an "Assignment Stress Injury" (ASI) evaluation protocol for journalists who may have mental health issues as "a consequence of trauma assignments in the field and subsequently in the newsroom with its added stress and demands." Based on her research studies with Canadian journalists, Keats' continuum ranges from "Acute Complaints" (single symptoms that interfere with daily functioning—such as anxiety, emotional exhaustion, and sleep problems) to "Psychiatric Conditions" (a group of symptoms under specific circumstances—such as panic attacks, acute stress, major depression, and PTSD). The ASI protocol material includes reference information: When to seek help? What kind of help to get—(1) self-help, (2) peer support, (3) professional help)? Where to get help?[10]

The Dart Centre's *Trauma & Journalism: A Guide for Journalists, Editors & Managers* lists steps for supervisors to provide effective trauma management before, during, and after stressful coverage. As Mark Brayne notes: "It's essential to brief and educate teams and individuals before they're sent on potentially traumatic stories; to support them during such assignments or projects; and to support them afterwards with practical and social support, and, where necessary, with expert trauma counseling."[11]

In a spring 2010 telephone interview, Sarah Ward-Lilley, managing editor, world newsgathering for the BBC, spoke of the challenges of implementing trauma journalism reform as part of culture shift for a 23,000-employee news organization. She described herself as sort of "a mad target" for trying to effect systemic organizational change. Ward-Lilley, who has been with BBC News for 21 years, is responsible for the training, safety, and well-being of its staff and freelancers both in the United Kingdom and abroad.

According to Ward-Lilley, the BBC provides several levels or layers of training, including a one-day trauma-awareness course to sensitize managers on requirements to establish a "safe" culture for employees. Since the mid-1990s and its coverage of the violence in Bosnia and surrounding regions, the BBC has offered hostile-environment training over five or six days, using former military personnel as instructors, to enable journalists to be physically protected and equipped to safely handle war zone conditions.

In the 108-page *Handbook for Journalists*, produced in 2009 by Reporters sans frontières, the BBC is described as going further than most news organizations in imposing strict rules to protect its staff and stringers, particularly in high-risk work (e.g., deployments to hostile environments, covert filming of dangerous groups, and covering events such as terrorist incidents, natural disasters, and pandemic diseases). At the outset, BBC staff are informed that they have a right to decline such dangerous assignments without penalty or "any other detrimental consequence." An extensive risk assessment procedure is followed including:

- recommended methods of operating
- individual and team security measures
- protective equipment, first-aid, and trauma equipment
- preventive health measures
- safety communications
- contingency planning.[12]

Longtime British war correspondent Kate Adie underwent hostile-environment training when she was reporting for the BBC. On the subject of journalists being accompanied by private security forces, she states: "It's totally mistaken to suppose that an armed escort is going to give a journalist any protection—on the contrary, journalists who turn up surrounded by armed personnel are just turning themselves into targets and in even worse danger."[13]

The BBC explains that its mission is to care for the psychological and emotional effects not only for staff in the field but also for those "editing and handling material back at base" as part of traumatic stress awareness. The training is provided to full-time BBC staffers as well as to freelancers (stringers). Once in the field on high-risk assignment, BBC reporters are governed by strict guidelines, including designation of team leaders and safety advisors. A high-risk operations team at BBC headquarters is charged with keeping producers and editors up-to-date with details on field conditions, providing security advice and information (including contingency plans), and coordinating and maintaining safety equipment and training programs.[14] After the kidnapping and murder of *WSJ* reporter Daniel Pearl in Pakistan in February 2002, major news organizations like the BBC began incorporating specialized training and contingency procedures for staff who were arrested, detained, or kidnapped.[15]

As described earlier, the BBC utilizes the TRiM model to support the emotional health of journalists working under stressful conditions. TRiM uses a combination of peer and management support to encourage a safe environment and to destigmatize the impact of trauma. A 1-hour structured interview (i.e., operational debrief) helps managers evaluate staff returning from critical incident coverage. Ten assessment questions are intended to be conversational and reassuring. "The process allows journalists' brains to decompress," says Ward-Lilley, noting that if any emotional issues linger after a month, then counseling will be recommended for the news media worker.

The BBC also encourages frank commentary from high-profile correspondents, such as David Loyn, who are willing to discuss their experiences, including the risks and aftermath. The goal is to have senior staff reassure younger employees about dealing with the effects of stress. Initially, comments were provided on videotape. In recent years, several veteran journalists have presented their personal stories in an open forum, where questions are answered and information on trauma training provided. "The theme of these presentations is: don't suffer in silence," says Ward-Lilley.

In his chapter, "We Have a Long Way to Go," published in *Sharing the Frontline and the Back Hills*, Chris Cramer, former president of CNN International Networks and current global, multimedia editor of Thomson Reuters, was outspoken in his criticism of news organizations, particularly in the United States, that were reluctant to provide comprehensive safety training "for journalists traveling into harm's way."[16] Among the few US news organization Cramer credited—CNN, NBC, and the *New York Times*.

Cramer, the honorary president of INSI, considers it dangerous and irresponsible for media companies to claim that providing training and support services for journalists is too expensive. On page 50 of the 2007 INSI publication *Killing the Messenger*, Cramer, who has spent almost forty years working in print and broadcast journalism in Europe and the United States, states:

> those of us who manage and assign have a greater than ever responsibility to ensure that we do everything possible for our staff. For the last few years, some of us in positions of responsibility have been urging the entire media profession to wake up to the issue of safety training for our staff. I have to tell you that for a long time, we felt our pleas were falling on deaf ears.[17]

When interviewed in May 2010, Will King, senior director of news operations for CNN International, quipped that there was a time when foreign correspondents prepared for covering wars and other conflicts by merely packing "water purification tablets and a road map." But after tragic deaths and injuries of staff in places like Somalia and Sarajevo, CNN has taken a leadership position in providing weeklong hostile-environment training for hundreds of its staff and by providing safety equipment (e.g., body armor), armored vehicles, and security personnel.

INSI director Rodney Pinder credits CNN, the BBC, the AP, and Reuters for committing tens of millions of dollars on news safety for their staff (including indigenous news workers in conflict zones). He says INSI's membership of some 120 media organizations contributes significantly from their own resources toward the safety of journalists—"whether through direct local investment in training and safety infrastructure or through humanitarian support for journalists and others who are the victims of violence."

An INSI website lists thirty security training providers worldwide. Nineteen are based in the United Kingdom; the United States, France, and Australia have two firms each; Germany, Switzerland, Kenya, Jordan, and the United Arab Emirates each list one training organization.[18]

Two of the best-known security training firms serving international print and broadcast news organizations are AKE (prominent client: CNN) and Centurion Risk Assessment Services (prominent client: the AP), both based in England. A weeklong hostile-environment training program is estimated at $2,500 per person, plus travel and accommodations. The training, which is typically conducted by former military personnel, includes classroom and field instruction, first-aid training, and PTSD information sessions—all designed to enhance a trauma journalist's awareness, preparedness skills, and self-sufficiency. According to AKE's website: "The training is delivered in a blend of lectures and practical scenarios, supported by video footage, demonstration, weapons and materials. The programme is comprehensive and interactive, culminating in a series of challenging and realistic training exercises where you put what you've learned into practice."[19]

The Centurion Risk Assessment Services website lists more than fifty news media, humanitarian aid agency, charitable organization, commercial business, and nongovernmental organization clients. It describes its mission as preparing people "mentally and practically for dangerous work in extreme conditions."[20]

Posted on the Centurion website is an article by Vincent Laforet of the *New York Times*, "Hostile Environment Training 101." This informative, entertaining first-person account describes how Laforet felt more like a soldier than a journalist during his week of 10-hours per day training sessions in classrooms and "on the cold and muddy grounds" under the direction of battle-tested Royal Marines. He praises the security training course for teaching "some basic steps that could very well save a colleague's life"—not to mention your own:

> You will be taught how to stop an arterial bleed, or "pumper" as well as something as common as shock. You will . . . re-enact actual gun shot scenarios, car accidents, and worse . . . . Other topics include kidnappings, weapons, artillery etc. . . . You will learn about different types of mines, as well as how to survive in both cold and hot climates. Border crossings and riot situations are also covered.[21]

A free resource for conflict reporters and other news personnel is journalists@risk (www.journalistsatrisk.org), described as an online community of media professionals with experience of work in hostile environments, including war zones. The website includes a community discussion board, a "KnowledgeBase," INSI Safety Tips, online maps, and other resources. A sample "Tip of the Day": "Never carry a weapon or travel with journalists who do. Be prudent in taking pictures. Seek the agreement of soldiers before shooting images. Know local sensitivities about picture-taking."[22]

In addition to proactive security training programs, CNN offers post-coverage intervention services with trauma psychiatrist Anthony Feinstein. Confidential counseling services are also provided to CNN employees "who are exposed either directly or indirectly to occupational related stress," according to a human resources department brochure titled "Turner Broadcasting System, Inc.: Post Traumatic Stress Disorder Program." The brochure notes the higher rates of psychological distress for journalists who have covered "war, natural disasters, and other tragic events" and describes comprehensive treatment services ("pre-deployment, during deployment and post-deployment") available for CNN employees and their families "where ever and when ever needed."[23] Information on PTSD programs and services is also provided via the CNN website, and counseling is offered face-to-face, by telephone, and online.

Will King, who started with CNN as a news video producer in 1980 (when the network began), manages the infrastructure of all CNN's thirty-three international news operations outside the United States. Like other veteran journalists, he refers to the PTSD program services as "head laundry," which may be required after stressful coverage. King says the traditional stigma once associated with mental health services for journalists is easing, particularly as younger employees enter the work force. He also notes how all managers receive awareness training regarding PTSD and related issues, and that employees are encouraged to talk with colleagues if they are experiencing any number of physical, behavioral, intellectual, or emotional symptoms as a result of exposure to a traumatic event.

"The 'Lou Grant' era has passed," King says, "and we're much better off."

Dr. Anthony Feinstein says that significant progress regarding trauma journalism services has been made, although a lot of work needs to be done to effect widespread change. He recalls speaking to a group of war correspondents less than a decade ago when a female reporter from New Zealand told him: "Psychotherapy is for pussies." Feinstein believes in the power of individuals to transform an entrenched culture like journalism.

He points to his work with CNN as illustrating the willingness of many staffers to participate in postevent debriefing sessions, such as the ones he conducted after the 2010 Haitian earthquake. Feinstein says the most common categories of "presenting issues" were anxiety, sleeplessness, and recurring (disturbing) images. He adds that some CNN employees asked questions like: "I am fine, so should I be worried?" Feinstein's answer: No. He stresses in his interactions with journalists that most are remarkably resilient after trauma coverage, and his views are supported through his seminal research on the emotional effects (psychological distress) of reporting on war and other crises and disasters. Feinstein continues to compile interesting data in the field, including the impact of exposure to trauma on a person's work, particularly among journalists, writers, and creative types. For example, "Does the trauma result in greater sensitivity and empathy or withdrawal and detachment?"

C. Danny Spriggs' involvement with crisis coverage is noteworthy because he isn't a journalist, researcher, or therapist. The vice president of global security for the AP since 2008 had spent twenty-eight years in the US Secret Service, progressing to the rank of deputy director, the organization's second-highest position. The one-time police officer and US Marine was recognized by the Department of Treasury with a Special Act Award for his meritorious performance during the March 30, 1981, assassination attempt on the life of President Ronald Reagan.

Today, Spriggs is concerned with the safety and welfare of some twenty-five hundred journalists in two hundred forty worldwide bureaus. He describes a three-pronged approach at the AP as including operational security, physical security, and a "post-mortem" experience. Approximately seventy to eighty staff annually participate in a five-day hostile-environment training course, and two-day refresher programs are required every three years. Specialized training is also provided for staff covering high-profile events such as the World Cup, the Olympics, and national political conventions.

Based on threat assessments from private and government sources, the AP will provide "both static and mobile security personnel on a case-by-case," says Spriggs. Under his direction, deployment of security guards has expanded during the past two years. Spriggs also notes the company's focus on the training and security needs of local (indigenous) journalists, in addition to the staff of foreign correspondents.

He adds, "The AP has enhanced its 'after-action' response to journalists by initiating forums for addressing Post-Traumatic Stress Disorder, along with the long-established Employee Assistance Program." As a complement to its hostile-environment training, the AP initiated a series of Global Speaker Initiatives (GSI) in 2010. These GSI forums feature peer-to-peer conversations by reporters and photographers about their experiences in covering tragedy and trauma, including discussion of the psychological effects of crisis coverage.

In an e-mail on May 11, 2010, Tom Curley, president and CEO of the AP, responded to an off-the-record claim that reporters at some media outlets were being fired when they confided to their supervisors that they were suffering from PTSD or severe emotional effects as a result of trauma coverage:

> I suppose anything is possible, and I can imagine a couple extreme situations where something like this might be interpreted as having happened. . . . All (news organizations) are so much more aware of what to look for, how to rotate people, when to reach out. An important new factor is pre-assignment training, which helps many think through issues. We also work people up a ladder of exposure to battlefield assignments as much as possible. I know all the major organizations who put people on the front line are very careful about every aspect of pre- and post-assignment care/check/vetting. I have seen bosses react negatively to other issues (e.g., alcoholism, separation anxiety).

Crime Coverage

The summer 2010 issue of the *American Journalism Review* highlighted an emerging area of concern for news organizations: how to protect investigative journalists operating in areas dominated by organized crime? The article "Playing Defense" by Sherry Ricchiardi opened with a dramatic anecdote about a reporter in Zagreb, Croatia, who was almost beaten to death by bat-wielding thugs trying to intimidate the journalist, who had been researching mafia activity in that region of Eastern Europe. Several other anecdotes described how investigative journalists and their families were targeted because of their work.[24]

Psychiatrist Frank Ochberg commented in the story how such "extreme and prolonged threats of reprisal" can be debilitating and demoralizing. He noted that if news managers are indifferent or insensitive to the plight of their affected reporters, severe psychological trauma could result.[25]

The *AJR* article explained that threats against the media in Eastern Europe have resulted in the deaths of reporters, including Anna Politkovskaya, who was killed in her Moscow apartment in October 7, 2006. "She had gained international recognition for her investigative reports into human rights abuses by the Russian military in Chechnya," Ricchiardi wrote. "Nineteen journalists have been killed in Russia since 2000 in retaliation for their work, making it one of the world's most hostile environments for the news media."[26]

The Organized Crime and Corruption Reporting Project (OCCRP) was established in 2007 in Sarajevo, the capital of Bosnia and Herzegovina, by Drew Sullivan, a former investigative reporter for the *Nashville Tennessean* and Paul Radu, cofounder of the Romanian Center for Investigative Journalism. The OCCRP works to implement safety and security policies for at-risk journalists in the region. The guidelines include procedures for attending dangerous meetings with sources, for travel in high-risk areas, and for how to handle threats. In the case of a murder of a fellow investigative reporter, "OCCRP reporters are committed to aggressively completing the work of a fallen colleague."[27]

Despite the efforts of news media organizations and advocacy groups, trauma journalists are ultimately responsible for their safety, health, and welfare. Melissa Manware described the impact of her "nearly 10 years of cops reporting" in "Overcoming Trauma" in the May 2008 issue of *Quill* magazine. She wrote how in her career she covered hundreds of deaths (nearly all violent), many of children and innocent victims—"people who were shot, smothered, stabbed, raped, burned and beaten."[28]

While discussing the emotional effects and enduring sadness of such work, she also commented on the role of empathy: "I also believe that a reporter who really cares about a story, who is emotionally touched by a story, will almost always do a better job of telling it." The former journalist concluded her article optimistically: "Stories change lives, they give voices to the voiceless and, most importantly, they remind all of us of our humanity."[29]

A sidebar to the Melissa Manware story featured "Tips for Overcoming Trauma," provided by the Dart Center for Journalism & Trauma (www.

dartcenter.org). The introduction stated, "Statistically, the more tragedies a journalist covers, the more likely that person is to experience psychological consequences." Among the tips for journalists to cope and stay healthy when covering difficult assignments: take breaks and try to pace your exposure to distressing images or documents; find a hobby, exercise, attend a house of worship, spend time with family and friends ("For people exposed to trauma, social support is the single best predictor of emotional resilience"); find someone you can talk to; focus on the importance of your work and the good it may do; and *know your limits* ("It's common to experience emotional distress in the weeks after witnessing a traumatic event. If the distress doesn't subside after a month, however, consider seeking professional help").[30]

Faces of Trauma Journalism: George Hoff

Photo by Patricia Collis

Veteran Canadian broadcast journalist George Hoff has experienced trauma firsthand by covering war, natural disasters, murder trials, and countless acts of violence in his journalistic career. But George has spent the bulk of his work years as a newsroom manager, assigning teams of reporters, videographers, editors, and producers, often putting people in dangerous situations. He understands that caring for others carries additional risks and responsibilities that extend beyond getting the story done well and on deadline.

The 61-year-old spoke at length about the lessons learned when he had to assign replacement staff in the CBC (Canadian Broadcasting Corporation) newsroom to edit videotape of the devastating December 26, 2004, tsunami that struck South Asia. December 26 is "Boxing Day," a national holiday in Canada. As a result, young, inexperienced people were on the job viewing and selecting videotape to air on newscasts. After a few days of working long hours, one of the replacement staffers came to George, disturbed by the repetitive viewing of images of death and destruction.

"I have to confess I hadn't thought about," he says with a sigh, reflecting on the encounter. "And yet I was asking young people in their twenties to watch this carnage of the effects of the tsunami for six hours a day and to pick their pictures. The viewer sees it once and can turn his eyes away if he chooses; the editor doesn't have that choice."

George, who prides himself on his strong work ethic and structured management style, says he felt guilty that he waited to initiate procedures to mandate breaks for people viewing and editing videotape—only after the conversation with the young troubled employee. He adds: "You can only do so much in that kind of situation."

What George experienced with the CBC newsroom staff regarding the emotional impact of repetitive viewing of traumatic video occurred more recently with coverage of the 2010 Haiti earthquake, resulting in trauma consultants being retained to talk to staff at major news organizations. But the issue of emotional care for editing and production staff has been a timely topic, dating back to the events of 9/11, the terrorist videotaped executions of Daniel Pearl and Nick Berg, and other troubling footage of war and disaster.

Although he is among the growing cadre of journalists advocating empathetic and ethical coverage of conflict, tragedy, and trauma, George is regularly reminded how the macho credo of "suck it up and do the next story" still predominates news media across Canada, the United States, and around the world. He says the impact of violence on a journalist's psyche is too often "kept in the closet," either because of organizational policies, fears of job losses, professional insecurities, or other "chilling" effects that block employees from discussing their emotional health.

The compact, ruddy-faced Vienna, Austria, native, grew up in Toronto (his current residence). He became a journalist in the 1970s and "got hooked on the rush of daily (breaking) news." During his years in the field, there was no trauma training by either the CBC or CTV Television Network. George recalls being sent to cover war, terrorism, riots, and disasters with just handshakes and well-wishes from colleagues. He worked on stories in Northern Ireland and England, Africa, Haiti, and the Middle East, among other postings.

"I used to come home from long trips, and I had a family of kids at the time," he says, recalling how he had to decide how much detail to share with his wife and two sons. "I had to fit myself back into this family." George says that over time he became aware of the emotional effects of trauma coverage, how the experiences started to "build" on him and the difficulties that caused. He says as his career progressed, he was offered counseling while working at the CBC. But he never utilized any therapeutic services.

The one thing I did ask for was time with my family after difficult and lengthy assignments. I always got a week or two. It was important to help me re-integrate with my family and was the most important piece in keeping the four of us in sync.

George and his wife for more than thirty years have raised two sons, now 30 and 27. On the job, he has tried to treat his staff like an extended family. The former managing editor of the CBC's Ottawa Bureau was responsible for knowing what the news teams, particularly in difficult reporting environments, were going through. He was regularly on call 24/7. Sometimes, he wouldn't leave the office, staying all night to demonstrate his concern, commitment to their safety, and to be available if a quick decision was required. He also made sure that his CBC teams knew that counseling was available. He would inform them of the services, tell them that he supported their utilization if necessary, but he drew the line at following up to see if an individual had sought counseling.

"It's an extremely touchy situation," he says describing the balancing act of caring while respecting a person's privacy. "Sometimes you just do it on instinct."

Colleagues who have worked with George at CBC TV News credit him for his editorial integrity and exemplary approach to complex ethical problems. Longtime CBC correspondent David Halton writes that George's "proven track record in news-gathering in war zones and other high-pressure situations . . . enabled him to command the respect of CBC reporters."

As the only Canadian journalist to be awarded a Dart Center Ochberg Fellowship, Hoff sees his advocacy role as extremely important. "There is a need for more journalists to come forward and openly discuss issues arising from the coverage of violence and trauma—," he wrote in an online article on September 27, 2009, for the Canadian Journalism Project. "—be it in Afghanistan, a child shot on a Canadian city street, the daily realities of aboriginal communities, sitting through a trial like (Robert) Pickton or (Paul) Bernardo, or covering natural disasters such as forest fires, floods and hurricanes in Canadian communities."[31]

George is concerned that the focus of much of today's discussion on hostile-environment training and related services has to do almost exclusively with foreign coverage. "There is no training for a local journalist (in Canada) who covers fatalities on a daily basis," he says, noting the cumulative impact of reporting on deadly traffic accidents, grisly murders, or grueling courtroom scenes like the infamous 1995 trial of Ontario (Canada) serial killer and rapist Paul Bernardo.

"You can be as affected by a trial as you can by covering a tsunami," George says.

He tells me that journalists who covered the Bernardo trial were "still marked" by the graphic testimony and extensive audio and videotape evidence a decade later. He says a journalist colleague wrote to him recently, telling George that, "I never really accounted for the impact it (trauma coverage) might have had on my less-than-perfect personal life."

While George is well aware of the strains reporting on stressful stories can have on a marriage, he says his family "always gave me strength." When home he would debrief with his wife. To relax he often turned to cooking, reading, and scrabble games. He also found time for solitude and reflection on long bicycle rides. For decades he has enjoyed visits to a family rustic cabin (i.e., no electricity or running water) by a lake in central Ontario. "This only works from May–November!"

Unlike the stereotypical correspondent who unwinds with his mates after a tough day in the field, George says he doesn't always socialize while working on difficult stories.

> I will either seek a quiet space or, if the conditions allow, go for a walk. As the team leader I have to pick these days. So it is a bit of a juggling act, but, in the end, if I need to process events, I initially do it alone.

He recommends that his fellow journalists be honest with themselves in trying to find ways to cope with the challenges of trauma coverage. He advises newsroom managers to listen very carefully to reporting teams in the field: How tired are they? Can you give them a day off? What do they need? "As a leader, it is important to listen to the editors who are in closer contact with the teams," he says. "If a journalist hesitates about taking on a risky assignment, don't push. Don't rush the decision."

He cites the recent experience of someone who had worked for and with him for decades. They discussed an upcoming war assignment, and George told him to take a couple of days to think it over. The man called back and said, "I don't think I want to do this anymore." George replied, "You've given to journalism a tremendous amount, and if you're done with that kind of work, that's OK."

But George has also experienced cases where a person accepts an assignment, and the job will be underway when conditions change, and it gets dangerous in the field. "Then the journalist wants to pull out, and my feeling is that's his decision," he says. "But I've not been necessarily thrilled by it. I realize it's difficult, but there's a job to do."

He speaks frankly to young journalists. While stressing that not all news coverage is about trauma and violence, he asks them to question their interests and motives for taking on dangerous assignments. "I am honest. Brutally honest. I don't make it easy," he says.

Now a freelance producer and instructor at Centennial College in Toronto, George tries to dispel any myths about glory-seeking crisis coverage:

> I think it is important that they [students] are told clearly and with examples that being in the field is not always fun. If you choose to be a reporter, a field journalist, you will witness death, injury, trauma, and

violence. I use quotes from other journalists, I use my own experiences, I use the experiences of young journalists. I lay it all out.

George's online article "'Suck It Up' Just isn't Enough" states that most current journalism programs in Canada give the coverage of violence and trauma "cursory treatment." However, his quotes can sound contradictory, ranging from optimistic ("There's a growing awareness." "It's cracking the lineup and getting into universities and into forums.") to frustrated ("In Canada, training is still a spotty thing." "Psychological issues are not delved into." "I wish we got to the point where newsroom managers understood what was going on.").[32]

He credits the work of people like Cliff Lonsdale, president of the Canadian Journalism Forum on Violence and Trauma, with promoting panel discussions about conflict coverage and related topics at media conferences. Lonsdale, former chief news editor for CBC Television and a documentary filmmaker, currently teaches journalism at the University of Western Ontario, specializing in television and international reporting. Ongoing dialogue about trauma journalism in Canada includes thorny issues such as the potential legal ramifications of journalists being diagnosed with PTSD even after receiving training (i.e., Could a news media company be liable for the emotional problems of a journalist affected by his or her coverage?).

George writes of the "considerations we as journalists make every day as we seek to report on events. It is part of our work, but how it is handled—the sensitivity used, the words chosen—can increase or alleviate the trauma of the victim and his/her family."[33] He closes a July 2010 e-mail, reiterating the significance of news media ethics:

The need to understand the issues from the victim's point of view is critical. That requires education. It really should be part of every journalism program.

CHAPTER SEVEN

News Reform 101

In any reform movement, leaders emerge to create, to advocate, and to implement change. Since the 1990s, many individuals have made notable contributions to remaking newsroom culture in response to the effects of high-risk, high-stress reporting. The four reformers highlighted in this chapter—Frank Ochberg, Chris Cramer, Cait McMahon, and Rodney Pinder—are emblematic of international efforts to humanize trauma journalism.

Frank Ochberg

In his online primer "PTSD 101 for Journalists," Dr. Frank Ochberg, founder of the Dart Center for Journalism & Trauma, discussed its definition, impact, and significance—"how to anticipate it, recognize it, and report it, earning the respect of your readers and your interviewees." Ochberg stated: "The recognition of PTSD and related conditions enhances not only a reporter's professionalism, but also the degree of humanitarianism brought to every victim interview."[1]

His article provides official diagnostic criteria for PTSD as defined by the American Psychiatric Association in its *Diagnostic and Statistical Manual of Mental Disorders, DSM-IV.*[2] As discussed in Chapter 2, Ochberg had pioneered the study of the condition in the 1970s and 1980s, noting that symptoms included recurring intrusive memories of the traumatic experience (e.g., where the person experienced a life-threatening situation, a violent assault, or other serious incident), a feeling of detachment and estrangement or psychological numbing, and a heightened sense of anxiety or a lowering of the "fear threshold."[3]

Ochberg offers guidelines as preparation for reporting on the impact of violence, disaster, and tragedy, specifically, where interviewing traumatized individuals may occur—both in the immediate aftermath of the event and in anniversary coverage. For example: "But you the journalist may be the cause of emotional injury, since this person was exposed to major traumatic stress and has reached some new adjustment state that you will disrupt. In a way, this is a more delicate, difficult situation."[4]

The trauma expert believes in cultivating a sense of caring for the emotional health of both *sources* ("give your interviewee a sense of respect throughout") and *news media workers* ("Journalists are candidates for Secondary Traumatic Stress Disorder, an empathetic response that affects us, therapists included, when our professional detachment is overwhelmed by certain life events."). In his conclusion, he quotes essayist and author Roger Rosenblatt who, as senior editor of the *New Republic*, wrote about journalists covering the genocide in Rwanda in the 1990s:

> Most journalists react in three stages. In the first stage, when they are young, they respond to atrocities with shock and revulsion and perhaps a twinge of guilty excitement that they are seeing something others will never see: life at its dreadful extremes. In the second stage, the atrocities become familiar and repetitive, and journalists begin to sound like Spiro Agnew: If you have seen one loss of dignity and spirit, you've seen them all. Too many journalists get stuck in this stage. They get bogged down in the routineness of the suffering. Embittered, spiteful and inadequate to their work, they curse out their bosses back home for not according them respect; they hate the people on whom they report. Worst of all, they don't allow themselves to enter the third stage in which everything gets sadder and wiser, worse and strangely better.[5]

As an author and popular conference speaker, Ochberg reaffirms his core belief that by discussing PTSD openly, people "disarm" the condition, which currently affects an estimated 3 to 4 percent of adults in the United States.

> We do not prevent it, but we minimize its degrading, diminishing effects. We help victims become survivors. We help survivors regain dignity and respect.[6]

In March 2010, the chairman emeritus discussed the Dart Center's genesis:

> Dart began with a focus on trauma rather than on tragic circumstances, such as poverty, prejudice and ignorance. We wanted to help journalists deal with human events that came up regularly in deadline reporting, and to have a scientific understanding of the vulnerability, resilience, impact, treatment and outcome.

At 70, he continues his private psychiatric practice and relishes his role as a networker extraordinaire. Quite simply: Ochberg, one of the pioneers of trauma science, uses his expertise and enthusiasm to connect people in both the therapeutic and journalistic communities. His vision for the future focuses on the role of higher education to establish "teaching centers of excellence" in trauma journalism. Though Ochberg is no Pollyanna. He recognizes there are still intransigent, insensitive editors, and he realizes that it will take decades for widespread reform to occur. "But," he says proudly, "we've passed the tipping point."

In the 1990s, when Dr. Frank Ochberg was establishing a "Victims and the Media" program at Michigan State University, Chris Cramer was a respected British journalist, a recovering victim of terrorism, and a manager intent on addressing trauma's impact on news coverage.

Chris Cramer

At the close of our telephone interview, Chris Cramer says in an upbeat, clipped British accent: "Take good care." Those words reflect the mission Cramer embarked on years ago to reform news operations by mandating hostile-environment training for reporters covering war and conflict, by instituting innovations such as 24/7 telephone crisis counseling for journalists in the field, and by cofounding the International News Safety Institute to advocate for protection of staff, freelance, and indigenous news media workers. He says, "Once you have changed the culture surrounding trauma and removed the stigma, it is possible to achieve a lot."

While admitting progress worldwide, particularly at "exemplars" such as the BBC, CNN, NBC, Reuters, the *New York Times*, and several British newspapers, the 62-year-old Cramer remains critical of the "pockets of resistance" among other media organizations. And he reserves his sharpest barbs for those companies trying to use the economic recession as an excuse to cut back on safety training. In Cramer's opinion: If you can't look after your staff, then don't cover the news.

Chris Cramer is most sensitive to those journalists who have been affected by their trauma coverage. He says, "I've been in that dark hole." According to published accounts, Cramer, then a reporter for the BBC, was taken hostage in the Iranian embassy siege in London in 1980. He had gone to the embassy seeking a visa to travel to Tehran to report on the American hostage drama. In the London terrorist assault, he was pistol-whipped by gunmen who were threatening to murder a hostage each hour before blowing up the building. After two days as a captive, Cramer faked a heart attack and was freed. The gunmen later murdered an embassy hostage.

Cramer was offered stress counseling by the BBC. But he refused any formal intervention then and for the next few years. He says he tried to shrug off his memories and anxieties and return to work. Instead of counseling, Cramer sought the "tried and true" remedy of drinking regularly after work with colleagues, believing that would reduce the stress. But his work and personal life suffered.

"By and large," Cramer was quoted in the book *Sharing the Frontline and the Back Hills*, "despite their apparent intelligence, members of the media believe they are immune from that which they cover."[8] In retrospect, Cramer realized he had been badly shaken by his hostage experience. But, he said, like many other trauma journalists, he was driven by the competitive nature of news reporting and afraid to admit he had any doubts about his ability to cover conflict stories.

> For years, journalists from all parts of the business had adopted the principle that you never refused an assignment, no matter how dangerous it might turn out to be; that doing so would run you the risk of losing some professional esteem. For men and for women, it was all a matter of "balls." And there was the added hazard many of us felt, that if you displayed a lack of courage to your bosses there was a real risk of losing the assignment.[9]

In *Journalists under Fire: The Psychological Hazards of Covering War*, Cramer acknowledged the impact of living in denial: "I did not want to be knowingly anywhere that was unsafe—at one point that could be a restaurant or the underground [subway]. I didn't want to be anywhere that put things outside my control."[10]

Less than a year after the embassy siege, Cramer left news reporting and entered the ranks of management at the BBC. But it would take an "epiphany" a decade later during the war in the Balkans—the shelling of the city of Dubrovnik, Croatia, in October 1991—before Cramer would realize the "madness" of sending news teams into war zones unprepared and unprotected. During the next year, Cramer and other news managers established policies for providing staff with proper equipment (e.g., flak jackets and armored vehicles), insurance coverage, training and related services, such as peer debriefing and confidential counseling (i.e., "head laundering"). In 2000, the BBC, CNN, and other members of the international news community, including Independent Television News (ITN), Reuters, and Associated Press Television News (APTN), would endorse a set of trauma-coverage guidelines for journalists and their supervisors.[11]

Through two decades, Chris Cramer has been one of the visionaries in global broadcast news and an outspoken change agent in trauma journalism. While admitting he "did some of the heavy lifting," he says getting widespread acceptance for safety training and other support programs and services, especially in the United States and among the print media, remains "a slow, uphill plod." Cramer believes that future success will be ensured by "embedding trauma journalism training in the DNA" of university education and professional skills development.

Cait McMahon

In the field of trauma journalism research, Melbourne, Australia, native Cait McMahon is believed the first to have targeted the relationship between posttraumatic stress and posttraumatic growth among news media workers. The dynamic 50-year-old is married and has "three beautiful sons who are quickly learning the 'ins and outs' of trauma and the world of journalism." McMahon's 2005 study of 100 Australian print and broadcast journalists, 73 percent of whom had more than eleven years of crisis coverage experience, revealed positive and negative "parallel trauma responses."[12]

In this study, posttraumatic growth referred to "positive outcomes of trauma exposure that result in dramatic enhancement of the individual" (i.e., higher functioning related to perception of self, others and/or attitude to life). Such a result among journalists was related to having the opportunity to share their experiences with supportive others (notably among war correspondents). McMahon, who has degrees in theology and psychology (she is a registered psychologist), explained the focus of her doctoral research in an e-mail response:

> One of my hypotheses is that negative effects and growth and resilience often sit side by side in a person, as they are actually different constructs—it is not necessarily either/or. A little like the concept that you may have a chronic illness, and whilst this is a terrible thing, you may feel a stronger, better person as a result of struggling with its reality.

Her study's findings included 24 percent of respondents (of which half were war reporters) meeting the criteria for PTSD, a percentage similar to the 29 percent of war correspondents with trauma effects in the 2002 research study by Anthony Feinstein and colleagues that revealed levels of journalist PTSD comparable with those of combat veterans.[13] McMahon's research also showed a significant difference in trauma experienced in a professional role (potential for posttraumatic growth) as opposed to the often-negative effect of personal-life traumas. In describing the methods of those covering tragic stories, she notes: "The job of journalists is to grapple with, on both an emotional and cognitive level, the trauma they are reporting on."

To date, McMahon is the only Australian psychologist to publish studies on journalism and trauma. But she is more than a trailblazing researcher.

McMahon has spent two decades facilitating trauma-related training with journalists, managers, editors, and executives in news organizations across the Asian Pacific region, in the United Kingdom, and in the United States. She began her media career working as an on-site newsroom counselor at the *Age* newspaper in the late 1980s and early 1990s. She explained her five and a half years at the Melbourne-based publication as "the chaplaincy model of employee assistance." She observed that journalists were "very cagey" about not revealing any negative effects of trauma coverage, due to professional pride, competition, and fear of disclosure. "Most folks see going for psychological help as a weakness," McMahon says.

Over time, however, there was progress in the newsroom as journalists began to confide more in her and participate in peer support efforts, including informal debriefings. McMahon's experience has been that those journalists who are more forthcoming about their emotional reactions to stressful assignments are better able to empathize with sources affected by tragedy and trauma and have potential to become more insightful, effective reporters.

She undertook her first clinical study of work-related trauma exposure on journalists in 1993. In 2001, McMahon published the results of research on the impact of secondary trauma for print media journalists reporting on disaster. Her findings showed that "a large majority (e.g., 35 percent) of the fifty-seven journalists surveyed experienced the intrusiveness, avoidance and depression symptoms [associated with PTSD] between one and three years following reporting on the traumatic story." A significant outcome of this 2001 research was that a majority of journalists expressed a desire to "download" or talk about their experiences.[14]

Since December 2004, Cait McMahon has applied her research, training, and counseling skills as managing director of the Australasia Dart Centre for Journalism and Trauma. She has coordinated crisis response teams, developed specialized training programs, and conducted international research presentations on trauma journalism. As a psychologist, McMahon has counseled Vietnam veterans and others diagnosed with PTSD, but she now works exclusively with the news media.

Rodney Pinder

As founding director of INSI, Rodney Pinder is committed to protecting journalists worldwide. He is particularly concerned with local news media workers (e.g., freelancers, stringers, and fixers) in developing countries and in those nations where journalists "operate under a blanket of fear"—often targeted because their reporting threatens powerful interests.

"In many countries, a free press is endangered," Pinder says, noting how the majority of journalist fatalities are not international reporters and camera people killed covering war but local journalists trying to investigate crime and corruption who are murdered in their own homeland. According to Pinder, many news media workers not only routinely face danger, such as threats of kidnapping and execution by criminals and terrorists, but also low pay and "shocking working conditions."

INSI was established in Brussels, Belgium, on World Press Freedom Day (May 3) in 2003 by major international news organizations (including the AP, the BBC, CNN, Reuters, and ITN—United Kingdom) out of growing concern for the rising incidence of attacks on news personnel. Among the precipitating events for the creation of the worldwide coalition and liaison network were the murders of celebrated journalists Kurt Schork and Miguel Gil Moreno in Sierra Leone in 2000 and the intensive level of violence that had been directed at those reporting on war in the Balkans in the 1990s. Journalist safety became a more visible and critical issue for news organizations during the Iraq War as insurgent groups targeted reporters for capture and killing. In recent years, the massacre of scores of journalists in the Philippines and high casualty rates for reporters in Mexico have become primary concerns for INSI, which in March 2007 published *Killing the Messenger*, an extensive global inquiry, "the first of its kind, into the causes of journalists deaths."[15] In 2006, INSI had worked with the International Federation of Journalists and the European Broadcasting Union to advocate for passage of a UN Security Council Resolution (1738) to protect the "safety of journalists in conflict."

In a spring 2010 interview, Pinder, 66, spoke emphatically of the fundamental right of journalists as citizens to be protected by their governments and the international community: "States must step forward and fund and support the programs that enable journalists to do their jobs safely and without fear."

Pinder spent more than forty years as a foreign correspondent covering wars and conflict in the Middle East, Northern Ireland, Rhodesia/Zimbabwe, South Africa, Indonesia, Iraq, and Iran. As a bureau chief for Reuters in Johannesburg during the "township wars," he sought protection for journalists reporting on horrific violence in the streets. He says he went to "too many funerals of too many good young people who were only trying to do their jobs."

In November 2009, Pinder was quoted in a *New York Times* article on the risks faced by novice journalists in conflict zones: "There's a lot of ignorance behind some of this behavior, because people don't realize how dangerous it's become for journalists in the world today."[16] He estimates that about 1,500 people have been killed while working for news organizations since 2000. What makes these casualty figures even more shocking, Pinder says, is the impunity that exists in many parts of the world for journalists' killers. He remains frustrated by the reticence of the news media to report on journalist deaths, assaults, and violence.

Pinder is realistic in discussing reform opportunities. He admits it is "almost impossible in some cultures to get journalists and their organizations to face up to the issues and to do something about it." To address these obstacles, INSI offers services directly to journalists, such as a confidential online traumatic stress self-test. INSI's members include major news organizations, media freedom groups, journalist unions, humanitarian organizations, and individual journalists. Member fees and donations subsidize INSI's provision of free basic safety training for news media workers who are unable to afford their own and otherwise would have little or no access to such services. Pinder says that in the past 7 years, INSI has helped train some 1,600 news media staff in 21 countries, including Iraq, Afghanistan, the Philippines, and Somalia. In addressing the needs for journalist safety internationally, INSI is aligned with the CPJ, other media advocacy groups, and stakeholders such as UNESCO (United Nations Educational, Scientific, and Cultural Organization).

Pinder believes that if journalists are going to have "society on our side and have people care about our futures," then the news media must bear responsibility for their reputation:

> Journalists need to ask themselves about their own behavior. What have we done in the West that society doesn't value us anymore? Maybe it's the way we behave.

Regarding the future of INSI, Rodney Pinder stubbornly opines that achieving change worldwide is a matter of "plugging away and slogging on."

Classroom Reform

In mid-June 2010, thirteen college educators from the United States, Canada, Germany, and Australia met for three days at Columbia University in New York City to explore the pedagogy of trauma journalism. These educators, most of whom had extensive professional experience as print or broadcast journalists, were members of the inaugural class of Academic Fellows, as selected by the Dart Center for Journalism & Trauma. The convivial but concerned group of men and women, whose ages ranged from barely 30 to the cusp of 70, sought ways to incorporate the teaching of ethics, interviewing, and the emotional effects of crisis and conflict coverage in their coursework. Their objective was to enhance the preparation, resiliency, and performance of student and professional journalists. Dart Center officials were eager to support the mission of these earnest instructors while hoping for its evangelical movement on trauma journalism awareness to spread globally.

Academic fellows represented large institutions, including the University of Arizona, Boston University, University of Nebraska, NYU, and UW, as well as smaller schools, such as Lyndon State College in Vermont and Harry Truman College in Chicago. The "Trauma Thirteen" group heard research presentations, viewed simulations, and engaged in free-flowing discussions on how to change newsroom and classroom cultures. Topics included the following:

- teaching about covering suicide, homicide, and accidental death
- building trauma scenarios for instruction
- preparing student journalists for disaster coverage
- covering minority/cultural issues, including Native American and Hispanic communities and
- keeping student journalists safe while covering tragedy and trauma.

Dan Williams, associate professor of English, philosophy, and film studies at Lyndon State College, discussed his one-credit special topics class, "Responding to Disaster," which is offered in cooperation with the Psychology and Human Services Department. The course is intended for journalism, television studies, and human services majors "who may be exposed to trauma themselves or deal with trauma victims in the workplace." Recently, the semiannual course has been run with technical assistance and about $2,500 in per-event funding from the Vermont Homeland Security Department. Community support has featured local police and fire departments and area paramedics, who perform their "training exercise" duties as if they were responding to a true disaster.[17]

Recent large-scale simulations at Lyndon State have included dormitory fires and campus shootings. More than a hundred people, including students and town residents, participate in these mock crises—many serving as hostages, patients, and victims with detailed injury reports and realistic wounds. Student journalists are briefed before the exercises and given regular updates. The goal of the trauma workshops is to teach young reporters how to identify and interview a traumatized person without causing additional harm or emotional damage. In addition, training organizers try to show student journalists how to lessen the risk of becoming a victim of secondary trauma as a result of their coverage.

Williams' interest in trauma dates back to his years working at CNN International under then-managing director Chris Cramer. In 2007, he and a Lyndon State College colleague, Professor Margaret Sherrer, conceived the trauma training module that features a 2-hour orientation, a 5-hour training session, and an 8-hour campus-wide disaster exercise, debriefing, and wrap-up. In 2009, Williams published a paper on his efforts titled

"Why Wait for Disaster When Your Local College Can Arrange One?" In the paper, he noted the existence of other university simulations or emergency drills that offer guidance for students on dealing with traumatized people. Williams described a six-week summer "boot camp" for graduate journalism students in the Newhouse School at Syracuse University in New York that for several years featured mock crisis coverage through a series of staged events on campus, conducted in cooperation with local public-safety officials.[18]

At North Carolina State University, Bradley Wilson, the coordinator for student media, has been staging campus emergency drills, such as simulated shootings or explosions, since the mid-1990s to help student journalists interact with traumatized people. Wilson, who has worked in emergency medical services for twenty years and is a trained medic, was editor of the 2010 Journalism Education Association's special edition *Covering the Unimaginable*, an eighty-page publication that serves as a crisis-planning compendium for educators confronted by disaster, violence, and a host of emergencies, notably student deaths and suicide. Several case studies and firsthand accounts are provided, as well as strategies and media relations guidelines. At the end, Wilson appeals for journalists to "respect and cover the human side of tragedy."[19]

Across the Atlantic, Gavin Rees, a journalist and filmmaker and director of the Dart Centre Europe, supervises disaster simulations with students at Britain's Bournemouth University Media School. He describes a soccer stadium bombing exercise in "Weathering the Trauma Storms":

> But 10 minutes before play started, an explosion ripped through the Shed end of Chelsea football ground. The first reporters on the scene were journalism students. They could see at once that there were significant casualties. People were streaming out of the stands on to the pitch. Some, despite being wounded and disoriented, wanted to talk; others preferred to lash out at the media. For many of the student journalists, this was their first professional encounter with extreme distress. By the end of the day, one thing had become clear: those who showed the most emotional savvy collected the best material.[20]

Rees explains that the workshop is intended to demonstrate that by being sensitive to the psychological aspects of crisis coverage, young journalists can be better prepared in their careers. By using actors in trauma-awareness training who behaved like real victims and survivors—exhibiting dramatic responses including dissociation, rage, and fear—educators forced students to confront their own uncomfortable reactions while experiencing the emotional distress of the victims.

In January 2010, Rees developed another scenario for Bournemouth students based on reporters' experiences covering the aftermath of Hurricane

Katrina, specifically the events at the Houston Astrodome, one of the evacuation sites for more than 10,000 Katrina survivors. Actual BBC-TV coverage of the devastating effects of the hurricane and the events that ensued in New Orleans and other Gulf Coast locales was used to prepare journalism students for their immersion in the simulation, which included 5 in-depth characterizations, based on real-life accounts of survivors, and a mock news conference with a FEMA official. Again, as in the soccer stadium bombing exercise, real actors played the roles of victims in detailed scripted drills. Throughout the course of the exercise, student journalists were surrounded by chaos and conflict and expected to perform under significant pressure.

At the Columbia University trauma journalism program, educators deliberated the pros and cons of such elaborate disaster simulations. Certainly, role-plays enable opportunities for coaching, feedback, and debriefings, not to mention trial and error. But some questioned how relevant such large-scale trauma scenarios were when training journalists who would be much more likely to cover community crises and conflicts, such as auto accidents, fires, and violent crime during their professional careers. Others admitted that at many universities, such exercises would be difficult if not impossible to stage successfully in journalism programs with large enrollments.

Modifying existing university journalism curricula is no easy task, as many academics could attest. Challenges, such as the detailed course-hour requirements facing accredited academic programs, become potential roadblocks for those seeking to add trauma journalism instruction at their institution. Such realities would help to explain why there are only a handful of designated trauma classes in journalism programs in the United States and other countries.

The University of Central Oklahoma features a regularly scheduled "Victims and the Media Seminar," a three-credit course described as "an intensive study of the interpersonal and psychological effects of trauma on journalists and the people they interview." According to its instructor, Professor Kole Kleeman, the course explores the concept of PTSD and its application to victims of significant violence and tragedy. Students examine the impact of media coverage of war, school shootings, violent crimes, natural disasters, and other events involving emotional and physical injury or trauma.[21]

Prior to joining the journalism faculty at the University of Missouri in 2009, Professor Jim MacMillan taught a three-credit course "Journalism and Psychological Trauma" at Temple University. The course syllabus described the class as an introduction to the "special challenges and responsibilities of covering traumatic events in the news."

Weekly discussions targeted: Crime, Murder, Suicide, and the Urban Gun Crisis; Disasters (natural and human-caused); War (emotional and moral injury, accurate reporting under stress); School Shootings (Columbine and before, anniversary coverage); Genocide, Justice, and Reconciliation

(Rwanda); Sexual Trauma, Domestic Violence, Children and Trauma; Local Beat Trauma (authorities and other first responders); Death Notifications (best practices); Self-Care for Journalists, Posttraumatic Therapy, Resilience and Posttraumatic Growth (finding therapists, effective treatments). Students were also assigned to interview a journalist who had covered traumatic news events. MacMillan, a career photojournalist before entering academia, explained that in his new position at the University of Missouri, he has only one class meeting to lecture on trauma in his convergence reporting and editing courses. But in the near future, he plans on teaching trauma journalism techniques to "Mizzou faculty and students."[22]

The University of Washington and Michigan State University boast two of the longest-running examples of trauma journalism instruction in existing college-level reporting and news writing courses. Since 1997, UW students have learned how to cover traumatic incidents by participating in extended interview simulations (e.g., professional actors from "Effective Arts," a Seattle-based training and development company, portray survivors of a fatal apartment fire). Prior to these classroom exercises, students undergo a 2-hour orientation to the role of emotions in reporting. Subsequently, student teams participate in a 2-hour scenario with the actors by conducting a series of 5-minute interviews with traumatized "sources" positioned around the classroom.[23]

The actors have specific information to reveal to the student reporters. But the students must learn how to deal with individuals who are angry and confrontational, overwhelmed and confused, or withdrawn and reticent. UW Professor Randy Beam explains that students read from the textbook *Covering Violence: A Guide to Ethical Reporting about Victims and Trauma* and consider questions such as: How would you start the interview with an individual who has experienced a traumatic reaction? If the person breaks down and starts to cry as you interview him or her, how exactly will you respond? If the person asks if you know the condition of a loved one, and if you know the loved one has been seriously injured, how will you respond? Journalism faculty at UW believe such experiential learning exercises are excellent preparation for the real world.

MSU's "Victims and the Media Program" was established in 1991 by professors William Coté and Frank Ochberg. According to Ochberg, educators worked with the Michigan Victim's Alliance to introduce journalism students to individuals who had been victimized by crime or other life-altering events. Some of the victims agreed to be interviewed. Others gave talks, including firsthand critiques of their treatment by insensitive news media. Additional participants in the program have included journalists, victim advocates, law enforcement and emergency medical personnel, and mental health professionals.

Rachele Kanigel is a journalism professor and student newspaper adviser at San Francisco State University. She is also author of *The Student*

Newspaper Survival Guide, a textbook for student journalists and their advisers.[24] Kanigel has conducted several workshops related to trauma, including "Covering Suicide," "Preparing for the Big Story," and "The Ethics and Practice of Student Journalism." Her recommendations for college media advisers include the following:

- develop a disaster plan
- train for the big story (e.g., natural disaster—weather related, manmade disaster—terrorism, major accident, serious crime, and major campus stories—resignation of official, scandal, suicide, disease outbreak)
- assemble a team
- plan a multistory package
- use interactive story features, such as maps and discussion boards
- establish a mobile alert system
- utilize social media, including Twitter feeds/posts and Facebook pages
- take care of your staff (e.g., utilizing campus counseling services, debriefing sessions, and accessing resources of organizations, such as the Dart Center for Journalism & Trauma)[25]

Kanigel writes compellingly how student media should cover a campus suicide. "Deciding whether and how to cover a suicide is one of the most common and most poignant ethical dilemmas a student editor may face," she states, noting that the professional media typically don't cover suicide unless there is a newsworthy angle or focus affecting the public at large (e.g., in connection with a homicide, kidnapping, or other serious crime). But for college students, suicide is a genuine social problem in their age group. Kanigel cites the US Department of Health and Human Services statistics listing suicide as the third-leading cause of death among 15- to 24-year-olds after accidents and homicide.[26] A suicide on campus may have a significant impact on a large segment of the student and faculty population of a college or university.

Media coverage of suicide is a controversial topic, given the documented effect of how certain "sensationalized" news media reports contribute to suicide contagion or "copycat" deaths. A 2010 report of the American Foundation for Suicide Prevention (AFSP) calls for the responsible coverage of suicide to educate audiences about likely causes, warning signs, trends in suicide rates, recent treatment advancements, and other preventions. The report notes how the AFSP has worked with the Annenberg Public Policy Center and participated in a workshop with the National Institute of

Mental Health, the Office of the Surgeon General, the Centers for Disease Control and Prevention, the Substance Abuse and Mental Health Services Administration, the American Association of Suicidology, the World Health Organization (WHO), and several other agencies to develop international media recommendations for reporting on suicide. How a news story is worded concerning the manner of death is one of the guidelines. For example, it is preferred by advocacy organizations to have the deceased described as "having died by suicide" rather than as "a suicide" or having "committed suicide."[27]

A report in 2000 by the WHO (*Preventing Suicide: A Resource for Media Professionals*) states: "Clinicians and researchers acknowledge that it is not news coverage of suicide per se, but certain types of news coverage, that increase suicidal behaviour in vulnerable populations. . . . Reporting of suicide in an appropriate, accurate and potentially helpful manner by enlightened media can prevent tragic loss of lives by suicide."[28]

The media are encouraged to play a constructive role by listing available mental health services, publicizing the warning signs of suicidal behavior, and conveying the message that depression is often associated with suicide (and depression is a treatable and not fatal condition).[29] In Australia, similar guidelines on the reporting of suicide have been supported by the issuance of two new (2010) reports in an advocacy campaign by the *Mindframe* National Media Initiative, "which provides advice to media and health professionals about portrayals of suicide and mental illness."[30] The goal is to minimize harm in news coverage (e.g., reducing the risk of contagion-type suicides).

Ian Richards, a journalism professor at the University of South Australia in Adelaide and a former print reporter, spoke at the June 2010 Academic Fellows program at Columbia University about media coverage of suicide and its effects particularly on young people. In an August 5, 2010, online article by Meg Spratt, director of Dart Center West (at UW), Richards explained how his university conducts a "Dealing with Death Day" with journalism students to help teach them about difficult reporting practices:

> intrusion into grief and interviewing the recently bereaved. Run in conjunction with the Australian Funeral Directors Association, the annual program deals with such topics as death, dying and children's concepts of death, and includes presentations from a bereavement counselor, a forensic scientist, and a representative of the State Coroner's Office.[31]

At the event, students join with experienced reporters in discussions about the ethical and practical issues involved in coverage of tragedy and trauma.

The Spratt article described how members of the Columbia University Trauma Thirteen shared their ideas for implementing journalism coursework, training modules, and special projects at their educational institutions.[32] Professors Yvonne Latty of NYU and Celeste Gonzalez de Bustamante of the University of Arizona have developed a joint program, "Beyond the Border." According to Bustamante, the immersive reporting experience for undergraduate and graduate students "is a cross-cultural and international project" focusing on the Arizona-Sonora region and New York City and "issues such as immigration, violence (e.g., ethnic and racial conflict), and environmental degradation."

Bustamante, an assistant professor at the University of Arizona School of Journalism, spent more than fifteen years working in public television. Her specialization is studying the history of news media in Mexico and the US-Mexico borderlands. Latty, a journalism professor at NYU's Arthur L. Carter Journalism Institute, directs multimedia graduate programs. An author of two books, including the critically acclaimed *We Were There: Voices of African American Veterans from World War II to the War in Iraq*, Latty worked for the *Philadelphia Daily News* for thirteen years, specializing in urban issues. She is currently producing and directing a documentary on uranium concentration on the Navajo reservation. Teresa Trumbly Lamsam, visiting professor, University of Kansas, has conducted research on "historical trauma in Indian Country" and Native American tribal media. Lamsam writes, "Trauma can be a result of war and disaster, but it can also be experienced in disadvantaged communities and through historical discrimination."[33]

International educator Barbara Hans, who participated in the June 2010 fellowship program, is a lecturer and researcher at Hamburg University in Berlin, Germany. She has worked as a reporter and editor for *Spiegel Online* and *Der Spiegel*, producing stories on poverty, violence, addiction, and sexual abuse. Hans plans to teach a future graduate journalism course in "Covering Catastrophes" as part of a media ethics unit.[34]

Cliff Lonsdale, a lecturer of information and media studies at the University of Western Ontario, and president of the Canadian Journalism Forum on Violence and Trauma, was the "dean" of the Trauma Thirteen group of Academic Fellows. His experience in covering conflict and violence dates back to the 1960 Civil War in the Congo. He was chief news editor and head of production for CBC Television and CBC News. Since 1993, he has been an independent documentary filmmaker. Lonsdale writes: "We need 'climate change' in our newsrooms and journalism schools—for greater recognition and understanding of the impact of troubling events on news gatherers, news makers, and news consumers. Emotional trauma is an integral part of the newsgathering process."[35]

As one of the Dart Center for Journalism & Trauma's Academic Fellows, representing Ball State University, I share Cliff Lonsdale's views on the need for "climate change" in our newsrooms and classrooms. Instruction on emotional effects of crisis coverage is directly related to raising awareness of the ethical implications of interviewing victims and their families and friends. Students need to know what is appropriate behavior for interacting with those affected by tragedy and trauma. Instruction on progressive techniques should include discussion of the role of emotion and empathy in critical incident reporting. By informing students of the effects of trauma journalism, we educators will help prepare them for what they will encounter, and, hopefully, enable them to be more resilient, responsible, and effective as news media professionals.

Lessons from VTU and NIU

College media advisers Kelly Furnas at Virginia Tech University and Jim Killam at Northern Illinois University weren't conducting simulations or role-plays when they had to direct their student journalists to cover real tragedies under intense emotional stress and international scrutiny. The horrific violence on April 16, 2007, at Virginia Tech that left thirty-two dead and twenty injured was followed less than a year later by the tragic Valentine's Day (February 14, 2008) shootings that killed six and wounded eighteen at Northern Illinois. Both Furnas and Killam were credited for guiding their student newspaper teams through the most extreme of crises. Each adviser kept his journalists focused on their mission of providing the "extended campus" community of readers with accurate, timely, and sensitive news coverage. But Furnas and Killam were also responsible for the safety, health, and welfare of dozens of student reporters, editors, photographers, designers, and support personnel at their respective papers, *Collegiate Times* (VTU) and the *Northern Star* (NIU).

In April 2009, Furnas and Killam wrote articles, posted on the Dart Center website, that included tips for college newsroom advisers. Some of these lessons may seem obvious, such as having contact information for all staff members in "redundant places" (e.g., hard copy, computer, and cell-phone lists, plus use of social media). But Furnas, who was named executive director of the Journalism Education Association (JEA) on August 1, 2010, also reminded advisers to:

- allow staff members, to shine, regardless of their position
- have policies in place for dealing with outside media
- consider who can have access to the newsroom
- be ready to specify in an agency photo contract the length of time the rights belong to the agency to sell and what uses, such as fellow college papers, are allowed.[36]

Jim Killam offered common-sense advice for advisers and teachers: "Before doing anything else, contact (your) loved ones."[37] He reminded faculty supervisors that they are often seen as parents by students during an emergency, and they need to be a calm, collected, and reassuring presence in the newsroom. But Killam also recommended that advisers "resist the urge to take charge" and "stay on the role modeling side."

Echoing Furnas, Killam noted: "Pay attention to everyone, not just those who are on the front lines of reporting."[38] He described how weeks and even months after the shootings, some of the NIU student journalists began experiencing PTSD-type symptoms, and his duties became more about "taking care of kids than challenging them." He also discussed how he processed his thoughts and emotions through writing about his experiences in e-mails to "our alumni group and to the College Media Advisers list."

Killam, who said he plans to incorporate formal crisis training for incoming newspaper staff, concluded his 2009 article with a request:

Pay it forward. Virginia Tech and The *Collegiate Times* staff were a huge support to us. What a fantastic example they set. The best way we can redeem all that's happened is to use the experience to help others— in our case, other journalists.[39]

Faces of Trauma Journalism: Judith Matloff

Photo courtesy of Columbia University

Like many trauma journalists, Judith Matloff had "absolutely no desire to cover violence" when she began her career in 1981 with a degree from Harvard in Latin American Studies. She was interested in politics and fluent in Spanish and Portuguese. She first worked for six months for UPI as a general reporter in Mexico City, editing stories from across Central America. By the early 1990s, she was a veteran correspondent for Reuters, having reported across Europe and Southern Africa. Her facility with Portuguese led to dangerous postings in Angola and Mozambique.

In 1992, after elections were contested in Angola, her bureau chief had told Judith: "Hang in there and get ready for the long haul. You've got a nice war ahead of you." The country's airports and ports quickly closed, and she found herself as the sole Western female covering the story. A year later, reporting on South African strife, she was issued the only red flak jacket in her news bureau; the men reporters all wore blue.

I wanted to be very macho like the guys. I was working with people who were seasoned, had done this for many years. Some had military experience. And I didn't want to seem like a wimp, so I kept a lot of stuff inside of myself.

The "stuff" that Judith refers to included emotions she felt upon witnessing the horrors of war, oppression, and genocide in assignments throughout Central and South Africa. "I wasn't mentally prepared for this level of violence, for this level of carnage," she says. But Judith pressed on for years, "sent hither and yon to places of conflict."

Decades later as I interview her by phone from her New York residence, the 52-year-old Matloff is friendly and upbeat as she recounts years of harrowing journalistic work. She speaks in fluid sonorous sentences. "Am I talking too fast?" she asks. Then in typical New York style, she answers her own question with a good-natured laugh: "I talk like a train." Listening to her describe her reporting adventures, I envision Sigourney Weaver portraying the slender dark-haired war correspondent—if Judith's story were to go Hollywood.

Today, Professor Judith Matloff teaches a "Covering Conflict" course in the Graduate School of Journalism at Columbia University, where she's been an adjunct faculty member since 2002. Prior to Columbia, she taught at NYU. Judith admits she is frank when advising her students about the risks of trauma journalism:

> Know your limits and motivations. Understand that it is normal to have extreme reactions to extreme events. Anticipate that you may feel very distressed; know the symptoms and get help if they appear. That was the biggest problem with my generation. We didn't have a word for "trauma." No one talked about "shellshock," or whatever it was called in those days. You went forth with a bottle of scotch and pretended to be really tough and macho and then had terrible nightmares that resonated during the day. Friends became alcoholics, got into car crashes, split with their wives. Two colleagues committed suicide. That wouldn't have happened if we understood trauma.

It seems reasonable to ask, why did Judith Matloff continue to put herself in harm's way? What were the rewards of such risk-taking and often self-destructive behavior? Why did the native New Yorker with the Ivy League degree spend so many years covering the "nasties" as she calls them—assignments in Angola, Mozambique, the Sudan, Rwanda, Burundi, Sierra Leone, and Chechnya?

"It gives you such a sense of mission," she says. "I felt I was serving some sort of higher cause." Judith explains that even the illusion of making a difference, such as influencing policy makers, can raise one's spirits. But the most fulfilling parts of Judith's work didn't pertain to speaking truth to those in power. It was being "humbled, listening to the stories of the people we covered." She speaks of hearing incredible tales of heroism in the most desperate environments. She notes how journalists reporting on life-and-death issues are regularly inspired by the resilience of the human spirit.

"This type of work, as draining as it can be, really is the ultimate journalistic experience," Judith says. "And the camaraderie you develop with colleagues is unparalleled. There's a tribe of us that have these incredible bonds that are unspoken. But they're so deep, and they're so satisfying." Her words about the unparalleled support of devoted colleagues call to mind the recollections of war veterans speaking of how friends got them through the tough times.

But, ultimately, there was a price to pay in Judith's career. She felt guilty leaving people whom she had interviewed behind, knowing they were likely to die. And her life was threatened as a result of her reporting. Although she rose in the media ranks to become *The Christian Science Monitor's* Africa Bureau Chief, responsible for coverage in forty-seven countries, and later the Moscow Bureau Chief, directing coverage of fifteen countries in the former Soviet Union, the stress was unrelenting. She had thought her last assignment in Moscow would revolve around more diplomatic stories. Instead, she once again found herself in the midst of chaos and conflict as she reported on the second Chechen war. By the cusp of 2000, Judith Matloff was "kind of burned out, sick of covering violence and wanted a change of pace."

To ease the emotional strain, she shifted her focus to personal rather than professional concerns. She sought the "life-affirming choice" of starting a family. She and her business writer husband returned to New York City, where her son would be born. But her hopes of a "normal life" were temporarily suspended as they discovered their row house in Harlem was a former crackhouse, located on a street dominated by an armed Colombian drug gang, with whom she and her husband would have to negotiate for safe passage. The tale of their eventual peaceful coexistence became the subject of her book *Home Girl: Building a Dream House on a Lawless Block*, published in 2008.[40]

Judith's first book was *Fragments of a Forgotten War* (a nonfiction account of the Angolan War), published in 1997.[41] She also contributed to another book, *Reporting Iraq: An Oral History of the War by the Journalists Who Covered It*, published in 2007.[42] That text was coedited by the *Columbia Journalism Review*, for which Judith has served as a contributing editor, addressing international conflict reporting issues, since 2005. She has written freelance articles for the *New York Times*, the *Economist*, *Newsweek*, WSJ.com and TIME.com, among other publications. Judith has also been a consultant on journalism safety and wrote guidelines for covering sexual violence for the United Nations.

In her article "Scathing Memory," published in the November/December 2004 issue of the *Columbia Journalism Review* (*CJR*), Judith discussed how the news media were facing up to the psychic costs of war reporting:

> This is a story about the invisible wounds that journalists often suffer when covering war. Anyone who has covered violence is aware of the psychic damage it can wreak—the guilt, the sense of being a parasite, the unbearable pettiness of daily life. . . . With a new wave of emotionally scarred reporters coming out of Iraq (many of them relative rookies), editors are realizing that it will take more than flak jackets and "hostile environment training" to keep correspondents healthy. Among other things, they are introducing confidential hotlines for journalists who need help, and scrutinizing e-mail for signs of distress.[43]

Judith cited several examples of journalists who had been severely affected by the danger and stress of conflict coverage in their careers, including Pulitzer Prize-winning photographer Greg Marinovich, who had witnessed "a gruesome period in South Africa's history in the early 1990s, when his daily routine involved taking pictures of people being shot or hacked to death." One of Marinovich's colleagues, Ken Oosterbroek, also a photographer, was shot to death in the same incident in which Marinovich was gravely wounded and nearly died. According to Judith's article, "He recovered, went back to work, and later buried two more colleagues who had committed suicide." Frank Smyth, the Washington, DC, representative of the Committee to Protect Journalists, was described in the *CJR* article as "tormented by nightmares in 1991 after being held for two weeks in Iraq's Abu Ghraib prison when he was covering the Kurdish rebellions that followed the first Gulf War." Smyth eventually recovered thanks to counseling and other methods, including acupuncture and yoga. John Laurence, CBS-TV correspondent during the Vietnam War, stated in Judith's story that counseling years later helped him cope with the "psychological costs of his career . . . heavy drinking, sleeplessness, paranoia, dependence on tranquilizers." But he "never felt cured."[44]

Judith ended "Scathing Memory" with self-disclosure about how the emotional impact of trauma journalism often "bleeds out over time":

> I put myself on autopilot when I was in Angola for a particularly rough six months in the early 1990s. I was nervous about a death threat, but distracted myself by working eighteen-hour days. When caught in sniper fire, I assumed a Zen-like state of denial. Landing at an airport that was being shelled, I busied myself with helping the wounded and collecting testimonies. Months later, after leaving the country, I had disturbing

dreams about limbless people whom I couldn't save. I developed a phobia about roads that reminded me of an ambush.

My catharsis came from writing a book about the war, which forced me to confront emotions. And, yes, I consulted a trauma expert.[45]

A member of the advisory council for the Dart Center, Judith Matloff believes the younger generation of journalists, particularly with more women serving as editors and bureau chiefs, is becoming emotionally sensitized to the effects of trauma journalism.

"The issue is cresting," she proclaims. "There's no stopping it now."

CHAPTER EIGHT

Culture of Caring

Kristin Millis had been working as city editor for a medium-sized (25,000-circulation) Western daily newspaper for about 18 months when her cops and courts reporter asked to be excused from an assignment. Near day's end, the young woman, one of the best on the staff, told Millis of a grisly death at a construction site. A man had been run over by a steamroller. The reporter asked, "Do I have to go?"

Millis, who was called the "newsroom mom," kind of smirked at the question. She recalls saying: "Come on, you're a newspaper reporter. What do you think?" So the reporter reluctantly went to the accident scene. She returned hours later and said, "Look at my shoes."

The blood of the dead man had washed over the reporter's white espadrille shoes during the area cleanup. Millis was startled at the sight. She used to tease the reporter about her stylish shoe choices, telling her she should keep a pair of sneakers in her trunk. But on this late afternoon in the summer of 2001, she never asked the woman how she was doing, if she was OK, or if she wanted to talk about what she saw. The reporter went to her desk to file the story, and Millis continued with her editorial duties.

Nine years later, the memory of that day still returns to trouble Millis, who is currently director of student publications at the University of Washington. The 43-year-old southern California native says she always considered herself a friendly, approachable, and empathetic person. But her assumed distanced role in the newsroom almost a decade earlier had seemingly blocked any emotional support for the troubled reporter. In a July 19, 2010, posting to the College Media Advisers (CMA) listserv, Millis wrote: "I didn't realize my responsibility as an editor to be aware of her mental health, or to reflect back resources or help her set healthy boundaries as necessary."

During a July 2010 telephone interview, Millis described how this 2001 newsroom incident became a turning point in her professional life. Months later, the reporter confided in Millis that she had been in counseling for about a year trying to deal with the emotional effects of her work. Covering court cases and hearing explicit details of sexual assaults and other violent crimes had become increasingly difficult for the woman.

"What makes me feel really sick about it is that she had asked for every Wednesday off between certain hours," Millis says, admitting: "I felt like I didn't take care of her. I felt horrible that she had to wander and find that (counseling) herself. . . . I didn't realize how much stress was affecting her."

In 2005, Millis, who had first reported for a daily newspaper (the *Times Independent* in southern Utah) as an 18-year-old, became student media adviser at UW. Roger Simpson, the founding executive director of the Dart Center, coauthor of the text *Covering Violence: A Guide to Ethical Reporting about Victims and Trauma*, and a UW faculty member, has helped train Millis' student reporters on the ethics of trauma journalism, including the responsibilities of editors to their staff during stressful news coverage.

Millis believes that journalists get "bombarded by the traumatic and the negative" and become very closed off emotionally over time. This disconnection contributes to the newsroom culture of being "hardened, angry, and unfeeling." She says she unintentionally became "a very cynical person in a short period of time" during her five years as a reporter and editor at daily and weekly newspapers and trade magazines after graduating from Utah State University. But she feels fortunate to have changed her outlook and to be able to help young journalists learn about their responsibilities as well as their rights.

"In order to be a truly effective reporter, you do have to be a person first," Millis says, describing how journalists can become so detached that they're not trusted by people. To be a successful storyteller, not just a news aggregator, she says requires more than just gathering facts. "You need the human element and the relevance and connection to community."

Kristin Millis' evolution into a self-described "compassionate journalist" is emblematic of the movement to reform newsroom practices. She illustrates the transformation in a profession that has been bound by century-old practices and an ethos described as rigid, uncaring, and even self-destructive.

Those journalists who have lost their lives in pursuit of a story, a photograph, or piece of film or video footage, are testimony to the adage that change is often born of tragedy. As with the civil rights movement in the United States and social justice efforts globally, sacrifice almost always precedes progress. Such was the case at the turn of the millennium when representatives of major news organizations met just months after the May

24, 2000, killings of two heralded trauma journalists: Kurt Schork and Miguel Gil Moreno in Sierra Leone. The September 20 conference, "Setting the Standard: A Commitment to Frontline Journalism; An Obligation to Frontline Journalism," was held in London and sponsored by The Freedom Forum European Centre. In the conference publication, Centre director John Owen described the meeting as "a gathering of leading international journalists and senior editors and news executives to focus on what practical things could be done, to help prepare journalists for assignments to dangerous conflict areas." Christiane Amanpour moderated a six-member panel. Members of Miguel Gil Moreno's family appealed to attendees to adopt "common or universal standards" governing news organizations' provision of insurance, mandatory safety training and equipment, postassignment assistance (e.g., counseling), and ongoing monitoring of hostile-environment criteria. Moreno's brother Alvaro's personal request was more succinct: "You have to change. Stop talking. Just do things."[2]

According to INSI's Rodney Pinder, a panelist at the September 2000 conference, a direct result was an "unprecedented" cooperative agreement reached in November 2000 between competitors in the broadcast news industry, CNN, BBC, ITN, Reuters, and APTN, resulting in comprehensive safety guidelines to protect journalists internationally. A decade later, these standards provide benchmarks for other news media . However, due to the recession and closing of hundreds of newspapers in the US in recent years, small- and medium-sized periodicals are unlikely to offer such assistance to their employees. And a broader question for newsrooms internationally is whether print and broadcast *domestic* trauma journalists will receive the type of training, security, and support services provided to *foreign* (e.g., war) correspondents?

I believe innovation will come incrementally as journalists and advocacy groups continue their efforts to secure progressive policies, procedures, and codes of conduct. News media workers will be more open about discussing emotional issues related to crisis coverage. Whether you call it a consciousness-raising or institutional reform, change is coming to newsrooms. Trauma journalism may not yet have reached zeitgeist proportions in the public discourse, but a critical mass of cross-disciplinary influence is building.

Laura Van Dernoot Lipsky, a former emergency room social worker, community organizer, educator for trauma victims/survivors, and coauthor of *Trauma Stewardship*, described her mission in words suited to a twenty-first-century trauma journalist:

I had to find some way to bear witness to trauma without surrendering my ability to live fully. I needed a new framework of meaning—the concept that I would eventually come to call "trauma stewardship."[3]

Columnist James Poniewozik discussed a new framework of meaning for journalism in the November 29, 2010, issue of *TIME* magazine.⁴ His analysis is very relevant to mentors like Kristin Millis who are trying to educate and enlighten young journalists that craft and compassion can coexist. Poniewozik wrote:

> News organizations are still beholden to a concept of objectivity that has little to do with the word's actual meaning. Real objectivity does not mean having no opinion or voicing no point of view. It means seeking, recognizing and interpreting facts even when they conflict with one's preconceptions or desires. What journalists and the people who talk about them call objectivity is more like neutrality—often a false and labored one—intended to avoid offending the audience or sources (or advertisers). . . . The days of pretending that journalists are dispassionate infobots are ending. And that's good: trust built on openness is stronger than trust built on an agreed-upon fiction. We are seeing the death throes of the unsustainable concept of "objectivity." Long live the real thing.

Trauma journalism reformers like Chris Cramer, Judith Matloff, Mark Brayne, Scott North, Sarah Ward-Lilley, and Joe Hight are striving to instill a culture of caring in newsrooms to replace monolithic industry attitudes, such as objectivity at the expense of emotion, and to confront narcissistic reporting masquerading as empathy. They are challenging those who insist that journalism has to be conducted according to certain stubborn precepts. They are working to raise awareness across geographic, demographic, and even artistic boundaries.

The recent Broadway drama *Time Stands Still*, starring Laura Linney, Brian D'Arcy James, Christina Ricci, and Eric Bogosian, demonstrated the growing awareness of trauma and news media issues in contemporary culture. Linney and James portrayed journalists dealing with the emotional aftermath of covering the Iraq War. On November 30, 2010, the performance of the play at New York City's Cort Theatre was a benefit for the Dart Center for Journalism & Trauma. After the performance, a panel discussion was hosted with Bob Woodruff, the ABC-TV correspondent who had recuperated from serious head injuries after a roadside bombing in Iraq, his wife, Lee, cofounder with him of ReMind. org and the Bob Woodruff Foundation (supporting injured service members, veterans, and their families), and psychiatrist Robert L. Lifton, who pioneered mental health studies of Vietnam veterans. This posttheatrical event "conversation" was designed to raise awareness of the closely aligned worlds of the journalist and the warrior—when each is exposed to stress, danger, and trauma.⁵

A final reflection: I have written this book as an outsider. A lifelong free-lancer, I have never worked in a newsroom. But I have immersed myself in the lives and narratives of fellow journalists. I have gathered their stories and grown from their wisdom and experience. My intent has been to study trauma journalism by interpreting facts, opinions, and insights of news media workers and managers, therapists, and scholars. My hope is that I have asked questions and explored issues that challenge the status quo and resonate with readers.

Faces of Trauma Journalism: Michelle Faul

Photo courtesy of Sayyid Azim

From the outset of my phone interview, I am struck by Michelle Faul's beautiful English accent. Hers is a distinctive theatrical voice. In dramatic, lyrical tones she punctuates anecdotes of the violence and carnage she has covered in almost forty years as a print and broadcast journalist, based primarily in Africa and the Caribbean. I hear her passion as she speaks of death, inhumanity, and institutional abuses. But what resonates after our call has ended are the regrets she recounted as a 54-year-old unmarried, childless woman once more on assignment in yet another conflict zone.

Before our conversation in mid-April 2011, Michelle had e-mailed career highlights, starting with her work as a teenage "cub" reporter:

1974: Joined the *Rhodesia Herald* in my native Rhodesia (later: Zimbabwe), straight out of high school. Covered the war there by 1976.

1979: Moved to London to cover negotiations that helped bring independence to Zimbabwe and ended a seven-year guerrilla war for black majority rule. Wrote scripts for *BBC Radio 4*.

1980: Chief correspondent and subeditor of the *Sunday Mail*, sister paper to the *Herald*.

1981: Correspondent for the *Zimbabwe Times* until the government shut it down.

1982: Freelancer (print and radio stringer) for *BBC African Service* and several newspapers, including the *Scotsman*, the *Australian*, and the *Yorkshire Post*.

1983: Joined the AP (print and radio reporting).

1984–85: Spent months covering the Ethiopian famine.

1986: Forced to leave Zimbabwe because of reporting on Gukurahundi, the killings by soldiers of thousands of people from the minority Ndebele tribe.

1986–88: Nairobi-based east Africa correspondent. Covered Uganda's civil war, Sudan-Ethiopia and Chad-Libya conflicts.

1988–89: Editor on the AP international desk in New York City.

1990–95: West Africa correspondent based in Abidjan. Covered civil wars in Liberia and Sierra Leone. Covered the Rwandan genocide, then spent weeks in Goma, writing about the resultant million-plus refugees. Briefly covered the conflict in Somalia.

1995–2005: Caribbean news editor and bureau chief, based in Puerto Rico. Covered Haiti's woes extensively and post-9/11 events in Guantanamo Bay, Cuba.

2005–Present: Chief Africa correspondent, based in Johannesburg. Covered the war in eastern Congo. Spent three months reporting on aftermath of Haiti's earthquake. Currently covering the conflict in the Ivory Coast (Cote d'Ivoire).

"I don't think any of us realized in the seventies, eighties, and early nineties what the cost of all this is to us personally," she says, disclosing that she was diagnosed a few years ago as suffering from severe PTSD, "exacerbated by the fact that I had never been treated." The cumulative impact of decades of crisis coverage has affected Michelle in deep and unexpected ways. She explains that her story published five years earlier in April 2006 on the bloody legacy of former Liberian dictator Charles Taylor triggered profound, awful memories. Michelle had covered Liberia's civil war and the related violence in neighboring Sierra Leone in the 1990s, when she was an AP West Africa correspondent.

The lead of her retrospective 2006 story (dateline: FREETOWN, Sierra Leone, AP) reads: "The chopped-off fingers clinging to the railing of a river bridge. The 12-year-old boy who drew a picture of a bloody serrated knife he had used to kill, trying to exorcise ghosts of those he had murdered. A day that started with a dog eating a corpse, and ended with a family eating their pet dog. I cried then and I cry now as I drag out of the shadows of memory the horrors of Charles Taylor's sieges of Monrovia." Michelle's article details how under Taylor's rule, an estimated 330,000 people were killed ("more hacked to death with machetes than gunned down") and some 40,000 died of starvation.

She says at the time of writing the story, she had found it "quite cathartic," but it set her thinking too much—"and probably contributed to a near mental breakdown that made me incapable of writing and left me in the hands of psychologists and psychiatrists for three months." Once such memories are uncovered, the toll can be significant. In Michelle's case: "All these things came up, and I started thinking. I started having nightmares about a room I saw in Rwanda."

The "room" in Michelle's dreams was a macabre place where a family of about a dozen people had been slaughtered and dismembered during the Rwandan genocide. Severed heads, torsos, arms, and legs were stacked neatly in sections of this blood-soaked room. "It seemed so tidy, yet psychopathic . . . bizarre, disorienting, scary," she says. In 2008, at the advice of her general practitioner, Michelle met with a psychologist who was appalled that in all her years covering wars and trauma she had never sought any therapeutic help.

I feel fine, Michelle recalls saying.
You don't feel fine, replied the psychologist. *I can hear the anger in your voice. I hear pain.*

Michelle says at first she listened skeptically to her diagnosis, while admitting at the time she was also "drinking and smoking much too much" in dealing with her anxiety, stress, and depression. She explains her initial resistance: "In Africa, we talk to each other about our problems; we're our own therapists. Seeing a psychologist is considered a Western phenomenon. But clearly that idea [avoiding counseling] didn't help me." Michelle also describes feeling isolated through the years when coming off a hard story because "family and friends don't want to hear about it—especially my fellow Africans. We're all so exhausted by the constant bad news that comes out of our continent."

To cope, Michelle will talk with fellow reporters after tough assignments ("I have made lifelong friends from a few days of shared fear"). In her free time, she unwinds by cooking, entertaining, and engaging in her lifelong appreciation of art, culture, and music. When asked if she draws strength from her faith, Michelle describes herself as a "failed Catholic. . . . After what I've seen, I'm sorry, but if God is up there, I don't understand how he can allow these horrors."

Today, Michelle credits counseling with making her aware of the need to deal immediately with the stress she is experiencing when covering a story. "We journalists don't realize what it [trauma] is doing to you," she says. "There are things you can do to make yourself feel better when you're in a really bad place." Michelle then chronicles the times she has seen vivid death scenes, encountered machine-gun fire, or has been held at gunpoint.

But her most recent account of a checkpoint in the Ivory Coast results in a great burst of laughter as she recalls the dialogue with a young armed rebel. When Michelle had explained she was a journalist, he took a long look at her and said: *You're so old. You must go home and rest. You're too old to be a journalist. It's time for you to retire.* In our phone interview, Michelle pauses and asks: "Can you imagine how insulted I was?" Then she laughs again deeply.

Michelle Faul has been blessed with a hearty sense of humor. But she attributes her remarkable resilience through the years to her mother, Ethel, who used to tell her when she was growing up in war-torn Rhodesia: "My darling, you can be whatever you want in the world. You just have to have the will." Michelle adds confidently: "She gave me the will."

Born in Embakwe Mission (Rhodesia—now Zimbabwe), she speaks warmly of her upbringing as one of five daughters in a multiracial home and credits her mother ("a wonderful, wonderful woman") and her stepfather, Michael, a white Englishman who helped nurture Michelle's classical musical training (her father had died in a hunting accident when she was just 3-years-old). The aspiring concert pianist also played violin and oboe and was a talented singer as a child. Both her parents were teachers, and she was supposed to go to college in England, where the family had lived for several years. However, plans changed when they relocated back to Rhodesia, where attending a university wasn't an option. She was en route to a secretarial college ("Because my mum used to tell me: 'Shorthand and typing are always useful.' ").

When she was finishing high school, an aunt, Francesca Bowers, showed her an ad for a "cub reporter" position at the white-run *Rhodesia Herald* newspaper. After scoring the highest of all applicants on the paper's entry tests, Michelle stood before the intimidating panel of male interviewers, who told her there were no openings on the "women's page." The sturdy teenager stood her ground, stating: "All I know how to do is write well." Though at the time, she had no idea about the difference between writing a poem or short story and being a journalist. Despite her naiveté, she was hired and soon became the first reporter of color to cover white stories for the paper. The young trailblazing journalist wrote about auto accidents and the drunken driving court, pet shows, and livestock before she eventually began reporting on her nation's civil war. As a combat zone journalist, Michelle was compelled by the Rhodesian government to be armed with (and know how to maintain and shoot) an Uzi submachine gun: "I used to slide mine under the seat and pray that if I were stopped by a guerilla ambush that they wouldn't notice, and I could talk my way out of it. . . . Fortunately, never ambushed, never had to respond."

Decades later, Michelle comments on the arc of her career, noting: "A total error; it wasn't planned that way. I'm not a war journalist or someone who seeks out conflict. I just happen to live on a continent where drama comes to you."

She says her greatest attributes are being a good listener and talker: "I can persuade you, if you are a rebel commander. I can tell you why it is good for you to tell me your side of the story and give me an interview. I can also talk my way out of situations, like through a roadblock."

Michelle's assignments have taken her across Africa to England, the United States, and to the Caribbean, where she covered years of strife in Haiti, long before the massive earthquake. She returned three days after the January 2010 disaster. While reporting on the devastation, she received long e-mails encouraging her and colleagues with the AP to talk to a counselor, by phone if necessary. Michelle says advocacy of such therapeutic interventions has been rare in her career. However, she acknowledges the importance of hostile-environment training she has received with the AP, completing two courses in recent years, most notably first-aid training. As a result of these courses, "You have the means to deal with horrible situations."

Michelle has survived countless life-threatening situations, but she would never subscribe to being an "adrenaline junkie." She finds it frightening the number of journalists who "get off on violence." Her motivation is not thrill seeking but truth-telling. She is driven to challenge the powers that be and report on the ignorance and injustices she encounters. Most recently, she was outraged by the failure of UN peacekeepers to protect innocent people in widespread violence in western Ivory Coast (Africa). While reporting on mass murders, estimated at 800 to 1,000 civilians, she was frustrated by editors who objected to her use of the word "massacre." They settled on "killings."

Michelle Faul is passionate about her work and the sacrifices she and others have made in covering risk-filled, dangerous stories for decades. She calls for medical coverage and pensions for trauma journalists and a limit on the days of continuous crisis coverage by news media workers. She also worries that in these "desperate times" in journalism, young, inexperienced freelancers ("stringers") are risking their lives for a chance at adventure and fame.

And she reflects on what was lost and what might have been in her own life.

"I'm not married because of my career," she says. "But it's work I needed and wanted to do. A bigger regret is never having children. I wish I had made the time. . . . But it just never happened. Just no time."

At the end of our conversation, I tell her an old Groucho Marx line to add a bit of levity to the call. It is nearing midnight now in Africa. I close by saying, "Take care of yourself." After a pause, her strong clear voice returns: "I always do."

Reuters correspondent Kurt Schork reports from a trench in Bitez, central Bosnia, September 22, 1993, during the Bosnian war. Schork was later killed in an ambush in Sierra Leone (Africa) on May 24, 2000, in an attack that also claimed the lives of Miguel Gil Moreno and four Sierra Leone Army soldiers.

Credit Line: REUTERS/Laszlo Balogh

ACKNOWLEDGMENTS

Although I owe my profound appreciation to many people, I begin with Katie Gallof, my editor at Continuum International Publishing Group. In August 2009, at a journalism educators' conference in Boston, Katie queried me about the research paper I was presenting on trauma journalism. She thought the subject sounded promising as a book idea. As a result of her advocacy and the strength of my work to date, I secured a contract later that fall. The Boston conference was also noteworthy because I met Terry Anderson there during my presentation. I have benefited from Terry's support and encouragement, as he has been one of several mentors along the way.

My research on this subject started in fall 2005. UW Professor Roger Simpson, author and then-executive director of the Dart Center for Journalism & Trauma, and Dr. Frank Ochberg, Dart Center founder, were the first sources to be contacted. Upon their recommendations, I interviewed several individuals, notably trauma psychiatrist, researcher, and author Dr. Anthony Feinstein and Joe Hight, president of the Dart Center and then-managing editor of the *Oklahoman* newspaper. Joe paved the way for me to visit Oklahoma City during the summers of 2006 and 2007 to talk with editors and reporters who had covered the 1995 tragedy and other critical incidents. But, more importantly, Joe took a leap of faith and permitted me to shadow him during his final year as Dart Center executive committee president with on-site, telephone, and e-mail access. I'm sure there were weeks when I came close to wearing out my welcome. But Joe stayed true to his word and gave me an insider's view of the emerging news media reform movement.

In 2009, I wrote an extended narrative nonfiction account ("Transformer") of this movement, the pivotal role of the Dart Center, and the efforts of Joe Hight, Frank Ochberg, and others to effect change in the coverage of tragedy and trauma. At the risk of inadvertent omission, the Hight-Ochberg connection has resulted directly and indirectly in assistance from (in alphabetical order): Randy Beam, Mark Brayne, Clytie Bunyan, Celeste Gonzalez de Bustamante, Penny Cockerell, Joan Connell, Chris Cramer, Ann DeFrange, Dawn Fallik, Henry Freeman, Deirdre Stoelze Graves, David Handschuh, Carla Hinton, George Hoff, Ed Kelley, Charlotte Lankard, David Loyn, Judith Matloff, Cait McMahon, Barb Monseu, Elana Newman, Scott North, Bryan Painter, Rodney Pinder, Natalie Pompilio, Gavin Rees, Sherry

Ricchiardi, Jody Santos, Bruce Shapiro, Elaine Silvestrini, Frank Smyth, Meg Spratt, Berry Tramel, and Sarah Ward-Lilley. My special thanks to all on this list and others noted in the Acknowledgments who generously gave of their time with in-depth interviews, reviews of excerpted material, and commentary on my text.

I acknowledge the contributions and support of colleagues at BSU: College of Communication, Information, and Media Dean Roger Lavery, former journalism department chairperson and author Jim Willis, Chairperson Emerita Marilyn Weaver, stalwart friend and Professor Emeritus Mark Popovich, Professor Emeritus Steve Bell (who introduced me to former ABC-TV correspondent Jim Wooten), and BSU faculty members John Strauss (who alerted me to the emblematic story of Kristin Millis, described in Chapter 8: Culture of Caring), Mary Spillman, Ryan Sparrow, Brad King, Jennifer Palilonis, and Phil Bremen, plus BSU alumni: Professor Fred Blevens and Gene Policinski, Julie Bisbee, and Anna Asatiani (who helped arrange my interview with Georgian journalist Tengo Gogotishvili). Thanks also to Marc Ransford, BSU's media relations manager.

As coordinator of the annual Eugene S. Pulliam National Journalism Writing Award, I have met many fine journalists. Two former winners who shared valuable information on trauma journalism were Amy Dockser Marcus (2005 winner, *WSJ*) and Janet Kelley (2007 winner, formerly with the *Lancaster New Era* (Pennsylvania)). Amy Dockser Marcus also assisted me in contacting Amy Farber (founder of the LAM Treatment Alliance). The 2011 Pulliam Award winner, Rukmini Callimachi, and her editor Mary Rajkumar of the AP referred me to colleague Michelle Faul. University of Kansas Professor Max Utsler provided introductions to Ridge Shannon, Dave Forstate, and Tim Twyman.

In April 2010, I attended an international conference on war, journalism, and history ("Covering Conflicts in the Modern World") at the University of Kentucky, upon the invitation of Terry Anderson. As a result, I was fortunate to meet and interview Molly Bingham and Steve Connors, who have been extremely supportive of my work. Other important contacts resulting from that conference included Tom Curley and Danny Spriggs of the AP and Will King of CNN International.

I thank the following organizations, publications, and individuals for granting me permission to use/reprint print, online, and video materials: Columbia University Press for excerpts from *Covering Violence* by William Coté and Roger Simpson (© 2006, reprinted with permission of the publisher); HarperCollins Publishers for brief quotes from *Dispatches from the Edge* by Anderson Cooper (© 2006 by Anderson Cooper); The Johns Hopkins University Press and Thomas Allen Publishers (Toronto, Canada) for excerpts of *Dangerous Lives: War and the Men and Women Who Report It* (2003) and *Journalists Under Fire: The Psychological Hazards of Covering War* (2006) by Anthony Feinstein, M.Phil., Ph.D., F.R.C.P.(C).

Foreword by Chris Hedges (pp. x–xi, 10, 18–19, 47, 80 excerpts) (© 2003, 2006, reprinted with permission of The Johns Hopkins University Press and Thomas Allen Publishers (Canadian rights)); Simon & Schuster, Inc. for selected excerpts from 2007 edition of *1 Dead in Attic: After Katrina* by Chris Rose (© 2005, 2007 Times-Picayune Publishing Corp., reprinted with permission of Simon & Schuster, Inc.); the Dart Center for Journalism & Trauma (for articles and other items cited in the Notes); the Dart Centre Australasia (for excerpts of the 2008 DVD *News Video & Trauma*, produced by Brett McLeod and Paul Webber); the Freedom Forum (for excerpts of the summer 2001 issue, "Front Lines and Deadlines: Perspectives on War Reporting," of *Media Studies Journal*, editorial director Christy Mumford Jerding: Used by Permission, 2011, First Amendment Center); the Nieman Foundation for Journalism at Harvard University (for excerpts of the winter 2009 issue, "Trauma in the Aftermath: Voice, Story, Character and Journalism," of *Nieman Reports*, editor Melissa Ludtke); Mark W. White, vice president, Manufacturing and Specialty Marketing, *U.S. News & World Report* (for excerpts of the 2004 article "A Fall from Grace" by Kit Roane); the *Oklahoman* newspaper (for stories cited in the notes); Barbara Kopple, director and coproducer, *Bearing Witness*, a 2004 film by Bob Eisenhardt, Barbara Kopple, Marijana Wotton, produced by Marijana Wotton and Barbara Kopple, produced by Magnum Films for A&E Network, Nancy Dubuc, executive producer (for excerpts of journalist profiles); Mike Walter, writer/director/producer of the 2008 documentary *Breaking News, Breaking Down* (for excerpts of journalist profiles and commentary); Ashland University Professor Gretchen Dworznik, Simon Fraser University Professor Patrice Alison Keats, Lyndon State College Professor Dan Williams, University of Missouri Professor Jim MacMillan, UCO Professor Kole Kleeman, San Francisco State University Professor Rachele Kanigel, and college (student) media advisers Jim Killam at Northern Illinois University and Bradley Wilson at North Carolina State University (for sharing their trauma journalism research and instructional materials). My thanks to author and University of Kentucky Professor Terry Anderson (for his poem "High Wire" and other selected excerpts of his 1993 book, *Den of Lions*). I also appreciate the assistance of writers Michael Howerton, Chris Williams, and Christine Haughney regarding their accounts of 9/11.

In closing, I am eternally grateful to my wife, Mykie, who transformed my life, thankful to family and friends for their love and kinship, and proud to honor the memory of my late parents, Peggy and Don. My final and most important expression of gratitude is to God for keeping me strong in body, mind, and spirit.

NOTES

"High Wire"

1 Terry Anderson, "High Wire," *Den of Lions* (New York: Ballantine Books, 1994), 33.

Chapter 1

1 Al Tompkins, "Help for Journalists under Stress," *Poynteronline*, September 14, 2001, www.poynter.org/content/content_view.asp?id=5837 (February 17, 2009).

2 Joe Hight and Frank Smyth, *Tragedies & Journalists: A Guide for More Effective Coverage* (Seattle: Dart Center for Journalism & Trauma, 2004), 29.

3 Anderson Cooper, *Dispatches from the Edge: A Memoir of War, Disasters, and Survival* (New York: Harper Paperback, 2007), 112.

4 Eric Daniel Metzgar, director, *Reporter* (New York: HBO Documentary Films, 2010), Thursday, February 18, 2010.

5 Marguerite Higgins, *News is a Singular Thing* (Garden City, NY: Doubleday, 1955), 76. Roger A. Simpson and James G. Boggs, "An Exploratory Study of Traumatic Stress Among Newspaper Journalists," *Journalism & Communication Monographs* (1999): 1(1), 1–26.

6 Anthony Feinstein, *Journalists under Fire: The Psychological Hazards of Covering War* (Baltimore: Johns Hopkins University Press, 2006), 173.

7 Jim Willis, column in *Publisher's Auxiliary*, National Newspaper Association, www.nnaweb.org, March 15, 1999.

8 Jody Santos, *Daring to Feel: Violence, The News Media and Their Emotions* (Lanham, MD: Lexington Books, 2009), xviii.

9 Anthony Feinstein and Mark Sinyor, "Women War Correspondents: They are Different in So Many Ways," *Nieman Reports* (Winter 2009): 63(4), 24, www.nieman.harvard.edu/reports/issue/100059/Winter-2009.aspx

10 Bill Kovach and Tom Rosenstiel, *The Elements of Journalism* (New York: Three Rivers Press, 2007), 88.

11 Alessandra Stanley, "Broadcast Coverage: Compassion and Self-Congratulation," *New York Times*, January 15, 2010, www.nytimes.com/2010/01/16/arts/television/16watch.html (January 18, 2010).

12 Cooper, *Dispatches from the Edge*, 56–7.

13 American Psychiatric Association, *Diagnostic and Statistical Manual of Mental Disorders, Fourth Edition (DSM-IV)* (Arlington, VA: American Psychiatric Association, 1994).

14 Jerome Aumente, "The Iraqi Shoe-Thrower: When Endangered Journalists Need Help," *Nieman Reports* (Winter 2009): 63(4), 23, www.nieman.harvard.edu/reports/issue/100059/Winter-2009.aspx

15 International News Safety Institute, www.newssafety.org (February 24, 2010).

16 Committee to Protect Journalists, *On Assignment: Covering Conflicts Safely*, 2003, 4, www.cpj.org/reports/2003/02/jounalist-safety-guide.php (March 30, 2010).

17 Kenna Griffin, "Preparing Journalists for Emotions," Dart Center, April 4, 2009, http://dartcenter.org/content/preparing-journalists-for-emotions (May 6, 2010).

18 Frank Ochberg, "Ochberg Fellowship Guidelines," Dart Center, 2009, www.dartcenter.org/fellowships/index.php (February 17, 2009).

19 Roger Simpson and William Coté, *Covering Violence: A Guide to Ethical Reporting about Victims and Trauma* (New York: Columbia University Press, 2006).

20 Jim Willis, *The Human Journalist* (Westport, CT: Praeger, 2003).

21 Feinstein, *Journalists under Fire*.

22 Harold Evans, *War Stories: Reporting in the Time of Conflict from the Crimea* (Charlestown, MA: Bunker Hill, 2003).

23 George Sullivan, *Journalists at Risk: Reporting America's Wars* (Minneapolis: Twenty-First Century Books, 2006), 6.

24 John Laurence, *The Cat from Hué: A Vietnam War Story* (New York: Public Affairs, Perseus Books Group, 2002).

25 Ian Stewart, *Ambushed: A War Reporter's Life on the Line* (Chapel Hill, NC: Algonquin Books, 2002).

26 Scott Anderson, "Prisoners of War: The Lure of Gunfire and the Enemy Within," *Harper's Magazine* (January 1997): 35–54.

27 Jackie Spinner, *Tell Them I Didn't Cry: A Young Journalist's Story of Joy, Loss, and Survival in Iraq* (New York: Scribner, 2006).

28 Barbie Zelizer and Stuart Allan, editors, *Journalism after September 11* (New York: Routledge, 2002), 21.

29 Chris Bull and Sam Erman, editors, *At Ground Zero: 25 Stories from Young Reporters Who Were There* (New York: Thunder's Mouth Press, 2002).

30 Ann S. Utterback, *Broadcasting through Crisis* (Los Angeles: Bonus Books, 2005).

31 Kim Lacy Rogers, Selma Leydesdorff and Graham Dawson, *Trauma and Life Stories* (New York: Routledge, 1999).

32 Judith Herman, *Trauma and Recovery* (New York: Harper Collins, 1992).

33 Mark H. Massé, "FRONTLINE: Dramatic Stories of Pain, Healing and Hope from a Community Crisis Intervention Team" (master's degree project, University of Oregon School of Journalism and Communication, June 1994).

34 Scott Reinardy, "It's Gametime: The Maslach Burnout Inventory Measures Burnout of Sports Journalists," Association for Education in Journalism and Mass Communication Annual Convention, Newspaper Division, San Antonio, Texas. Conference paper presented August 2005.

35 The Freedom Forum, www.freedomforum.org/ (June 8, 2010).

36 Committee to Protect Journalists, www.cpj.org/reports/2008/07/journalists-killed-in-iraq.php (June 8, 2010).

37 Carlos Conde, "Toll Rises to 46 in Philippine Election Unrest," November 25, 2009, www.nytimes.com/2009/11/25/world/asia/25phils.html?_r=1&ref=philippines (February 10, 2010).

38 Elisabeth Bumiller, "Video Shows U.S. Killing of Reuters Employees," April 5, 2010, www.nytimes.com/2010/04/06/world/middleeast/06baghdad.html (April 7, 2010).

39 Richard Sambrook, editor, *Killing the Messenger: Report of the Global Inquiry by the International News Safety Institute into the Protection of Journalists* (Brussels, Belgium: INSI, March 2007), 38.

40 Ibid., 47.

41 Ibid., 44.

42 Peter Maass, "Deadly Competition," *Brill's Content*, September 2000, www.petermaass.com/articles/deadly_competitition/ (April 15, 2010).

43 Committee to Protect Journalists, www.cpj.org/ (March 31, 2010).

44 Christiane Amanpour, "Natalya Estemirova," *TIME*, December 16, 2009: 168.

45 Sonali Samarasinghe Wickrematunge, "When They Come for Us," *Nieman Reports* (Winter 2009): 63(4), 18, www.nieman.harvard.edu/reports/issue/100059/Winter-2009.aspx

46 "A Journalist's Death," *Washington Post*, August 11, 2007: A-16.

47 Norman Sims, *True Stories: A Century of Literary Journalism* (Evanston, IL: Northwestern University Press, 2007), 247.

48 Hunter S. Thompson, *Hell's Angels* (New York: Random House, 1967).

49 Joan Didion, *Salvador* (New York: Simon & Schuster, 1983).

50 Sims, *True Stories*, 254.

51 Ibid., 254–5.

52 Ibid., 257.

53 Ibid., 252.

54 Ibid.

55 Eric James Schroeder, *Vietnam, We've All Been There: Interviews with American Writers* (Westport, CT: Praeger, 1992), 40.

56 Truman Capote, *In Cold Blood* (New York: Random House, 1965).

57 Gerald Clarke, *Capote: A Biography* (New York: Simon & Schuster, 1988), 402.

58 Sims, *True Stories*, 241.

59 Ibid., 257.

60 Jim MacMillan, Proposal Review Questionnaire, Continuum International, September 19, 2009.

61 Adam Yeomans, "AP Chief: Journalists Need Access to Battlefront," Associated Press, April 8, 2010, www.ap.org/pages/about/whatsnew/wn_040810a.html (April 12, 2010).

62 Ibid.

63 Terry Anderson, *Den of Lions* (New York: Ballantine Books, 1994), 48.

64 Ibid., 39.

65 Ibid., 393.

Chapter 2

1 "Morning of Terror: City Struggles with Shock of Deadly Bombing," *Oklahoman*, April 20, 1995: A-1.

2 Mark A. Hutchinson and Ron Jackson, "Mother Sacrifices Life for Son," *Oklahoman*, May 8, 1999: A-15.

3 Hight and Smyth, *Tragedies & Journalists*, 38.

4 Frank Ochberg, "PTSD 101 for Journalists," Gift from Within, www.giftfromwithin.org/html/ptsd101.html (July 9, 2006).

5 Sherry Ricchiardi, "After the Adrenaline," *American Journalism Review*, November 2001, 5 of 7, www.ajr.org/article_printable.asp?id=2382 (September 7, 2006).

6 Sherry Ricchiardi, "Confronting the Horror," *American Journalism Review*, January/February 1999, 7 of 7, www.ajr.org/article_printable.asp?id=825 (May 12, 2006).

7 Ibid., 4.

8 Ibid., 3.

9 Ibid., 6.

10 Ibid., 2.

11 Ibid., 6.

12 Ibid., 2, 6.

13 Ron Steinman, "Trauma: Journalism's Hidden Malady," *Digital Journalist*, October 2005, 1 of 6, http://digitaljournalist.org/issue0510/steinman.html (November 20, 2006).

14 Hight and Smyth, *Tragedies & Journalists*, 20.

15 Steinman, "Trauma: Journalism's Hidden Malady," 5 of 6.

16 Simpson and Coté, *Covering Violence*, 197.

17 Simpson and Boggs, "An Exploratory Study of Traumatic Stress Among Newspaper Journalists," 1–26.

18 Courtney Lowery, "The Journalist and the Human Response," *Montana Journalism Review* (Summer 2002): 32, 4 of 6, www.umt.edu/journalism/MJR/MJR_2002/stories/tragedy.html (September 7, 2006).

19 Simpson and Coté, *Covering Violence*, 2.

20 Ibid., xi.

21 Charlotte Lankard, *It's Called Life: Living, Loving, Hurting, Changing* (Mustang, OK: Tate Publishing, 2007), 100–1.

22 Tom Lindley, "Police Increase Training to Deal with Mentally Ill," *Oklahoman*, December 2, 2001: 1-A.

23 Ibid.

24 Tompkins, "Help for Journalists under Stress."

25 Feinstein, *Journalists under Fire*, 147.

26 Willis, *The Human Journalist*, 148.

27 Joe Hight, "Local Tragedy, National Spotlight," December 26, 2006, www.dartcenter.org/articles/special_features/hight_amish.html (January 4, 2007).

28 Joe Hight, " 'Hokie Pride' Motivates Virginia Tech Student Paper's Coverage of Tragedy," May 23, 2007, http://dartcenter.org/content/8220hokie-pride8221-motivates-virginia-tech-student-papers-coverage-tragedy (May 30, 2007).

29 Joe Strupp, "Tragic Link: Twin Cities Papers Get Care Package from Roanoke," *Editor and Publisher*, http://business.highbeam.com/4130/article-1G1-167625103/tragic-link-twin-cities-papers-get-care-package-roanoke (August 14, 2007).

30 Gretchen Dworznik and Max Grubb, "Preparing for the Worst: Making a Case for Trauma Training in the Journalism Classroom," *Journalism & Mass Communication Educator* (Summer 2007): 205.

31 *Bearing Witness*, a film by Bob Eisenhardt, Barbara Kopple, Marijana Wotton, produced by Marijana Wotton and Barbara Kopple, produced by Magnum Films for A&E Network, Nancy Dubuc, executive producer, © 2004.

32 "Barbara Walters Talks with Molly Bingham, a Photojournalist Recently Released from an Iraqi Prison," *ABC News*, April 4, 2003, http://abcnews.go.com/print?id=123733 (May 4, 2010).

33 Molly Bingham, "Dispatch: Eight Days in Abu Ghraib," *Digital Journalist*, July 2003, http://digitaljournalist.org/issue0307/dis_bingham.html (May 4, 2010).

34 Sambrook, *Killing the Messenger: Report*, 44, 47.

35 Molly Bingham, "Ordinary Warriors," *Vanity Fair*, July 2004, www.vanityfair.com/politics/features/2004/07/iraq200407?prin (May 14, 2010).

36 Molly Bingham, "Home from Iraq: Journalist Urges Americans to Search for Truth, Freedom," *Courier-Journal*, May 9, 2005, www.commondreams.org/cgi-bin/print.cgi?file=/views05/050 (May 14, 2010).

Chapter 3

1 Bruce Shapiro, "In Search of an 'Inside Narrative'," *Nieman Reports* (Winter 2009): 63(4), 74, www.nieman.harvard.edu/reports/issue/100059/Winter-2009.aspx

2 Herbert N. Foerstel, *Killing the Messenger: Journalists at Risk in Modern Warfare* (Westport, CT: Praeger, 2006), 8.

3 Ibid., 9.

4 Sullivan, *Journalists at Risk*, 6.

5 Evans, *War Stories*, 42.

6 Committee to Protect Journalists, "Iraq: Journalists in Danger," http://cpj.org/killed/mideast/iraq (June 8, 2010). International News Safety Institute, www.newssafety.org/ (June 15, 2010).

7 Timothy J. Kenny, "In the Bleeding Fields," *Media Studies Journal* (Summer 2001): 15(1), 90.

8 Ibid., 94.

9 Ibid.

10 Ibid.

11 Hight and Smyth, *Tragedies & Journalists*, 20.

12 Kit R. Roane, "A Fall from Grace," *USNews.com*, May 9, 2004, www.usnews.com/usnews/culture/articles/040517/17photog_ (4 of 11) (March 23, 2010).

13 Ibid., 1.

14 Ibid., 5.

15 Ibid.

16 Ibid., 6.

17 Ibid., 6, 7.

18 Ibid., 7.

19 Ibid., 8.

20 Evans, *War Stories*, 84.

21 Feinstein and Sinyor, "Women War Correspondents," 24–5.

22 Ibid., 25.

23 Refer Chapter 2, n. 31

24 Ibid.

25 Ibid.

26 Ibid.

27 Ibid.

28 Ibid.

29 Ibid.

30 Gary Knight, "Up Close and Deadly," *Media Studies Journal* (Summer 2001): 15(1), 104.

31 Ibid., 105.

32 Anthony Feinstein, John Owen, and Nancy Blair, "A Hazardous Profession: War, Journalists and Psychopathology," *American Journal of Psychiatry* (2002): 159(9), 1570–5.

33 Greg Mitchell, "Not Fade Away: Joe Galloway, War Reporter, Retires," *editorandpublisher.com*, May 25, 2006, http://editorandpublisher.printthis. clickability.com/pt/cpt?action=cpt&title=Not+Fade+Away%3A+Joe+Gallowa y%2C+War+Reporter%2C+Retires&expir (June 26, 2006).

34 "We Were Soldiers," www.weweresoldiers.net/joes-story.htm (March 8, 2010).

35 Steve Inskeep, "A Retiring War Correspondent Returns from Iraq," *npr.org*, June 26, 2006, www.npr.org/templates/story/story/.php?storyId=5494800 (June 26, 2006).

36 *War Torn: Stories of War from the Women Reporters Who Covered Vietnam*, introduction by Gloria Emerson (New York: Random House, 2002).

37 Lori Runkle, "War Reporter Kate Webb Visits Iowa State March 3–4," *Greenlee School of Journalism and Communication*, March 4, 2005, www.jlmc.iastate.edu/news/2005/spring/KateWebbPreview.shtml (June 26, 2006).

38 "Being Where the Action is," *The Correspondent: The On-line Publication of the Foreign Correspondents' Club of Hong Kong*, December 2001–January 2002, www.fcchk.org/correspondent/corro-dec01/dec-kate1.htm (June 26, 2006).

39 Ibid.

40 Robert Sam Anson, *War News: A Young Reporter in Indochina* (New York: Simon & Schuster, 1989), 139.

41 Ibid., 219.

42 Ibid., 301.

43 Laurence, *The Cat from Hué*, 9.

44 Ibid., 25.

45 Ibid., 37.

46 Ibid., 55.

47 Ibid., 77.

48 Ibid., 87.

49 Ibid., 89.

50 Ibid., 837.

51 Judith Matloff, "Scathing Memory: Journalism Finally Faces Up to the Psychic Costs of War Reporting," *Columbia Journalism Review* (November/December 2004): 43(4), 19–21.

52 Ibid.

53 Ibid.

54 Yael Danieli, editor, *Sharing the Front Line and the Back Hills: International Protectors and Providers: Peacekeepers, Humanitarian Aid Workers and the Media in the Midst of Crisis* (Amityville, NY: Baywood, 2002), 296.

55 Feinstein, *Journalists under Fire*, x.

56 Ibid., 44, 142.

57 Ibid., 143.

58 "Reporting America at War," PBS—WETA, 2003, www.pbs.org/weta/ reportingamericaatwar/reporters/hedges/ (April 28, 2010).

59 Ben Lando, "The Moment: 1/25/10 Baghdad," *TIME*, February 8, 2010: 11.

60 Feinstein, *Journalists under Fire*, x.

61 Ibid., x–xi.

62 Ibid., 8–9.

63 Ibid., 10.

64 Ibid., 80.

65 Spinner, *Tell Them I Didn't Cry*, 67.

66 Ibid., 133, 135.

67 Ibid., 158, 160.

68 Ibid., 248.

69 Ibid., 249.

70 Ibid., 251.

71 Simpson and Coté, *Covering Violence*, 14.

72 Ibid., 16.

73 Ibid., 15.

74 Ibid., 16.

75 Donatella Lorch, www.donatellalorch.com/bio.html (July 29, 2010).

76 Evans, *War Stories*, 42.

77 Donatella Lorch, "Surviving the Five Ds: A Writer Struggles with the Emotional Aftermath of Covering Brutality in Africa," *Media Studies Journal* (Summer 2001): 15(1), 99.

78 Ibid., 100.

79 Ibid., 101.

80 Ibid.

81 Ibid., 103.

82 Donatella Lorch, www.donatellalorch.com/bio.html (July 29, 2010).

83 Feinstein, *Journalists under Fire*, 18–19.

84 Ibid., 19.

85 Ibid., 47.

86 Ibid.

87 Stewart, *Ambushed: A War Reporter's Life*, 13.

88 Ibid., 17.

89 Ibid., 25.

90 Ibid., 302.

91 Cooper, *Dispatches from the Edge*, 119–20.

92 Willis, *The Human Journalist*, 135.

93 Don Corrigan, "When Murder Strikes a Small Community," *Nieman Reports* (Winter 2009): 63(4), 7–9, www.nieman.harvard.edu/reports/issue/100059/Winter-2009.aspx

94 Ibid.

95 Ibid.

96 Ibid.

97 Ibid.

98 Simpson and Coté, *Covering Violence*, 222.

99 Ibid., 223.

100 Ibid., 224–5.

101 Brett McLeod and Paul Webber, producers, *News Media & Trauma: Stories from Australian Media Professionals about Reporting Trauma* (Willoughby [Sydney]: Dart Centre for Journalism & Trauma, Australasia, 2008).

102 Ibid.

103 Ibid.

104 Ibid.

105 Ibid.

106 Ibid.

107 Ibid.

108 Audrey Lott Watkins, "How Covering Jonesboro Changed a Reporter," Dart Center, 2010, http://dartcenter.org/content/how-covering-jonesboro-changed-reporter (June 21, 2010).

109 Ibid.

110 Ibid.

111 Ibid.

112 Ibid.

113 Simpson and Coté, *Covering Violence*, 245.

114 Andrew Freinkel, Cheryl Koopman, and David Spiegel, "Dissociative Symptoms in Media Eyewitnesses of an Execution," *American Journal of Psychiatry* (September 1994): 151(9), 1335–9.

115 Yamamoto Tsunetomo (translated by William Scott Wilson), *Hagakure: The Book of the Samurai* (Tokyo: Kodansha International; New York: Harper & Row, 1979).

116 Scott North, "Faith and Friendship," *Daily Herald*, October 13, 2002: A-1.

117 Scott North, "A Truth Beyond," *Daily Herald*, August 10–17, 2008, www.heraldnet.com/apps/pbcs.dll/article?AID=/20080810/N (June 13, 2010).

118 Ibid.

119 Ibid.

120 Ibid.

121 Ibid.

122 Ibid.

123 Ibid.

124 Ibid.

125 Ibid.

126 Ibid.

127 Ibid.

Chapter 4

1 Audrey Lott Watkins, "Columbine: Reporter's Perspectives, Part I," Dart Center, 2000, http://dartcenter.org/contents/columbine-reporters-perspectives-part-i (June 23, 2010).

2 Audrey Lott Watkins, "Columbine: Reporter's Perspectives, Part II," Dart Center, 2000, http://dartcenter.org/contents/columbine-reporters-perspectives-part-ii (June 23, 2010).

3 Larry Zalin, "Stress on the Press: The Media and Violence," *Columns*, March 2001.

4 Dave Cullen, *Columbine* (New York: Twelve/Hachette Book Group, 2009), 271.

5 Meg Moritz, director, *Covering Columbine* (Boulder, CO: University of Colorado and Rocky Mountain PBS, 2003).

6 Cullen, *Columbine*, 362.

7 Simpson and Coté, *Covering Violence*, 53.

8 Dirck Halstead, "Bill Biggart's Final Exposures," DigitalJournalist.org, 2004, www.digitaljournalist.org/issue0111/biggart_intro.htm (October 5, 2005 by Roger Simpson). Simpson and Coté, *Covering Violence*, 53, 286.

9 Simpson and Coté, *Covering Violence*, 54–5.

10 Mike Walter, "Tears are Part of Telling the Story," *Nieman Reports* (Winter 2009): 63(4), 11, www.nieman.harvard.edu/reports/issue/100059/Winter-2009.aspx

11 Ibid.

12 Bull and Erman, *At Ground Zero*, 10–11.

13 Ibid., 19.

14 Ibid., 19–21.

15 Ibid., 21–2.

16 Ibid., 162.

17 Ibid., 164.

18 Ibid., 290–1.

19 Ibid., 293.

20 Ibid., 297.

21 Ibid., 300–1.

22 Ibid., 302.

23 Ibid., 351.

24 Ibid., 355–6.

25 Ibid., 357.

26 Ibid., 362.

27 Ibid., 361.

28 Ibid., 363.

29 Ibid., 364.

30 Ibid., 365–6.

31 Ben Brown, "Covering the Tsunami," Dart Center, 2005, http://dartcenter.org/content/covering-tsunami-2 (June 23, 2010).

32 Ibid.

33 Ibid.

34 "Covering the Tsunami: A Frontline Club Discussion," Dart Center, February 22, 2005, http://dartcenter.org/content/covering-tsunami-0 (June 23, 2010).

35 Ibid.

36 Brian MacArthur, "Journalists Find Ways to Cope with Tsunami," *The Times*, January 7, 2005, http://business.timesonline.co.uk/tol/business/industry_sectors/media/article409100.ece (August 10, 2010).

37 Ibid.

38 Matt Ironside, "Journalism and the Tsunami," Dart Center, 2005. http://dartcenter.org/content/journalism-and-tsunami-0 (June 23, 2010).

39 Kimina Lyall, "The Emotional Toll of Disaster Reporting," Dart Center, March 1, 2005, http://dartcenter.org/content/emotional-toll-disaster-reporting-0 (August 10, 2010).

40 Ibid.

41 Ibid.

42 Cooper, *Dispatches from the Edge*, 32–3.

43 Jim Willis, *The Mind of a Journalist* (Thousand Oaks, CA: Sage, 2010), 217.

44 Ibid., 218.

45 Cooper, *Dispatches from the Edge*, 133.

46 Ibid., 141.

47 Ibid., 188.

48 Ibid., 202.

49 Chris Rose, *1 Dead in Attic: After Katrina* (New York: Simon & Schuster, 2007), xv.

50 Ibid., 52.

51 Ibid., 107.

52 Ibid., 109.

53 Ibid., 275.

54 Ibid., 76.

55 Ibid., 324.

56 Ibid., 328.

57 Ibid., 330–1.

58 Ibid., 327, 331.

59 Ibid., 342.

60 Melissa Ludtke, editor, "Trauma in New Orleans: In the Wake of Katrina," *Nieman Reports* (Winter 2009): 63(4), 40, www.nieman.harvard.edu/reports/issue/100059/Winter-2009.aspx

61 Ibid., 40–1.

62 Mike Walter, writer/director/producer, *Breaking News, Breaking Down* (Fairfax, VA: Walter Media, 2008).

63 Ibid.

64 Ibid.

65 Ibid.

66 Ibid.

67 Ibid.

68 Liz Halloran, "For a Moment, We are All the Hokie Nation," *U.S. News & World Report*, April 30, 2007: 14.

69 Amie Steele, "Story of Their Lives," *Journalist* (Society of Professional Journalists), 2007: 13.

70 Ibid., 10, 12.

71 Joe Hight, "'Hokie Pride' Motivates Virginia Tech Student." (See Chapter 2, n. 28.)

72 Kelly Furnas, "Virginia Tech: Tips from a Newsroom Adviser," Dart Center, April 20, 2009, http://dartcenter.org/content/virginia-tech-tips-from-newsroom-adviser (June 23, 2010).

73 Joe Grimm, "Massacre on a Managing Editor's First Day," May 21, 2007, *Poynteronline*, www.poynter.org/latest-news/top-stories/82415/massacre-on-a-managing-editors-first-day/ (May 30, 2007).

74 Ibid.

75 Steele, "Story of Their Lives," 11.

76 Amie Steele, "Virginia Tech: Tips from Student Journalists," Dart Center, April 20, 2009, http://dartcenter.org/content/virginia-tech-tips-from-student-reporters (June 23, 2010).

77 Ibid.

78 Meg Spratt, "Covering School Shootings," Dart Center, April 20, 2009, http://dartcenter.org/content/school-shooting-package (June 23, 2010).

79 Stephen J. A. Ward, "Emotion in Reporting: Use and Abuse," The Canadian Journalism Project, January 19, 2010, www.jsource.ca/english_new/detail.php?id=4693&PHPSESS (June 23, 2010).

80 Ibid.

81 James Nachtwey, "Out of the Ruins," *TIME*, February 8, 2010: 24.

82	Ibid.

83	Donna Boen, editor, "The Reporter," *Miamian*, Spring 2010: 8.

84	Jon Lee Anderson, "Neighbors' Keeper," *New Yorker*, February 8, 2010: 27.

85	Ward, "Emotion in Reporting: Use and Abuse."

86	Bruce Shapiro, "Haiti Quake: Watchful Waiting," Dart Center, January 21, 2010, http://dartcenter.org/content/managing-haiti-story (June 23, 2010).

87	Ibid.

88	Amy Dockser Marcus, "A Wife's Struggle with Cancer Takes an Unexpected Toll," *Wall Street Journal*, September 8, 2004, www.pulitzer.org/archives/6846 (March 10, 2010).

89	Amy Dockser Marcus, "After Leukemia, Family Struggles to Define 'Normal,'" *Wall Street Journal*, June 9, 2004, www.pulitzer.org/archives/6848 (March 10, 2010).

90	Amy Dockser Marcus, "New Approach to Lung Cancer: Being Aggressive," *Wall Street Journal*, June 29, 2004, www.pulitzer.org/archives/6847 (March 10, 2010).

91	Amy Dockser Marcus, "The Loneliness of Fighting a Rare Cancer," *Health Affairs*, January 2010: 203–6.

92	Amy Dockser Marcus, *The View from Nebo: How Archaeology is Rewriting the Bible and Reshaping the Middle East* (Boston: Back Bay Books, 2000); Amy Dockser Marcus, *Jerusalem 1913: The Origins of the Arab-Israeli Conflict* (New York: Viking, 2007).

Chapter 5

1	Freinkel, Koopman, and Spiegel, "Dissociative Symptoms in Media Eyewitnesses," 1335–9.

2	Simpson and Boggs, "An Exploratory Study of Traumatic Stress," 1–26.

3	Fruake Teegen and Maike Grotwinkel, "Traumatic Exposure and Post-Traumatic Stress Disorder of Journalists: An Internet-Based Study," *Psychotherapeut* (2001): 46(3), 169–75.

4	Cait McMahon, "Covering Disaster: A Pilot Study into Secondary Trauma for Print Media Journalists Reporting on Disaster," *Australian Journal of Emergency Management* (2001): 16(2), 52–6.

5	Feinstein, Owen, and Blair, "A Hazardous Profession," 1570–5.

6	Caroline Pyevich, Elana Newman and Eric Daleiden, "The Relationship Among Cognitive Schemas, Job-Related Traumatic Exposure, and Posttraumatic Stress Disorder in Journalists," *Journal of Traumatic Stress* (2003): 16(4), 325–8.

7	Elana Newman, Roger Simpson, and David Handschuh, "Trauma Exposure and Post-Traumatic Stress Disorder Among Photojournalists, *Visual Communication Quarterly* (Winter 2003): 58(1), 4–13.

8 Hal Himmelstein and Perry E. Faithorn, "Eyewitness to Disaster: How Journalists Cope with the Psychological Stress Inherent in Reporting Traumatic Events," *Journalism Studies* (November 2002): 3(4), 537–55.

9 Howard J. Osofsky, Harry Holloway, and Allison Pickett, "War Correspondents as Responders: Considerations for Training and Clinical Services," *Psychiatry* (Fall 2005): 68(3), 283–93.

10 Patrice Keats and Marla Buchanan, "Journalists' and Photojournalists' Suggestions about How to Address the Psychological Effects of Traumatic Stress," paper presented to the Canadian Journalism Forum on Violence and Trauma, London, Ontario, February 2008.

11 Gretchen Dworznik, "Journalism and Trauma," *Journalism Studies* (2006): 7(4), 534–53.

12 Dworznik and Grubb, "Preparing for the Worst," 190–210.

13 Gretchen Dworznik and Stan Wearden, "Factors Contributing to PTSD and Compassion Fatigue" (under review), 2009.

14 Neil Greenberg, Matthew Gould, Vicky Langston, and Mark Brayne, "Journalists' and Media Professionals' Attitudes to PTSD and Help-Seeking: A Descriptive Study," *Journal of Mental Health* (2009): 18(6), 543–8.

15 Randal A. Beam and Meg Spratt, "Managing Vulnerability: Job Satisfaction, Morale and Journalists' Reactions to Violence and Trauma," *Journalism Practice* (2009): 3(4), 421–38.

16 Yung Soo Kim and James D. Kelly, "Public Reactions toward an Ethical Dilemma Faced by Photojournalists: Examining the Conflict between Acting as a Dispassionate Observer and Acting as a 'Good Samaritan'," *Journalism & Mass Communication Quarterly* (Spring 2010): 87(1), 23–40.

17 Ibid., 35.

18 Stan Alcorn, "New Tool for Journalism and Trauma Research," Dart Center, October 31, 2010, http://dartcenter.org/content/new-tool-debuts-for-trauma-research (November 4, 2010).

19 Bull and Erman, *At Ground Zero*, 1.

20 David Handschuh, "A Lens on Life and Death," *Poynteronline*, January 8, 2002, www.poynter.org/uncategorized/1846/a-lens-on-life-and-death/ (June 15, 2010).

21 Simpson and Coté, *Covering Violence*, 64.

22 David Handschuh, "Helping Another Breed of Foot Soldier," American Press Institute, November 25, 2001, www.beta.americanpressinstitute.org/content/p1413_c1383.cfm?print=yes (June 15, 2010).

23 Newman, Simpson, and Handschuh, "Trauma Exposure and Post-Traumatic Stress Disorder Among Photojournalists," 4–13.

24 Simpson and Coté, *Covering Violence*, 65, 69.

Chapter 6

1 Melissa Ludtke, editor, "How to Do an Interview—When Trauma is the Topic," *Nieman Reports* (Winter 2009): 63(4), 56, www.nieman.harvard.edu/reports/issue/100059/Winter-2009.aspx

2 Ibid., 57.

3 Lori Luechtefeld, "Interviews with the Interviewers: Dealing with Sensitive Issues," *IRE Journal*, May/June 2003: 14.

4 Joe Hight, "Five Steps to Covering a Disaster Effectively," Dart Center, 2007, http://dartcenter.org/content/five-steps-to-covering-disaster-effectively (July 25, 2007).

5 "Interviewing Service Members," Dart Center and Association of Health Care Journalists, May 2007, http://dartcenter.org/content/interviewing-service-members and www.healthjournalism.org/resources-articles-details.php?id=11 (June 4, 2007).

6 Ruth Teichroeb, *Covering Children & Trauma: A Guide for Journalism Professionals* (Seattle: Dart Center for Journalism & Trauma, 2006), 5–10.

7 Mark Brayne, editor, *Trauma & Journalism: A Guide for Journalists, Editors & Managers* (London, England: Dart Centre for Journalism & Trauma, 2007), 1–28.

8 Ibid., 11–12.

9 "How is Your Emotional Health? Test Yourself," International News Safety Institute, 2009, www.newssafety.com/stories/insi/ptsd.htm (February 24, 2010).

10 Patrice Keats, "Assignment Stress Injury," presented at the Canadian Association of Journalists Conference, Vancouver, BC, May 2009.

11 Brayne, *Trauma & Journalism*, 13.

12 *Handbook for Journalists* (Paris, France: Reporters sans frontières, 2009), 44.

13 Kate Adie Quotes, *Brainy Quote*, www.brainyquote.com/quotes/authors/k/kate_adie.html (May 14, 2010).

14 *Handbook for Journalists*, 45–8.

15 Ibid., 51.

16 Danieli, *Sharing the Front Line and the Back Hills*, 277.

17 Sambrook, *Killing the Messenger: Report*, 50.

18 "Training," International News Safety Institute, 2010, www.newssafety.org/index.php?option=com_content&view=category&layout=blog&id=243&Itemid=100121(February 24, 2010).

19 "Surviving Hostile Regions Training Course," AKE, 2010, www.akegroup.com/training/hostile-environment-training/ (May 12, 2010).

20 "What We Do," Centurion Risk Assessment Services, 2009, www.centurionsafety.net/About/What_We_Do.html (May 12, 2010).

21 Vincent Laforet, "Hostile Environment Training 101," Centurion Risk Assessment Services, 2009, www.centurionsafety.net/About/Centurion_in_the_Media/Host (May 12, 2010).

22 "Journalist Safety Community," Journalists@Risk, 2010, www.journalists atrisk.org/?article=18 (April 15, 2010).

23 *Turner Broadcasting System, Inc.: Post Traumatic Stress Disorder Program*, CNN brochure.

24 Sherry Ricchiardi, "Playing Defense," *American Journalism Review*, Summer 2010: 42–7.

25 Ibid., 46.

26 Ibid.

27 Ibid., 44.

28 Melissa Manware, "Overcoming Trauma," *Quill*, May 2008: 20.

29 Ibid.

30 Ibid.

31 George Hoff, "'Suck It Up' Just isn't Enough," The Canadian Journalism Project, September 27, 2009, www.j-source.ca/english_new/detail.php?id=4309 (March 3, 2010).

32 Ibid.

33 Ibid.

Chapter 7

1   Ochberg, "PTSD 101 for Journalists."

2   American Psychiatric Association, *Diagnostic and Statistical Manual of Mental Disorders*.

3   Ochberg, "PTSD 101 for Journalists."

4   Ibid.

5   Roger Rosenblatt, "Battle-Scarred Journalists: Rwanda Therapy," *New Republic*, June 6, 1994: 16.

6   Ochberg, "PTSD 101 for Journalists."

7   Feinstein, *Journalists under Fire*, 7.

8   Danieli, *Sharing the Front Line and the Back Hills*, 275.

9   Ibid., 276.

10 Feinstein, *Journalists under Fire*, 7.

11 Danieli, *Sharing the Front Line and the Back Hills*, 277.

12 Cait McMahon, "Journalists and Trauma: The Parallel Worlds of Posttraumatic Growth and Posttraumatic Stress—Preliminary Findings," proceedings of the 40th Australian Psychological Society Annual Conference, Australian Psychological Society, Melbourne, Victoria, Australia, 2005, 188–92.

13 Feinstein, Owen, and Blair, "A Hazardous Profession," 1570–5.

14 McMahon, "Covering Disaster," 52–6.

15 Sambrook, *Killing the Messenger: Report*.

16 Ian Austen, "For Novice Journalists, Rising Risks in Conflict Zones," *New York Times*, November 30, 2009, www.nytimes.com/2009/11/30/business/media/30somalia.html (June 23, 2010).

17 Chris Heide, "Staging Trauma," Dart Center, March 31, 2010, http://dartcenter.org/content/practicing-disaster (April 1, 2010).

18 Dan Williams, "Why Wait for Disaster When Your Local College Can Arrange One?," paper presented to the fifteenth annual Newspapers and Community-Building Symposium, Mobile, Alabama, September 25, 2009.

19 Bradley Wilson, editor, *Covering the Unimaginable* (Manhattan, KS: Journalism Education Association, 2010), 80.

20 Gavin Rees, "Weathering the Trauma Storms," *British Journalism Review* (June 2007): 18(2), 65.

21 Dr. Kole Kleeman, "Victims & the Media Seminar" syllabus, University of Central Oklahoma, Fall 2009.

22 Professor Jim MacMillan, "Journalism and Psychological Trauma" syllabus, Temple University, Spring 2009.

23 Migael Scherer, "Training Steps," Dart Center, October 31, 2008, http://dartcenter.org/content/training-steps (January 4, 2010). Sue Lockett John and Kevin Kawamoto, "Simulated Trauma in the Classroom," Dart Center, March 31, 2010, http://dartcenter.org/content/simulated-traumai-0 (January 4, 2010).

24 Rachele Kanigel, *The Student Newspaper Survival Guide* (Hoboken, NJ: Wiley-Blackwell, 2006).

25 Rachele Kanigel, "Planning for a Crisis" and "Covering Trauma," SlideShare, 2009, www.slideshare.net/rkanigel/planning-for-a-crisis; www.slideshare.net/rkanigel/covering-trauma (February 22, 2010).

26 Rachele Kanigel, "Covering Suicide," The Student Newspaper Survival Blog, August 30, 2007, http://collegenewspaper.blogspot.com/2007/08/covering-suicide.html (February 22, 2010).

27 "For the Media: Reporting on Suicide," the American Foundation for Suicide Prevention, 2010, www.afsp.org/index.cfm?page_id=0523d365-a314-431e-a925c03e13e762b1 (February 12, 2010).

28 *Preventing Suicide: A Resource for Media Professionals* (Geneva, Switzerland: Department of Mental Health, World Health Organization, 2000), 6, www.who.int/mental_health/media/en/426.pdf (March 1, 2010).

29 Ibid.

30 "Support for Continued Caution in Reporting Suicide," SANE Media Centre, March 11, 2010, www.mindframe-media.info (August 6, 2010).

31 Meg Spratt, "Dart Academic Fellows Talk about Teaching Trauma," Dart Center, August 5, 2010, http://dartcenter.org/content/dart-academic-fellows-talk-about-teaching-trauma (August 6, 2010).

32 Ibid.

33 Ibid.

34 Ibid.

35 Ibid.

36 Furnas, "Virginia Tech: Tips from a Newsroom Adviser."

37 Jim Killam, "NIU: Tips for Advisers and Teachers," Dart Center, April 19, 2009, http://dartcenter.org/content/niu-tips-for-advisers-and-teachers (June 23, 2010).

38 Ibid.

39 Ibid.

40 Judith Matloff, *Home Girl: Building a Dream House on a Lawless Block* (New York: Random House, 2008).

41 Judith Matloff, *Fragments of a Forgotten War* (New York: Penguin, 1997).

42 Mike Hoyt, John Palattella, and *Columbia Journalism Review*, editors, *Reporting Iraq: An Oral History of the War by the Journalists Who Covered It* (Brooklyn, NY: Melville House, 2007).

43 Matloff, "Scathing Memory," 19.

44 Ibid., 19–20.

45 Ibid., 21.

Chapter 8

1 College Media Advisers, July 19, 2010, www.collegemedia.org (July 19, 2010).

2 "Setting the Standard: A Commitment to Frontline Journalism; An Obligation to Frontline Journalism," Freedom Forum European Centre, September 20, 2000: 2, 20.

3 Laura van Dernoot Lipsky and Connie Burk, *Trauma Stewardship* (San Francisco: Berrett-Koehler, 2009), 4–5.

4 James Poniewozik, "The End of Objectivity," *TIME*, November 29, 2010: 71.

5 Bruce Shapiro, "A Benefit Performance for the Dart Center," Dart Center, November 11, 2010, http://dartcenter.org (November 11, 2010).

6 Michelle Faul, Associated Press Writer, "Memories of Taylor's Tyranny: Drugged-Out Child Soldiers, Dogs-Eating Corpses, Hacked off Limbs," *Associated Press*, April 3, 2006.

BIBLIOGRAPHY

American Psychiatric Association. *Diagnostic and Statistical Manual of Mental Disorders, Fourth Edition (DSM-IV)*. Arlington, VA: American Psychiatric Association, 1994.

Anderson, Terry. *Den of Lions*. New York: Ballantine Books, 1994.

Anson, Robert Sam. *War News: A Young Reporter in Indochina*. New York: Simon & Schuster, 1989.

Brayne, Mark, editor. *Trauma & Journalism: A Guide for Journalists, Editors & Managers*. London, England: Dart Centre for Journalism & Trauma, 2007.

Bull, Chris and Sam Erman, editors. *At Ground Zero: 25 Stories from Young Reporters Who Were There*. New York: Thunder's Mouth Press, 2002.

Capote, Truman. *In Cold Blood*. New York: Random House, 1965.

Clarke, Gerald. *Capote: A Biography*. New York: Simon & Schuster, 1988.

Cooper, Anderson. *Dispatches from the Edge: A Memoir of War, Disasters, and Survival*. New York: Harper Paperback, 2007.

Cullen, Dave. *Columbine*. New York: Twelve/Hachette Book Group, 2009.

Danieli, Yael, editor. *Sharing the Front Line and the Back Hills: International Protectors and Providers: Peacekeepers, Humanitarian Aid Workers and the Media in the Midst of Crisis*. Amityville, NY: Baywood, 2002.

Didion, Joan. *Salvador*. New York: Simon & Schuster, 1983.

Emerson, Gloria. Introduction to *War Torn: Stories of War from the Women Reporters Who Covered Vietnam*. New York: Random House, 2002.

Evans, Harold. *War Stories: Reporting in the Time of Conflict*. Charlestown, MA: Bunker Hill, 2003.

Feinstein, Anthony. *Journalists under Fire: The Psychological Hazards of Covering War*. Baltimore: Johns Hopkins University Press, 2006.

Foerstel, Herbert N. *Killing the Messenger: Journalists at Risk in Modern Warfare*. Westport, CT: Praeger, 2006.

Giovanni, Janine di. *Madness Visible: A Memoir of War*. New York: Alfred A. Knopf, 2003.

Handbook for Journalists. Paris, France: Reporters sans frontières, 2009.

Hedges, Chris. *War is a Force That Gives Us Meaning*. New York: BBS/Public Affairs, 2002.

Herman, Judith. *Trauma and Recovery*. New York: Harper Collins, 1992.

Higgins, Marguerite. *News is a Singular Thing*. Garden City, NY: Doubleday, 1955.

Hight, Joe and Frank Smyth, *Tragedies & Journalists: A Guide for More Effective Coverage*. Seattle: Dart Center for Journalism & Trauma, 2004.

Hoyt, Mike, John Palattella, and *Columbia Journalism Review*, editors. *Reporting Iraq: An Oral History of the War by the Journalists Who Covered It*. Brooklyn, NY: Melville House, 2007.

Kanigel, Rachele. *The Student Newspaper Survival Guide*. Hoboken, NJ: Wiley-Blackwell, 2006.

Kovach, Bill and Tom Rosenstiel. *The Elements of Journalism*. New York: Three Rivers Press, 2007.

Lankard, Charlotte. *It's Called Life: Living, Loving, Hurting, Changing*. Mustang, OK: Tate Publishing, 2007.

Laurence, John. *The Cat from Hué: A Vietnam War Story*. New York: Public Affairs, Perseus Books Group, 2002.

Lipsky, Laura van Dernoot and Connie Burk. *Trauma Stewardship*. San Francisco: Berrett-Koehler, 2009.

Loyd, Anthony. *My War Gone by, I Miss It So*. New York: Atlantic Monthly Press, 1999.

Marcus, Amy Dockser. *Jerusalem 1913: The Origins of the Arab-Israeli Conflict*. New York: Viking, 2007.

———. *The View from Nebo: How Archaeology is Rewriting the Bible and Reshaping the Middle East*. Boston: Back Bay Books, 2000.

Matloff, Judith. *Home Girl: Building a Dream House on a Lawless Block*. New York: Random House, 2008.

———. *Fragments of a Forgotten War*. New York: Penguin, 1997.

Preventing Suicide: A Resource for Media Professionals. Geneva, Switzerland: Department of Mental Health, World Health Organization, 2000.

Rogers, Kim Lacy, Selma Leydesdorff and Graham Dawson. *Trauma and Life Stories*. New York: Routledge, 1999.

Rose, Chris. *1 Dead in Attic: After Katrina*. New York: Simon & Schuster, 2007.

Sambrook, Richard, editor. *Killing the Messenger: Report of the Global Inquiry by the International News Safety Institute into the Protection of Journalists*. Brussels, Belgium: INSI, March 2007.

Santos, Jody. *Daring to Feel: Violence, The News Media and Their Emotions*. Lanham, MD: Lexington Books, 2009.

Schroeder, Eric James. *Vietnam, We've All Been There: Interviews with American Writers*. Westport, CT: Praeger, 1992.

Simpson, Roger and William Coté. *Covering Violence: A Guide to Ethical Reporting about Victims and Trauma*. New York: Columbia University Press, 2006.

Sims, Norman. *True Stories: A Century of Literary Journalism*. Evanston, IL: Northwestern University Press, 2007.

Spinner, Jackie. *Tell Them I Didn't Cry: A Young Journalist's Story of Joy, Loss, and Survival in Iraq*. New York: Scribner, 2006.

Stewart, Ian. *Ambushed: A War Reporter's Life on the Line*. Chapel Hill, NC: Algonquin Books, 2002.

Sullivan, George. *Journalists at Risk: Reporting America's Wars*. Minneapolis: Twenty-First Century Books, 2006.

Teichroeb, Ruth. *Covering Children & Trauma: A Guide for Journalism Professionals*. Seattle: Dart Center for Journalism & Trauma, 2006.

Thompson, Hunter S. *Hell's Angels*. New York: Random House, 1967.

Tsunetomo, Yamamoto (translated by William Scott Wilson). *Hagakure: The Book of the Samurai*. Tokyo: Kodansha International; New York: distributed in the United States by Harper & Row, 1979.

Utterback, Ann S. *Broadcasting through Crisis*. Los Angeles: Bonus Books, 2005.

Willis, Jim. *The Mind of a Journalist.* Thousand Oaks, CA: Sage, 2010.
———. *The Human Journalist.* Westport, CT: Praeger, 2003.
Wilson, Bradley, editor. *Covering the Unimaginable.* Manhattan, KS: Journalism Education Association, 2010.
Zelizer, Barbie and Stuart Allan, editors. *Journalism after September 11.* New York: Routledge, 2002.

BIOGRAPHY

MARK H. MASSÉ is a professor of literary journalism at Ball State University. A freelancer for more than 30 years, Massé has published articles, essays, and stories in international, national, and regional periodicals, as well as creative writing collections. He is author of *Inspired to Serve: Today's Faith Activists* and *Delamore's Dreams*, a novel. A New York native, he has degrees from the University of Oregon and Miami University (Ohio).

INDEX